MW01062015

RACE AND NATURE FROM TRANSCENDENTALISM TO THE HARLEM RENAISSANCE

SIGNS OF RACE

Series Editors: Phillip D. Beidler and Gary Taylor

Writing Race across the Atlantic World: Medieval to Modern
Edited by Phillip D. Beidler and Gary Taylor (January 2005)

Buying Whiteness: Race, Culture, and Identity from Columbus to Hip-Hop
By Gary Taylor (January 2005)

English and Ethnicity
Edited by Janina Brutt-Griffler and Catherine Evans Davies
(December 2006)

Women & Others: Perspectives on Race, Gender, and Empire
Edited by Celia R. Daileader, Rhoda E. Johnson, and Amilcar Shabazz
(September 2007)

The Funk Era and Beyond: New Perspectives on Black Popular Culture
Edited by Tony Bolden (August 2008)

Race and Nature from Transcendentalism to the Harlem Renaissance
By Paul Outka (August 2008)

RACE AND NATURE FROM TRANSCENDENTALISM TO THE HARLEM RENAISSANCE

Paul Outka

RACE AND NATURE FROM TRANSCENDENTALISM TO THE HARLEM RENAISSANCE
Copyright © Paul Outka, 2008.

All rights reserved.

First published in 2008 by
PALGRAVE MACMILLAN®
in the US—a division of St. Martin's Press LLC,
175 Fifth Avenue, New York, NY 10010.

Where this book is distributed in the UK, Europe and the rest of the world,
this is by Palgrave Macmillan, a division of Macmillan Publishers Limited,
registered in England, company number 785998, of Houndmills,
Basingstoke, Hampshire RG21 6XS.

Palgrave Macmillan is the global academic imprint of the above companies
and has companies and representatives throughout the world.

Palgrave® and Macmillan® are registered trademarks in the United States,
the United Kingdom, Europe and other countries.

ISBN-13: 978–0–230–60296–0

Library of Congress Cataloging-in-Publication Data

Outka, Paul.
    Race and nature from transcendentalism to the Harlem
Renaissance / Paul Outka.
        p. cm.—(Signs of race)
        ISBN 0–230–60296–7 (alk. paper)
        1. Racism—United States—History—19th century. 2. Racism—
United States—History—20th century. 3. African Americans—
Race identity. 4. Whites—Race identity—United States.
5. Philosophy of nature—United States—History. 6. Wilderness
areas—Social aspects—United States—History. 7. Wilderness
areas—Political aspects—United States—History. 8. Environmentalism—
Social aspects—United States—History. 9. Environmentalism—
Political aspects—United States—History. 10. United States—Race
relations. I. Title.

E185.61.O88 2008
305.800973—dc22   2008000235

A catalogue record of the book is available from the British Library.

Design by Newgen Imaging Systems (P) Ltd., Chennai, India.

First edition: August 2008

10 9 8 7 6 5 4 3 2 1

Transferred to Digital Printing in 2010.

Contents

ILLUSTRATIONS

Series Editors' Preface

The first thing you see when you enter the permanent exhibits at the Birmingham Civil Rights Institute is a pair of drinking fountains. Over one hangs a sign that says "White." Over the other hangs a sign that says "Colored."

To the extent that every social identity is to some degree local, the meanings of race in Birmingham, Alabama, necessarily differ, in some demographic and historical particulars, from the meanings of race in North Dakota and Northern Ireland, New York and New South Wales, Cape Town, and Calcutta. But the same questions can be asked everywhere in the English-speaking world.

How do people signal a racial identity?

What does that racial identity signify?

This series examines the complex relationships between race, ethnicity, and culture in the English-speaking world from the early modern period (when the English language first began to move from its home island into the wider world) into the postcolonial present, when English has become the dominant language of an increasingly globalized culture. English is now the medium of a great variety of literatures, spoken and written by many ethnic groups. The racial and ethnic divisions between (and within) such groups are not only reflected in, but also shaped by, the language we share and contest.

Indeed, such conflicts in part determine what counts as "literature" or "culture."

Every volume in the series approaches race from a transracial, interdisciplinary, intercultural perspective. Each volume in the series focuses on one aspect of the cross-cultural performance of race, exploring the ways in which "race" remains stubbornly local, personal, and present.

We no longer hang racial signs over drinking fountains. But the fact that the signs of race have become less obvious does not mean that they have disappeared, or that we can or do ignore them. It is the purpose of this series to make us more conscious, and more critical, readers of the signs that have separated, and still separate, one group of human beings from another.

Those signs are often versions of "No Trespassing," the assertion that certain territories "belong" to one set of people but not another. Members of our species routinely transform neutral "spaces" into social "places," in ways that lend themselves to racial coding. So it should surprise no one that the American fascination with "nature" has always been entangled in the American obsession with "race."

Thus, although Paul Outka's project focuses on American literature in the decades between Crèvecoeur (1782) and Hurston (1937), it begins much closer to home, in 1991, with a very public clash between antiracist and conservation activists, between black liberation theology and white ecocriticism. Outka reexamines our past in order to disentangle the threads that have led us to our knotted present. In that respect, Outka resembles most scholars currently working in critical race studies or in ecocriticism.

What distinguishes Outka is his ambition, and ability, to unite the two fields. He speaks with equal authority about Immanuel Kant and Frederick Douglass, Henry David Thoreau and Harriet Jacobs, Charles Chestnutt and John Muir. Such pairings retrace the relationship between aesthetic genres (sublimity and pastoral, slave narratives and transcendental nature writing) that have traditionally been segregated in different parts of our bookstores and our brains. Moreover, Outka connects those aesthetic categories to shifting racial categories (white and black, before and after the Civil War) and changing landscapes (from the originally forested eastern seaboard to the monocultural plantation system and its ecologically devastated postwar aftermath).

Race and Nature is not simply an act of critical bravura, an interdisciplinary tour de force (though it is that, too). Outka reweaves such seemingly diverse materials into a single narrative by showing us that they were, in fact, always part of the same story, a story that depended in part on systematically suppressing certain relationships. He retells that story by performing the most difficult critical feat of all: looking very closely at, and describing very precisely, what has been in front of us all along. In this case, what's in front of us are passages from many of the classic texts of America's multiracial literature. Outka reads, in America's texts and the places outside those texts, signs pointing to "moments of emptiness, possibility, and connection." Those signs have in the past often been used to "greenwash" American racism; Outka is not naively optimistic, and in fact he recognizes the impossibility of "purity," ethical or political, in any discussion of race. But Outka's rereading of our past, of the possibilities that lurk in emptiness, urges us and teaches us "to see black and white in green." And those are signs worth following.

Phillip D. Beidler and Gary Taylor

ACKNOWLEDGMENTS

This book would never have been completed without the generosity and support of a range of people and institutions. I began writing it a few years ago while teaching at the University of Maine at Farmington, and learned hugely from the comments and conversation of a range of colleagues and friends there, especially Gretchen Legler and Michael Johnson who both gave me valuable comments on early drafts. I also benefited greatly from discussions about the project and other environmental issues with Eric Brown, Daniel Gunn, Christine Darrohn, Michael Burke, Jeffrey Thomson, Ruth Hill, and many others. Doug and Judy Rawlings in particular taught me how rich and beautiful rural life can be, and how kind.

While at Maine, I had the great good fortune to be awarded a full-year American Council of Learned Societies/Andrew W. Mellon Junior Faculty Fellowship. With the grant and the generous additional support of UMF, I was able to take a full year off from teaching to work on the book. That one year saved me many, and I will always be grateful to the ACLS and the Mellon Foundation for giving me the chance to devote myself full-time to my scholarship. I owe a particular debt to friends and colleagues who wrote in support of my fellowship, including, especially, Mark Edmundson, my untiringly supportive and unfailingly insightful graduate director.

I also want to thank my current institution, Florida State University, for its generous support in helping me finish the manuscript, in particular for granting me a half-time teaching fellowship during my first and third semesters and for awarding me a First Year Assistant Professor grant as well to support scholarship over the summer. Special thanks are due my chair here, Ralph Berry, and my mentor and friend Andrew Epstein, who have both made the adjustment to life in a quite different sort of university both easy and exciting. I also want to thank in particular my colleague Gary Taylor, the editor of the "Signs of Race" series of which this book is a part. Gary has been supportive of the project from the very beginning of my time at

Florida State, and offered critically important help when I needed it most.

A number of other institutions and people have also helped greatly. I spent a summer in Charlottesville, Virginia, writing the prospectus for the book, and benefited there from library privileges extended to me by the University of Virginia. I moved from Farmington to Portland, Maine, in the course of writing the book, and relied on the assistance of the librarians at the University of Southern Maine. The librarians at the Digital Media Center at Florida State's Strozier Library provided invaluable aid in securing and preparing the images for the manuscript. I also had a very stimulating research trip early in the project to the Schomburg Center for Research in Black Culture at the New York Public Library, and I am grateful for the help I received there. For help with permissions I want to thank Itty Mathew at the New-York Historical Society, Julie Sopher at the Shelburne Museum in Vermont, and Erin M.A. Schleigh at the Museum of Fine Arts, Boston. I am especially grateful to Mason Stokes at Skidmore College for his very generous engagement with the project, and to Jahan Ramazani at the University of Virginia for his wonderful and ongoing support of my work. Finally a particular thanks is due David Wyatt at the University of Maryland who read drafts of most of the book, and did so out of sheer generosity, kindness, and his own intellectual curiosity. His suggestions and encouragement were invaluable to its development. I owe him much, a debt I hope to repay in part by trying to be as good to another junior scholar sometime in the future as David was to me.

Finally, I want to thank my family without whom I cannot imagine myself, much less the drafting and redrafting of this book. My parents, Gene Outka and Carole DeVore raised me in an intensely intellectual and imaginative environment, and have been there with love, support, friendship, and good advice throughout this long compositional process. My younger sister Jacqueline has been a smart, funny, and warm part of my life since I began graduate school. Thanks also to Lucy who walked ahead from graduate school to Florida. My wife's family has taken me to their heart in a way that begins to explain how kind and loving a sister and daughter they produced; my heartfelt thanks and love to Gerry, Radha, Jyoti, Michael, and Shakti. No one could have a finer sister, better friend, or more brilliant interlocutor than Elizabeth Outka. She read and reread most everything here, and certainly is, in large measure, responsible for whatever is good in it. My two-year-old son, Isaac, gives me more joy than I thought humanly possible; to him I owe some of the very happiest moments of my life. Finally, this book is dedicated to my wife, Uma, my closest friend, the love of my life, and the first and last reader of everything.

1

INTRODUCTION: THE SUBLIME
AND THE TRAUMATIC

In 1991, an umbrella organization of environmental justice activists sent a sharply critical open letter to ten of the largest environmental organizations in the United States, accusing them of "environmental racism." The letter charged that the groups focused monothematically on wilderness preservation, paid scant attention to the vastly unequal exposure of minority communities to toxic waste, diesel particulates, agricultural pesticides, and lead contamination, and were indifferent to the almost entirely white composition of their workforce. Most of the groups that received the letter (particularly Greenpeace and the Sierra Club) responded positively, subsequently paying greater attention to environmental justice concerns and recruiting people of color to serve on their professional staffs. Still, the letter exposed a much deeper racial fault line in American environmentalism than could be mended by shifting priorities and altering hiring practices.[1] As the black liberation theologian James Cone laments,

> Until recently, the ecological crisis has not been a major theme in the liberation movements in the African American community. "Blacks don't care about the environment" is a typical comment by white ecologists. Racial and economic justice has been at best only a marginal concern in the mainstream environmental movement. "White people care more about the endangered whale and the spotted owl than they do about the survival of young blacks in our nation's cities" is a well-founded belief in the African American community. (138)

Although both people of color and whites are deeply engaged in environmental struggles, the nature each group is concerned with remains markedly different.[2] One environment is inhabited, toxic; the other is uninhabited, wild, pure, untouched except by the gaze of the privileged visitor. American wilderness in all its empt(ied) glory remains a largely white preserve, while urban, polluted landscapes have long been identified with people of color.

This book analyzes the cultural history of the racialized split between an ahistorical and vulnerable wilderness ever in need of defense and a degraded and exploitable "other" nature. Race and nature have been profoundly entangled—and bitterly divisive—constructions since the first European colonization of the "New" World. This simultaneous division and imbrication, I argue, is an often hidden but always formative thematic of the slave narratives and transcendentalist abolitionism. The thematic emerges explicitly in late nineteenth- and early twentieth-century America with the founding of the conservation movement and the so-called Great Migration in the wake of the failure of Reconstruction. The book is divided into eight interlocked chapters that examine this immensely complex period of natural and cultural transition. I argue throughout the book that sublimity and trauma represent two racially disjunct resolutions of a similar moment when a given subject's identity merges with the nonhuman natural, and that the racial and environmental schism marked by that disjunction is central to the tangled ways nature and racial subjectivity have been constructed in America.

In the last few years, a number of ecocritics have pointed out that far from being natural, the wilderness is a racially and culturally particular construction with intellectual and aesthetic origins in Romantic sublimity and American transcendentalism, a construction institutionalized by the late nineteenth-century conservation movement of Muir, Pinochet, and Roosevelt that created the national park system.[3] Under such readings, "wilderness" functions in almost definitionally ideological terms. It marks a dehistoricized space in which the erasure of the histories of human habitation, ecological alteration, and native genocide that preceded its "wild" valorization is, literally, naturalized. As Stuart Hall notes, "the hope of every ideology is to naturalize itself out of History into Nature, and thus to become invisible, to operate unconsciously."[4] Such unconsciousness is reflected, for example, in John Muir's journal entry celebrating the wildness of his lakeside camp in Yosemite—"no foot seems to have neared it"—written almost on the spot where Chief Tenaya of the Yosemite Miwok people was captured by Major Savage (really) of the Mariposa Brigade twenty-five years earlier.[5] The absence of people of color from a nature defined by the absence of people—except, of course, for the leisured Romantic observer—is perhaps unsurprising. It is certainly at the

root of the larger, racially tinged, antiurbanism that afflicts mainstream environmentalism to this day.

The brutal history of the "removal" of Native Americans from the
natural places they inhabited and shaped has been extensively examined, and the ways Native subjectivity was constructed by whites as
synonymous with the "savage" American wilderness has also received
significant critical attention. Similarly, Annette Kolodny's important
work in the 1970s established a critical tradition of aligning American
nature with a feminized and domesticated pastoral, a landscape
"framed" by men in ways that mirrored disciplinary gender relations.
Her work reflected a larger insistence in ecofeminism on the intersection between ecological violence and an often racially marked misogyny, an analysis generally predicated on an alliance of the natural with
the female.[6] Only recently, however, have a few essays appeared that
address how the wilderness is constructed as a white-only space.[7] And
while the role of the natural sublime in the construction of both valorized wilderness and white male American identity has been celebrated
since (at least) Teddy Roosevelt's presidency, we still do not have a
sustained analysis of the ecological effects of the sublime and its mul-
tifaceted relation to the construction of race.[8]

That the intersection of nature and race—perhaps the two most
perniciously reified constructions in American culture—has yet to be
thoroughly examined underscores the longstanding, often normative,
whiteness of ecocriticism.[9] It also suggests a much harder fought
anthropocentrism in critical race studies that inverted the terrible historical legacy of making people of color signify the natural, as a prelude to exploiting both. This legacy—in which whites viewed black
people as part of the natural world, and then proceeded to treat them
with the same mixture of contempt, false reverence, and real exploitation that also marks American environmental history—inevitably
makes the possibility of an *uncomplicated* union with the natural world
less readily available to African Americans than it has been to whites
who, by and large, have not suffered from such a history. To have "the
survival of young blacks in our nation's cities" come in second to the
"endangered whale and the spotted owl" in the regard of some white
environmentalists thus implicitly references, indeed repeats, a much
older trauma. For Cone, this split fundamentally distorts both the
struggle for racial justice and for the environment: "People who fight
against white racism but fail to connect it to the degradation of the
earth are anti-ecological—whether they know it or not. People who
struggle against environmental degradation but do not incorporate in
it a disciplined and sustained fight against white supremacy are

racists—whether they acknowledge it or not" (138). While Cone goes further than I would—or at least I take a much longer historical route in what follows to get there—clearly the time for a critical dialogue between those interested in deconstructing "nature" and in those engaged by deconstructing "race" is long overdue.

Mainstream environmentalism, ecocriticism, deep ecology, ecofeminism, and other largely (though not exclusively) white forms of environmentally engaged writing generally agree that nature is valuable in itself, that an association between the human and the natural is salutary, at least for the human, and that the human/natural binary needs to be questioned, if not entirely done away with. All well and good. But these are principles that uncritically assume a much less fraught relation between the natural world and the human than that experienced by many African Americans. Such a view refuses to recognize the racial privilege arguably inherent in the blanket notion that "Nature is sacred." Which is not to say that Nature isn't (or is) or that people of all "races" do not often find great emotional and spiritual value in their relation to the nonhuman natural. But it is to call explicit attention to the very different ways that a relation to the natural has historically signified along sharply divided racial lines. It is to insist that critics, especially ecocritics, pay attention to the human as well as natural history of the ground we stand on when we speak. Looking down, there may be bones and ashes; breathing in, a sickly sweet smell; listening, the sound of dogs; looking out, strange fruit. When we can see this, as well as the mountain, we may be seeing something that looks more like the American landscape in all its contradictory nature, rather than a mystical and romanticized construction writ sublimely large.

This book attempts such double-vision, such historicized seeing, in an examination of how natural experience became racialized in nineteenth- and early twentieth-century America. I am fundamentally interested in the history of the intersection between the construction of racial identity and natural experience, in what sort of ecological and human consequences have flowed from the conjunction of differing racial subjects and particular nonhuman natural environments in this period.[10] In focusing on the historic intersection between the construction of racial identity and natural experience I strive to make neither race nor nature a privileged term, to avoid the twin errors of either a racial anthropocentrism or an ahuman "deep" ecology. Put another way, my own commitments to the natural world and to antiracism both inform the book's analysis and place some important boundaries on what I consider. These boundaries focus the book on race and nature, on the construction of whiteness and blackness, and on a particular period in American history, and each carries certain risks, as I examine below.

First, while my approach is influenced by ecofeminism's insistence on a constitutive link between intrahuman oppression and ecological violence, throughout the book race, rather than gender, provides the fundamental analytic category. In making race primary, I mean neither to overlook how gender inflects both racial and natural experience, nor to argue that race is somehow more important than gender in understanding how natural experience has been constructed, nor, certainly, to render normative white male experiences of the natural world. Quite the opposite; indeed this project is perhaps most profoundly engaged by denaturalizing those white male experiences and the white male subjectivity that emerges from them. So I examine a wide variety of texts produced by both women and men and pay close attention to the ways that gender inflects both natural and racial experience, in, for example, an analysis of the pastoral and the twinned figures of the slave concubine and the white Southern belle, or the ways real and imagined male sexual violence is naturalized, or the way gender inflects sublimity. While throughout my analysis I am acutely conscious of how racial subjects are always also gendered and classed subjects, the fact remains that race has often been slighted in ecocritical conversation. I want to engage that specific problem in a way that does not replicate the important work that ecofeminism has already performed.

To use "race" as an analytic category is always to risk reductive description, however central such reductive descriptions were to the period of American history with which I am concerned. Such distortions are to some extent unavoidable, a traumatic echo of the violence and distortion that marks the history of the construction of race in America. Writing about race (or gender, or class, or sexual preference/practice, or the many other categories we employ to group subjects) privileges it in a way that risks (at least) subsuming other ways identity is marked and shaped. I do hope to mitigate that distortion in part by engaging many different texts and authors, and I remain throughout explicitly self-conscious about the dangers of suppressing difference in favor of intellectual tidiness. And my formative insistence in this project that race and nature should always be understood as historically interdependent constructions itself works against reifying either nature or the white/black binary. As Margo Crawford insists in her Preface to the March 2005 issue of *American Literature, Erasing the Commas: RaceGenderClassSexualityRegion*, an "intersectional" approach to these all-too-privileged signifiers as "both the method of analysis and the content most worthy of analysis" is an approach that "testifies that enactments of race, gender, class, sexuality, and, also, region cannot be separated" (1). This project's insistence on the imbrication of natural experience, environmental violence, and the reification of black and white racial identity (in particular) attempts a form of such "intersectionality." Although my emphasis on "region" incorporates the nonhuman natural in ways that perhaps Crawford may not have intended, and race and nature are explicitly privileged in my analysis over other intersections, this book is nevertheless deliberately located at what Crawford calls the contemporary "critical juncture" that "uncover[s] how the constructs of race, gender, class, sexuality, and region construct *each other*" (1).

The challenge of Crawford's call for intersectionality is two-fold. First, and most important, she is right to see these five terms (at least) as always already entangled in any subject position. A focus on any of them in isolation threatens what she calls "pure logocentrism, the recreation of the old tired binaries" (1). But, second, the impossible exponential demands of attending to the interaction of all five variables means that any intersectional project must privilege a few points of intersection at the expense of a wide range of other vitally important combinations. An explicit consciousness of how that privileging inevitably leads us away from the first point is vital. I am certainly aware of this project's vast scope and consequent incompleteness, a limitation that haunts all intersectional projects. I neither mean to, nor could, offer an exhaustive study of the various critical theories, literary texts, and authors that I take up. Certainly I do not claim universal applicability for this critical narrative. My goal is more modest: to say something interesting and broadly "right" about a topic that, at least in its initial formulation here, demands such an expansive treatment.

Even though this project springs in part from the environmental justice movement's contemporary observation that the wilderness experience celebrated by mainstream environmental groups has traditionally excluded people of color generally, the second limit of the analysis is my focus on a particularly important racial binary: the construction of whiteness and blackness. Such a focus is not intended to make blackness uncritically synonymous with race, to make the white/black racial binary the only color line, or to ignore the important ways that naturalized white supremacy has constructed other racial subjects. Indeed, for most of American history, statements about race were usually also statements about nature, about "natural" racial differences, whether created by God or evolution. Racism—whether directed against African Americans, Native Americans, Chinese laborers, or Irish immigrants—almost always asserts the supposedly subhuman or "animal" qualities of its object in contradistinction to white/human supremacy, and thus its violence resonates both eco-critically and intersubjectively.

While my focus on black and white racial experience narrows the study, a much broader focus on "race and nature" would risk conflating the very different forms of various racial experience in American history, or, at least, approaching each superficially. I choose to emphasize the intersection between white and black natural experiences for two primary reasons. First, under slavery the conflation of African Americans and nature took a uniquely physical form. A metaphor became, for whites, literal. Rather than being a quick and dirty way of intensifying a slur—the Irish were often called "vermin," for example—slavery was a systematically materialized ontology. While nineteenth-century ethnography had elaborate classificatory schemes that emplaced various "racial" groups according to their distance from the bestial, the "Anglo-Saxon" or "Teutonic," or "Aryan" almost always occupied the top and the African the bottom, the place nearest the animal.[11] Even though whites claimed superiority over just about everyone, for most of American history, they reserved slavery for black people, and they did so because of this supposedly absolute "natural" inferiority.

Second, slavery explicitly connected racial violence and environmental degradation. Under slavery, whites frequently conflated African Americans with domesticated animals and pastoral agriculture, an association that morphed in the so-called hard racism of the postbellum period into the figure of the Black Beast that signified in part the degeneration of that antebellum pastoral. This association between human subjects and a commodified nature existed in sharp contradistinction to the other central intersection between white supremacy and environmental practice: the association between Native Americans and the precapitalist "untouched" savage wilderness. This association hardly proved salutary for either the wilderness or for the Native peoples, but—cold comfort—nevertheless afforded greater respect to both than did an association with the slave pastoral. Slavery's conflation of African Americans and the natural world is, I would argue, the clearest point where racial violence and a modern, commodifying environmental violence reveal a common root.

The third limit is temporal, and perhaps less controversial: the book is largely concerned with nineteenth- and early twentieth-century U.S. history and culture. This period encompasses, for example, the intersections among transcendentalism, slavery, and abolition before the war; among Reconstruction, "scientific racism," clear cutting, species extinction, and the founding of the national park system in the

postbellum period; and among lynching, Jim Crow, the so-called
Great Migration and the Harlem Renaissance, and the founding of
the conservation movement after Reconstruction and in the early
twentieth century. While I incorporate earlier and later work, and
believe my analysis sheds light on our contemporary moment, these
hundred-odd years are clearly essential for understanding the entangled constructions of whiteness, blackness, and nature.

The rest of this book is devoted to examining those intersections, how
they echo each other, how the parties involved engage in rituals of
purification in which their interconnections are repressed. Following
this introduction, my second and third chapters, "The Colonial
Pastoral, Abolition, and the Transcendentalist Sublime" and " 'Behold
a Man Transformed into a Brute': Slavery and Antebellum Nature"
analyze the interlocked construction of race and nature before the
Civil War. I begin by examining how whiteness became associated
with the conversion of the wilderness into the pastoral in the eyes of
early European settlers. This identification of whiteness and the pastoral came under enormous pressure in the antebellum period when slavery became central to the national discourse. I read transcendentalism's
Romantic sublime embrace of the wilderness and its emphasis on freedom and individual self-creation as an attempt to reconstitute whiteness's identification with nature in the context of slavery. My
examination of slave narratives focuses on how slavery depended in
part on a racialized association of the subject with a degraded and
commodified pastoral, particularly with domesticated animals and
monoculture agriculture. I show how this traumatic reduction echoes
through writers like Douglass and Jacobs, and how they struggle to
turn natural identification in a more salutary direction.

Chapters four through eight examine representations of entwined
ecological and racial violence that erupted throughout African American
and white cultural production during Reconstruction, Jim Crow,
and the Great Migration. I am particularly engaged with the
racially saturated construction of two vitally important landscapes in
late nineteenth-century America—the plantation pastoral and the
wilderness sublime. Chapter four, "Trauma, Postbellum Nostalgia,
and the Lost Pastoral," takes up the reductive pastoral nostalgia of
"Lost Cause" writers like Thomas Nelson Page and Joel Chandler
Harris, and the blackface ex-slave narrators they use to rewrite the
traumatic history of the antebellum plantation as a racially harmonious Garden. Chapter five, "Trauma and Metamorphosis in Charles
Chesnutt's Conjure Tales," reads Chesnutt's work as intervening on

this tradition, insisting, in the central trope of conjuration, on the profound dangers a merge with the natural world posed to African-American subjects before and after the war. The sixth chapter, "Strange Fruit," explores how the vicious cultural logic of racist evolutionary theory produces a series of evermore threatening images of blackness, from the "missing link" to the "Black Beast Rapist," a series that terminates in the surreal, ghastly hybridization of the land, and the black body that the song's title has named for more than fifty years. "White Flight," the seventh chapter, argues that we should see the ahistorical ecstasy of the Western sublime and the early conservation movement, particularly the awestruck writing of John Muir, as in part a recoil from the terrible brutality required to establish and maintain the color line, an attempt to shift the axis of the country from north and south, to east and west. The identification of whiteness in this period with a sublime landscape at once transcendent and vulnerable was central to whiteness's emergence as an ahistorical, racially unmarked normative identity. The final chapter, "Migrations," takes up the often overlooked ways that the relationship between blackness and nature was renegotiated in African-American cultural production in and around the Great Migration. Specifically, I examine the intersection between racial terror and nature in two stories by Angelina Weld Grimké, the figuration of the Great Migration in Toomer's *Cane,* and Hurston's engagement with the pastoral, the sublime, and the history of naturalized racial degradation in *Their Eyes Were Watching God.*

As this list of chapter topics demonstrates, to form and maintain two landscapes and two races—one endlessly exploitable, traumatized, and enslaved, and one unspoiled, sublime, "outside" of race, culture, and history, eternally free—out of a single place and a single species necessitates a wide-ranging and ever-renewed ideological police action. This book works against that action, works to blur the border between those racialized natures and those naturalized races in the hope that by trying to see green in black and white, we might eventually come to see black and white in green.

The chapters that follow are shaped by my readings in a range of different theoretical discourses, including sublimity, trauma theory, ecocriticism, and critical race theory, particularly whiteness studies. Before turning to an analysis of specific literary and cultural texts, I want in the remainder of the Introduction to clarify how I understand these discourses, and to outline how they relate to my larger concerns with the intersecting constructions of nature and race.

GROUNDING THE COLOR LINE

By insisting on the profound imbrication of natural and racial experience, among other things I hope to avoid the tautological binary choice between essentialist and antiessentialist positions that often afflicts attempts to analyze the color line from within its own logic. Samira Kawash calls this "a central paradox of the color line: [that] it essential-izes racial difference even as such difference can be shown to have no essence," and asserts that "the play of racial identity and hybridity must be considered in some way that avoids the over-burdened critical oppo-sition of essentialism and anti-essentialism" (14). To assert an antiessen-tialist critique from within a closed system that views blackness and whiteness as mutually constructing difference risks re-essentializing each term in its relational definition, most commonly in a reinscription of blackness as essentially not-whiteness.[12] As Kawash notes acutely:

> The doubled aspect of the color line, as both a historical location of domination and struggle and as a seemingly external, absolute com-mand, suggests that the question of essentialism with regard to race must always be suspended in an uneasy tension: on the one hand, there can be no essential black identity, but, on the other hand, blackness is always determined as an essence insofar as its very existence is dependent on its being essentially (although not necessarily in any particular property) different from whiteness, and it is precisely this essential difference that is continually founded and conserved by the color line. Thus, the essential-izing moment of the color line cannot simply be dismissed as error. The critical task, then, is to confront the essentialism of the color line without resorting to yet another version of essentialism that would function as a naturalizing explanation for the way things are.... Therefore, it must be addressed doubly, as both the origin of an absolutely real division and as the project of an utterly false and impossible distinction. (19–20)

In demonstrating how the color line has been historically grounded in nature and natural experience and how race has often marked the sorts of natural experience available to a given subject, I hope both to break open the entrapping binary logic of the color line while still attending to the unfortunate ways blackness and whiteness have managed to appear historically as mutually constituting essences. Seeing race and nature as fundamentally entwined reveals a key source of the "natural-izing explanation for the way things are." By focusing on how racial experience intersected with nature, we can avoid oscillating between the construction of white and black identity and instead begin to trace the historical narrative by which whiteness became an unmarked normative "humanity" and blackness solidified into a clearly marked racial essence. These two processes occurred not simply in a negotiation internal to themselves, but through reference to a third term—nature—a larger context that grounded (literally) both, while continuously enacting its own disappearance into the (literal) background. And not only did nature provide a critically important origin for the production of an essential blackness and a largely invisible whiteness, the naturalization of race allowed race and racial hierarchy to piggy-back on and recursively influence a preexisting and absolute human/natural hierarchy in ways that ecocritics are only beginning to consider.

As should be clear by now, I do not understand either whiteness or blackness as natural, but as constructions that I, among many others, both "white" and "black," would like to see pass genuinely, and not just putatively, out of an association with pigment and "biology," and into the ungrounded realm of culture.[13] In focusing on one origin story for the naturalization of black and white racial identities, I hope to acknowledge the tenacity of those constructions while avoiding what Paul Gilroy sharply notes is the "pious ritual in which we always agree that 'race' is invented but then are required to defer to its embeddedness in the world and to accept that the demand for justice requires us nevertheless innocently to enter the political arenas it helps to mark out" (*Against Race*, 52). Such racial "innocence" is not attainable to the extent one understands oneself as an historically constituted subject; at its base, to seek such innocence is to seek a place from which to speak outside of one's historical and cultural context. Indeed, the point of such a "pious ritual," especially for whites, is often to establish a politically and morally extraracial "pure" or "right" position, an authorial voice emanating not only from within race but also from without it—what Mike Hill memorably calls "the epistemological stickiness and ontological wiggling immanent in whiteness," or what Vron Ware and Les Back call "being in two places at once," both "tie[d] historically into a system of race privilege from which it is hard to escape" and, "by providing a critique of whiteness,...situate[d]...outside that system" (29).[14] It doesn't seem to me possible to resolve this contradiction, and, moreover, I am wary of spending too much time making it—me—the subject. Nevertheless, calling explicit and uncomfortable attention to the historical reasons behind that contradiction is vital, and certainly preferable to falling silent or just not worrying about it.

My interest is largely in the *unmarking* of whiteness, its literal and figurative naturalization—what Toni Morrison calls the "fishbowl," the "structure that transparently (and invisibly) permits the ordered life it contains to exist in the larger world"—and less so in the more straightforward ways that whiteness named itself openly when in conflict or dialogue with racial others (*Playing*, 17).[15] So I am not as engaged in what follows by the ultimately "successful" struggles of a variety of immigrant groups—the Irish in the nineteenth century, for example, as Noel Ignetiev has documented so effectively—to be classified as white, or by similar struggles by poor whites to distinguish themselves in absolute racial terms from African Americans. In focusing on what I will call whiteness's "transparence," I appreciate the danger of what Annalee Newitz and Matthew Wray in their work on "white trash" call "essentialist multiculturalism and racial theory, which posits that whites are a monolithic and unified group wielding absolute, racist power across lines of class, gender, sexuality, and other forms of difference" (183). But while *whites* may not be a "monolithic and unified group" in their various forms of embodiment that often cross other (unfortunately) determinative categories like class, gender, and sexuality, *whiteness* in its unmarked power continues to function in its own right, in ways subject to recognition and critique.

While the critique is broadly easy, the recognition is paradoxically more difficult. The temptation is to move from the correct recognitions that (1) race is a construction that has historically posed as an essence, some shifting set of qualities that supposedly adheres in those deemed "not white" and (2) that this historical construction of race as being "not white" leaves whiteness unmarked, normative, to the incorrect assertion (3) that whiteness is "really" a racial identity, at least in the same way that being "of color" is. The unmarking of whiteness does not hide some positive racial content that needs to be revealed; that unmarking "is what it is," the limning of a shaped absence. The reference of whiteness is a cultural space *intentionally* left blank, a frictionless surface for the racially unencumbered, largely visible and non-mysterious exercise of political and economic power. Piercing whiteness's veil, unmasking it as "really" another form of racial identity is to miss much of whiteness's force. Whiteness is that which creates the "problem" of race in Others; in itself it is how it feels *not* to be a problem.[16]

This is not to say, of course, that "whiteness" doesn't have a reference, or that white power is not utterly real, or that "white culture" does not arguably have recognizably distinct features, especially when viewed from a position outside of it.[17] Nor is it to say that blackness is "really" a race either. Neither is an essence, and neither was simply invented in relation to the other. I am only asserting that they were constructed differently in form as well as content, and that it is easy for critics to lose sight of that formal difference. In what follows I hope to analyze one important way that the fictional "reality" of blackness as a race was instantiated, and to do so without reinscribing whiteness as "really" a race "too." This necessitates not only a clear look at how white and black were defined in relation to each other, but how that binary was itself constructed within a largely unacknowledged natural context. In this I share Mason Stokes's "central contention...that, whiteness works best—in fact, that it works only—when it attaches itself to other abstractions" (13).[16] If "whiteness studies" is to avoid, even partially, instantiating whiteness in the same gesture that tries to do away with it, I think it has to see whiteness as emerging not simply *from* the white/black racial binary or *despite* other determinative forms of subject construction, but, in Stokes's words, "to yoke whiteness to other normative structures" (187–88). Accordingly, this study is not intended to be another attempt generally to retheorize "whiteness" or so-called whiteness studies.[19] Instead, I focus on the specific material intersection between racial construction and natural experience as a central "normative structure" in producing white—and black—racial identity in nineteenth-century America. I am concerned to examine how blackness and whiteness were historically produced in and through particular sorts of environmental practices, from agriculture to hiking, from slavery to sublimity.

My analysis focuses on moments of transformative instability in the relation between human and natural, times when the division between the subject and nature breaks down and the identities of both become uncertain. This breakdown, when the human is poised on the brink of a collapse into the natural, is also a moment of unspeakability, of blankness, a linguistic collapse that depends in an absolutely material way on the nonhuman natural. To be "like" nature is, at least temporarily, to be speechless, outside of the text, to be connected to someThing that, however much it is a human invention, is also not one.[20] As ecocriticism has been pointing out for some time, "nature" is both a construct and isn't; the term refers at once to a product of human culture and language, and to an unknowable realm outside of any text. Our theoretical accounts of nature must have, as Lawrence Buell declares succinctly, "a dual accountability to matter and to discursive mentation" (*Environmental Imagination*, 92). Claims for nature's Reality outside of human construction are, of course, essentialist, or can be, but *not*—emphatically—in the same way as an essentialist assertion of an intrinsic black/white/male/female/etc. identity is. The latter is

entirely false, the former is only half so. Indeed, the historical conflation these two quite different essentialist claims is precisely, I will
argue, what made blackness and whiteness such persistently "natural" constructions—the constructedness of race was obscured by its
association with unconstructed nature, an operation carried out
under the cover, as it were, of a moment of genuinely unrepresentable instability in the relation between human and natural.

The challenges of writing about such moments are manifold. Most
important, at least for my purposes, is to preserve a distinction
between the eruptive experience of a natural world existing outside of
human representation, a world of which—nevertheless, utterly and
fatally—we are irrevocably a part, and the myriad ways that ambiguity
is resolved, generally to ground some all-too-human political, cultural, or racial construct. When we say "nature" we reference two
quite different things simultaneously: something we know exists but
cannot talk about (at least without rendering it textual in the process),
and something we cannot stop talking about and (should) know does
not necessarily exist outside of our talking. To conflate the two is one
of the oldest tricks in the ideological book. Accordingly, at the core
of this book's argument is an examination of how such moments of
instability and representational collapse resolve or fail to resolve and
of what sort of racial identities and truths are instantiated, empowered, and naturalized in the wake of these intensely ambiguous
confrontations between human and natural.

Two primary theoretical modes—sublimity and trauma—govern this
transition from ambiguity to naturalized definition, each marking one
end of a continuum of possible resolutions of such moments. I insist
on both their linkage and difference, viewing each as historically
simultaneous resolutions of the in-fact irreducibly open question of
the relation between human identity and the nonhuman natural. Such
a linkage suggests that any critical analysis of race or nature in isolation
from the other is fundamentally incomplete. But while both sublimity
and trauma are discourses of unrepresentability, naming intensely
meaningful experiences that in some way exceed the subject's descriptive powers or refuse symbolic encoding in memory, they are also quite
different for the racially (un)marked subjects who experience them.

THE SUBLIME

Despite its manifest importance as a template for constructing nature
and natural experience, the theoretical tradition of the sublime has

received little sustained attention from ecocritics.[21] While the sublime's historical and cultural centrality to nineteenth-century conceptions of nature is regularly noted, such invocations rarely engage the complex and contradictory meaning of sublimity, both historically and in contemporary philosophy and literary theory. Part of the difficulty lies in the inherent ambiguity of the term; "the sublime" references a very loose and very wide array of experiences in which a subject is overwhelmed in a way that seems intensely meaningful. And in the several hundred years of theoretical speculation on sublimity in the West, that meaning has ranged equally widely, from Romantic profundity to Jamesonian postmodernism, from St. Theresa's ecstasy to Burke's terror, from the immediacy of Lyotard's avant-garde to Kant's inconceivability of the infinite. Both cigarettes and sweatshops are (apparently) sublime.[22] The difficulty of understanding the term is compounded further by the fact that sublimity functions both as an experiential mode—hiking the mountain—and as a textual mode—the painting of the mountain or other forms of nature "writing." It encompasses engagement and voyeurism, participation and observation, praxis and theory, both the rush of experience and the representation of it afterwards.

My initial interest here is to clarify the referent of the sublime as applied to the natural world and natural experience, without shutting down the powerful ambiguity that is central to it, an ambiguity that will ultimately prove vital to my argument about the applicability of the sublime both to ecocriticism and to the construction of race. Let me begin broadly then, calling the sublime an experience of potent uncertainty, a moment in which the identities of self and world become energetically interpenetrative. While this definition has clear affinities with versions of the Romantic sublime offered by Thomas Weiskel and others, I want to emphasize the distinction between the eruptive moment of radical uncertainty that my definition names, and its resolution, a resolution in which that initial ambiguity is converted into a conclusive meaning. While traditional narrative models of sublime experience—that move first from quiescence, then to eruption, and finally to resolution—helpfully organize the chaos of the experience, they also embed the intense atemporality of the eruptive moment in a larger sequential framework of emergence from some generally unexamined and therefore normative state, and effectively make the telos of the eruption the final reflective conclusion. The sublime's eruptive moment is bracketed between an unexamined and naturalized origin it breaks out from and a resolution that exemplifies the "real" meaning of the experience. The eruption becomes an unruly middle child, a transition between realities. This narrative bracketing threatens to obscure how the sublime functions *both* as an anti-idealist and an idealist discourse, conjoining the very different moments when the unrepresentability of the natural world presents itself forcefully to the human subject, and the resolution of that unrepresentability in a retextualization of the world as the sign of a newly empowered subjectivity. By separating the sublime's phenomenological effect from its ontological "meaning," I want to see it as both, but not simultaneously, experiential and truth producing.

This distinction is vital to an ecocritical reading of the sublime, preserving the important moment of "contact" with an extratextual nature at the center of the experience against its conversion back into textuality. Thus understood, the sublime might be useful to contemporary ecocritical debates over how we can understand nature as both extra-human materiality and as human construct, offering a powerful model for blending a sense of nature as text with the sense of it also existing independently, unrepresentably outside our textual constructions, with claims and rights of its own. Indeed, one definition of the natural sublime might be the moment when nature-as-extratextual-materiality and nature-as-human-representation intersect, both the indescribable recognition of a subtextual living world that includes the human but is not exhausted by it, and the massive reification of nature as a symbol of whatever ideology tagged along on the hike.

To insist, ecocritically, that the natural Other matters fundamentally in the sublime experience, and shouldn't be simply folded into an anthropocentric resolution, intervenes in the tradition of speculation on the sublime in an important way. The sophisticated attention the sublime has recently received from critics like Ferguson, Ashfield, de Bolla, Freeman, Lyotard, and many others, rarely sees the disorienting engagement with the nonhuman natural world at the center of the sublime as ultimately important in itself, but largely as it manifests the ways language, gender, ideology, and the like construct subject and world.[23] While such work is certainly worthwhile, the failure of representation at the heart of sublime experience offers ecocritical resources lost to such an anthropocentric analysis.

This generally unnoted anthropocentrism arguably has its source in the enormous influence of Kant's *Critique of Judgment* in structuring contemporary understandings of sublimity. For Kant, the profound uncertainty at the moment of sublime eruption is merely the starting point of the analysis. This state of uncertainty is brought about either by the "mathematical sublime"—something that suggests the infinite, such as the night sky full of stars, or the ocean—or, closer to Burke, the "dynamical sublime"—something fearful that suggests physical power much greater than we possess, such as a mountain or a storm. In both cases, the mind is initially overwhelmed by the seeming incomprehensibility of the object before it. Infinity makes the mind reel when one tries to imagine it literally rather than as a concept. The sight of immense power can similarly be difficult to grasp in itself, stunning us by its sheer disproportion with our own physical abilities. But this feeling of being overwhelmed is not the sublime, but the precondition for it. The Kantian sublime occurs in the *resolution* of this feeling, in the conversion of a moment of profound uncertainty in the relation between subject and world into a moment of utter disconnection:

> Now, in the immensity of nature and in the insufficiency of our faculties to take in a standard proportionate to the aesthetical estimation of the magnitude of its *realm*, we find our own limitation, although at the same time in our rational faculty we find a different, nonsensuous standard, which has that infinity itself under it as a unity, in comparison with which everything in nature is small, and thus in our mind we find a superiority to nature even in its immensity. And so also the irresistibility of its might, while making us recognize our own physical impotence, considered as beings of nature, discloses to us a faculty of judging independently of and a superiority over nature, on which is based a kind of self-preservation entirely different from that which can be attacked and brought into danger by external nature. Thus humanity in our person remains unhumiliated, though the individual might have to submit to this dominion. In this way nature is not judged to be sublime in our aesthetical judgments in so far as it excites fear, but because it calls up that power in us (which is not nature) of regarding as small the things about which we are solicitous (goods, health, and life), and of regarding its might (to which we are no doubt subjected in respect of these things) as nevertheless without any dominion over us and our personality to which we must bow where our highest fundamental propositions, and their assertion or abandonment, are concerned. Therefore nature is here called sublime merely because it elevates the imagination to a presentation of those cases in which the mind can make felt the proper sublimity of its destination, in comparison with nature itself. (*Critique of Judgment*, 101)

Kant's sublime consists of the act of rejecting the external—nature—as a source of the sublime. Faced with the confusion brought on by the infinite or powerful, we recover our stability and achieve sublimity through our recognition of our own essential superiority to, and difference from, the natural world that created the confusion. Despite Kant's density and complexity, the underlying moves of his sublime are quite simple, if not indeed reductive, at least from the perspective of a reader deeply interested in the natural world that Kant so definitively rejects. In Kant's view, we are overwhelmed by some "object" presented to our senses. We recognize that there is something in us that is superior to anything sensory. The sublime begins and ends with this recognition. Nothing specific about the object is fundamentally important to the experience or changes its texture or flavor. Moreover, what the mind recognizes as "the proper sublimity of its destination, in comparison with nature itself," is always the same destination: the supersensible or noumenal, an utterly mysterious realm of pure freedom, a freedom that only expresses itself in our sensible world as moral law, defined as that which we would do if we were not caught in the causal, phenomenal world. We can know nothing about this supersensible realm, however, except that (1) it exists (as "a mere negative presentation" [*Critique of Judgment*, 115]) and (2) that nothing else, nothing "sensible" ultimately matters in itself, but only as it references the supersensible.

Kant's account of sublimity has shaped the subsequent tradition in (at least) two fundamental ways. First, after Kant, critics tend to understand the sublime in terms of its resolution. The sublime is not the potent ambiguity of its eruptive moment, but what happens afterward— the truth that the moment reveals or fails to reveal. The sublime becomes fundamentally a reflective rather than experiential mode. Second, Kant's influence leads critics to accomplish that resolution in a way structured by his noumenal/phenomenal distinction, *either* by asserting that the sublime is "really" transcendent or at least somehow ineffable, *or* that the sublime is "really" something much more ordinary—a punitive superego, a refusal to acknowledge one's temporality or to give up God, an ideological cover-up for various forms of oppression. Both claims often lead to important readings, and I will employ a version of the latter when I argue for the importance of sublimity in the construction of whiteness. But what I want to note here is how both forms of resolution generally dispense with the nonhuman natural that initiated the sublime. The phenomenal resolution does so by turning the uncertainty in the borders between self and nature into a repressed symbol of a human social, political, or psychological concern. What I am calling the noumenal claim—that the sublime names something fundamentally mysterious—dispenses with nature by "de-hypostatizing" that eruptive experience, rendering it conceptual at the cost of the particularity and importance of the (natural) object.[24] The *experience* of profound ambiguity becomes the *concept* of undecidability.[25]

Kant made the sublime ultimately productive of T/truth and a subject radically empowered at the expense of the landscape. To make ecocriticism useful to theories of the sublime, however, extratextual nature must not be reduced to a metaphysically disposable "out there," to mere materiality awaiting human transformation into anthropomorphized meaning. Such a reductive model replicates the history of exploitation of the wilderness quite precisely. To make sublimity useful to ecocriticism, the Kantian telos must be reversed, the eruptive stage of sublimity deployed against its resolution. While nature is as heavily textualized and invested a term as there is in the language, that does not mean that its referent is simply a human linguistic projection. Nature also does not *mean* anything; its importance for humans lies in part in the way it unmakes our constructions, an unmaking at the heart of the sublime. The point, emphatically, is not to choose between nature as Real and nature as construction, but to distinguish between the two.

To say, then, as I will, that the American wilderness sublime is white, is both "true," and a deeply problematic historical construction that has nothing to do with the wilderness, part of what Laura Doyle calls the sublime's "pivotal and strategic doubleness" (26). This dual construction is not simply an American innovation, but already implicit in the structure of Kant's sublime. The subject's assertion of categorical difference from the landscape at the peak of the Kantian sublime is also a form of self-assertion, of self-definition. Indeed it is a triumph of human dignity over physical power, a moment when the "humanity in our person remains unhumiliated, though the individual might have to submit to...dominion," the evocation of "that power in us (which is not nature) of regarding as small the things about which we are solicitous (goods, health, and life), and of regarding its might (to which we are no doubt subjected in respect of these things) as nevertheless without any dominion over us and our personality to which we must bow where our highest fundamental propositions, and their assertion or abandonment, are concerned." Such a moving assertion of human freedom and dignity, however, depends not only on our separation from a nature encoded as enemy rather than friend, but also on the ability of the subject to perform the sublime itself, to achieve his or her separation from the natural world. While the ability to produce the sublime is a triumphant mark of the subject's intrinsic freedom, Kant's earlier writing makes it clear that he does not view that ability as universal. The failure to produce the sublime is, accordingly, a mark of the subject's bondage and degradation. Hence, in an earlier speculation on the sublime, Kant's 1764 *Observations on the Feeling of the*

Beautiful and the Sublime, this failure becomes a sign of black racial inferiority.[26] Kant writes:

> The Negroes of Africa have by nature no feeling that rises above the trifling. Mr. Hume challenges anyone to cite a single example in which a Negro has shown talents, and asserts that among the hundreds of thousands of blacks who are transported elsewhere from their countries, although many of them have even been set free, still not a single one was ever found who presented anything great in art or science or any other praiseworthy quality, even though among the whites some continually rise aloft from the lowest rabble, and through superior gifts earn respect in the world. (Eze, 55)

Here "the Negroes of Africa" fail to produce the sublime, and do so because they have "by nature no feeling that rises above the trifling." This failure is then conjoined with a more generic form of racist hearsay in a way that assumes without argument that the failure to achieve sublimity is part and parcel of the more widespread failure of blacks to "present[] anything great whether in art or science or in any other praiseworthy quality," a failure explicitly contrasted with whites pulling themselves up by their (hiking) bootstraps.

Moreover, this inability of Africans to produce the sublime itself reflects the constitutively degrading influence of their (supposedly) tropical environment. As Kant writes in his essay "On the Different Races of Man," "damp heat promotes strong growth in animals in general; in short, the Negro is produced, well suited to his climate; that is, strong, fleshy, supple, but in the midst of the bountiful provision of his motherland lazy, soft, and dawdling" (Eze, 46). This earlier version of the explicitly racially marked sublime is, as Meg Armstrong notes, obscured by the "transcendental" account of natural sublimity in the third *Critique,* an account in which the appearance of the natural sublime object is "symptomatic of an erasure of cultural, national, and gender-based differences which had previously been a more prominent part of Kant's discussion of the sublime" (226).[27] But while obscured, it still continued to function as an implicit, and supposedly neutral, test of humanity, one Kant had already predicted Africans would fail en masse. When this Kantian test was applied to the conflation of African Americans and the natural world in slavery and subsequent forms of white American racism, the result, then, was preordained: both the assertion of the sublime as a primal scene for the construction of white identity and the assertion of absolute difference between the sublime white subject and its opposite in the "strong, fleshy, supple, lazy, soft, and dawdling" black/natural followed "naturally."[28]

Trauma, and the Sublime

In her deservedly influential collection, *Trauma: Explorations in Memory*, Cathy Caruth offers a straightforward definition of Post-Traumatic Stress Disorder (PTSD): "a response, sometimes delayed, to an overwhelming event or events, which takes the form of repeated, intrusive hallucinations, dreams, thoughts or behaviors stemming from the event, along with numbing that may have begun during or after the experience, and possibly also increased arousal to (and avoidance of) stimuli recalling the event" (3). PTSD is not defined simply as terrible grief in the face of some catastrophe; indeed, one clinical predictor of PTSD is emotional "numbness" when the event is actually occurring. Rather, the disorder is marked by the repeated eruption of traumatic stress *later*, a confusion fundamental to the disorder, and captured in the ambiguity of the very phrase "post-traumatic stress."

This delayed reaction often takes the form of a repetition compulsion, a quite literal reexperiencing of the initial trauma—a car backfires and the Iraqi war vet dives for cover in the city street, a sexual abuse survivor is terrified to leave the apartment after dark, a Holocaust survivor cannot bear to see trains depart sixty years later. Such moments of recollection are generally absolutely literal ("as if it occurred yesterday") rather than the repressed symbolic material of fantasy. This literality makes their reexperiencing itself traumatic, reinscribing the original unbearable moment in a kind of agonized feedback loop. PTSD can be particularly severe when the originating event erupts unexpectedly, catching its subject unawares. The result is frequently hypervigilance, what Freud calls *angstbereitschaft*, or the "readiness to feel anxiety."[29] When a severe blow catches a subject off guard, it often cannot be processed at the time, but returns again and again, in a repetition marked by a pathological anxiety produced as a sort of ex-post-facto readiness for the originary event.

Traumatic experience is literally unbearable when it actually occurs, impossible to assimilate into the structure of the mutually constituting representations of identity and world that define subjectivity. It is what Shoshanna Felman calls a "crisis of truth," Dori Laub "a record that has yet to be made," Henry Krystal "a void, a hole," in the psyche where "a registration" should be found (Caruth, *Trauma*, 6), Christina Zwarg, "thinking the 'unthought'" (67), and, more fully, Dominick LaCapra an "uncanny, radically destabilizing excess that threatens the breakdown not only of 'literary' conventions but of all conventions of language use, indeed the possibility of breakdown in every sense" (199). This breakdown sunders the subject; Caruth observes "something…that seems oddly to inhabit all traumatic experience [is] the inability fully to witness the event as it occurs, or the ability to witness the event fully only at the cost of witnessing oneself…. The force of this experience would appear to arise precisely, in other words, in the collapse of its understanding" (*Trauma*, 7). The failure of witnessing and the "collapse in understanding" in traumatic experience finds analogues in the sublime's definitional experience of potent ambiguity, including Longinus's ancient "vaunting joy," Burke's "overwhelming terror" and the collapse of the Imagination in Kant's account of the sublime in the *Critique of Judgment* in the Enlightenment, the eruption of "radical indeterminacy" central to Thomas Weiskel's analysis of Romantic sublimity (23), and François Lyotard's understanding of the sublime as "bearing pictorial or otherwise expressive witness to the inexpressible" in a postmodern analytic (*Inhuman*, 93). Like sublimity, trauma names a textual break or a limit in the ability of a subject to understand his or her world, a break that erupts suddenly and that reformulates both subject and world in its image subsequently. The traumatic event initiates what Judith Butler calls "a series of paradoxes": that "the past is irrecoverable and the past is not past," that "the past is the resource for the future and the future is the redemption of the past," that "loss must be marked and it cannot be represented," that "loss fractures representation itself and loss precipitates its own modes of expression" (467).

In noting this similarity between sublimity and trauma, however, it is important not simply to fold them into each other as different flavors of the unimaginable extratextual. Such a move, as Dominick LaCapra suggests in his writing on the Holocaust, can lead to an "(an)aesthetics of the sublime that indiscriminately valorizes the un(re)presentable or the experimentally transgressive" (223), assimilating the specific historical event or natural setting that produces the sublime/traumatic moment into a larger critically narcissistic discourse of unrepresentability and the limits of (comprehensible) textuality.[30] Where the natural sublime enshrines a representational disjunction, a moment when the material Otherness of the world pierces its linguistic representation, trauma retains an absolute materiality, initially in a hyperencoding of the literal details of the event coupled with an emotional "numbness" that refuses to incorporate it into the subject's self-construction, and the event's subsequent recurrence in all its raw, literal, immediacy. Trauma's materiality repeatedly disrupts the ongoing linguistic interplay between the construction of self and the construction of world that defines what it means to be in the present.

In this sense trauma inverts the Kantian framework for sublime experience found in the *Critique of Judgment*. Rather than its "truth" being found in its resolution of the flux in the subject/material other relation, a truth that rewrites the subject in an empowered form at the expense of that material other, trauma's "essence" is found in its *failure* to resolve, in the repeated and shattering intrusion of that extra-subjective world into the subject's self-construction. In trauma the original confusion between self and world is first perceived "numbly," as if it were a concept or text, what Geoffrey Hartman calls an event "registered rather than experienced.... that seems to have bypassed perception and consciousness, and fall[en] directly into the psyche" (537). Only later (and repeatedly) does that numbness give way to the materiality of the originary experience itself. The return to an experi-ence that wasn't "experienced" when it "happened," that at some level didn't occur when it occurred but only afterward, repeatedly injects the subject with something external that he or she can't incorporate, can't render textual, an unassimilable shard. Instead of retrospectively defin-ing the "meaning" of the initial confusion sublimely, the traumatized subject is defined by it, in a violation so primary Dori Laub calls it the "true meaning of annihilation," the "loss of the capacity to be a witness to oneself" (Caruth, *Trauma*, 67). If the sublime's resolution generally occurs in a choice between conceptual ineffability (where the sublime experience represents the concept of undecidability generally) and demystifying phenomenality (where the sublime really is a cover up for something more ordinary), trauma's failure to resolve incorporates an oscillation between ineffability and materiality, between an impossible event not experienced when it occurred, and its devastating return later, not as symbolic repression or dream, but as a terrifying literality.

Laub's emphasis on how trauma forecloses the possibility of "witnessing" oneself suggests another important distinction between the sublime and the traumatic. For Burke, Kant, and many others, the terror, anxiety, or even exhilaration generated by the sublime object is carefully modulated, sufficiently strong to pierce the ordinary textual-ity of the moment, but not so powerful that the subject's capacity to observe the event is permanently undermined. The sublime is, famously, the experience of something we are frightened of *seen from a position of relative safety*.[31] Under such a reading, the sublime might be seen as a secondary effect or voyeurism of the traumatic, a view of suffering from a position just outside its emotional event horizon. Or more precisely, since trauma is marked by an initial numbness to the event, the border between sublimity and trauma might be defined as the border between the possibility of emotionally experiencing the traumatic event from a position (just, and often precariously) external to it, and the point when a distinction between an interior, feeling, observing self and the exter-nal world has utterly collapsed. While both sublimity and trauma involve a moment of instability between subject and world sufficiently potent to precipitate a representational break, sublimity ultimately defines a limit to that instability behind which the self shelters, trauma an unmanageable excess that consumes the self.

RACIAL AND NATURAL ENTANGLEMENTS

This profound interlinkage between sublimity and trauma suggests that sublimity may in fact be a sign of, or repression of, trauma. In what follows, I will argue that moments when a white subject enjoys a profound and difficult-to-represent identification with the landscape—whether the traditional landscape of the sublime the Southern pastoral—often signify another profound and ambiguous traumatic identification, and that both such moments are part of how racial identity has been historically constructed. Certainly the racialized subjectivity that emerges from moments of unrepresentable human/natural flux has in general proven sharply divergent in a way marked by race. The sublime transforms such moments into an empowered subjectivity and a romanticized nature that manifests the truth of the observer's power. The white Romantic or transcendentalist subject almost definitionally leaves such events having found some transcendent Reality outside of the artificialities of urban and suburban life, having recovered the Truth of his (or, less often, her) own nature in ecstatic contact with the peak or gorge.[32] Such subjects expect power, wisdom, and self-recovery from their contact with nature, not degradation; they leave the dross of society behind on the hike, (supposedly) stepping outside history and culture and recovering a genuine identity in contact with the wild. While this, of course, doesn't always happen, the Romantic stereotype persists, a readily identifiable preconstructed mold for white natural experience. This stereotypical experience of Romantic sublimity, of a powerful unmarked subjectivity "naturally" outside of history, culture, and race, serves as an important idealized version of white racial experience generally.[33] Indeed, as a range of critics of whiteness have noted, one essential move of white supremacy involves such a suspension of context (though they don't as a rule, connect such suspension to natural experience), what George Yancy calls, "whiteness...com[ing] to signify that which is transhistorical, nonaccidental, that which exists in virtue of itself" (10). In this move, whites typically assume the normative first term in a binary that defines the black Other as difference from that white normativity. To "get away from it all" then, is also to return to the very center. The natural sublime can all too easily serve to "greenwash" white identity, removing the historical and cultural context that establishes white supremacy, and substituting for it a dehistoricized white individuality and a luminous present moment of fantasized escape from culture, race, and time itself. Sublimity references purity, origin, the timeless norm; in its resolution, whiteness can assume those values.

By contrast, rather than expanding the possible identities of subject and nature, trauma violently limits those possibilities, collapses the distinction between the subject and nature, makes human subjects into natural objects, which then are available for exploitation. If sublimity names a pure empowering natural space outside of human history, trauma references environmental damage, a violent link between past, present, and future, the intersection between a degraded world and a degraded subject. For African Americans, moments of instability between self-identity and the natural world have historically often been violently reductive, producing the traumatic inverse of white sublimity, rendering both the subject and nature abject, commodified, subaltern. Indeed, the conflation of blackness and nature served as the principle "justification" for chattel slavery in antebellum America. In racially identifying slaves with the agricultural pastoral, especially with domesticated animals, a terrible sort of transitive algebra allowed whites to conjoin racial and ecological violence. Since whites could do whatever they wanted to nature, and since African Americans were considered part of nature, both land and slave were made utterly instrumental to white desire, objectified as natural resources to be exploited and "improved" in the same gesture. As James Cone observes, "[t]he logic that led to slavery and segregation in the Americas, colonization and apartheid in Africa, and the rule of white supremacy throughout the world is the same one that leads to the exploitation of animals and the ravaging of nature. It is a mechanistic and instrumental logic that defines everything and everybody in terms of their contribution to the development and defense of white world supremacy" (138). This transformation from human into natural object was central to how many slaves experienced their bondage, as Mia Bay documents in her recent work.[34] When Frederick Douglass, for example, writes in his *Narrative*, "Behold a man transformed into a brute," to describe being beaten into submitting to a slave identity, the moment of human/natural intersection produces an essentialized degradation that simultaneously threatens to racialize nature and naturalize race (58). Instead of the alliance with nature providing an empowering identity supposedly "outside" of race, as it might for the white romantic naturalist, Douglass receives race in the process of that transformative alliance, receives his slave identity as a reduction to the status of the ur-natural "brute." The sublime white subject possesses the scene; the traumatized black subject is possessed by it. This violent chiasmus creates split black and white racial and ecological identities in the act of repressing their interdependence.

If the sublime landscape served as an implicit image of white subjectivity, images of environmental devastation—the farmed out cotton field or the clear-cut, for example—provide a sort of sculptural representation of the failure of encoding at the onset of trauma and the repeated emergence of that failure later. That sublimity and environmental trauma should be historically marked by race should come as no surprise: (white) America has been "nature's nation" for as long as racial trauma and the natural world have been artificially, brutally, and thoroughly entangled. It would be easy to make the error of seeing race as an essence that uncomplicatedly precedes such moments of sublimity and trauma, or conversely, seeing the sublime or pastoral landscape as Nature rather than as a human construction of nature. But as we can never point out often enough, race is something made, not found, a set of characteristics grafted onto pigmentation or the idea of pigmentation. Nature is similarly a human construction, though one grafted onto an in-fact existent extratextual materiality of which we are irrevocably a part. The sublime and traumatic moments of exchange, then, are moments within a larger context of white supremacy in which the "reality" of race and the "reality" of nature, as constructions, are produced in a mutually reinforcing process that grounds the ungrounded as the Real.[35] Such moments serve to manufacture the subject as either fundamentally like the utterly free sublime wilderness or fundamentally like the utterly compliant pastoral in a process that constructs both white and black as natural. But, and simultaneously, the racial subjectivity produced in such moments serves the persistent eco-ideological function of splitting nature into two places, one forever wild and one infinitely exploitable, a split that has long allowed the American landscape to function both as a pure sign of American exceptionalism and as a garbage dump/raw materials superstore. In these endlessly repeated moments of double transformation the fate of both the American landscape and the American people has been entangled, and mostly for the worse.

2

THE COLONIAL PASTORAL, ABOLITION, AND THE TRANSCENDENTALIST SUBLIME

> I walk toward one of our ponds, but what signifies the beauty of nature when men are base?
> —Henry David Thoreau, "Slavery in Massachusetts"

COLONIAL WHITENESS AND THE NEO-EDENIC PASTORAL

When the first European settlers confronted the huge eastern forest of the Atlantic coast that stretched unbroken from Maine to Georgia, they saw a landscape belated rather than primordial, a nature that had fallen away, in every sense, from an originary divine pastoral. What might well seem to contemporary Americans, at least in their imagination, as a breathtaking view back to an untouched, uncreated natural beauty, was something quite different to most of these early settlers.[1] Rather than an originary pristine landscape, they saw an unredeemed in-between state, predated by a biblical origin story for the wilds before them. This vision of European-style civilization and a "tamed" neo-Edenic continent—with them having Adamically "subdued the earth" and taken "dominion over the animals and the beasts of the field"—served as its ecological telos.

Thomas Cole's 1828 painting, "Expulsion from the Garden of Eden," captures this substitution of a postlapsarian origin for the "American" wilderness well. Inside Cole's Garden, the viewer glimpses the divine pastoral, a profoundly tame, anthropocentric landscape of flowers, endless sunshine, cleared fields and abundant food produced without need of cultivation, and from which predation has been eliminated. In the center, two white figures, Adam and Eve, flee God's wrath across a natural bridge (a symbol of the American

Figure 1   Expulsion from the Garden of Eden, 1828. Thomas Cole, American (born in England), 1801–1848. Oil on canvas 100.96 × 138.43 cm (39 3/4 × 54 1/2 in.). Museum of Fine Arts, Boston. Gift of Martha C. Karolik for the M. and M. Karolik Collection of American Paintings, 1815–1865 47.1188.

Source: Photograph © 2008 Museum of Fine Arts, Boston.

sublime since Jefferson) into a howling wilderness, complete with towering volcanoes, plunging cataracts, old growth forest, and the return of predation in the figure of a wolf eating a stag and a vulture waiting for the remains.

But while the painting's explicit narrative reads from right to left, in reading more conventionally from left to right, the American viewer is invited to undo the Fall in his her contemporary history, to return the wild landscape to the Edenic original, to resolve the sublime in favor of the beautiful, and bring those white figures back to their "natural habitat" in the Garden.[2] For the early white settlers, the wilderness was not a Romantic place where they found their "true" selves, but a place of exile and punishment, an unimproved, un-Christian, and generally hostile wasteland with value only in its possibility of being converted into something else: a divine city on a hill, forts, towns, crops, money.[3] Whether explicitly religious or not, these early settlers were trained to see the wild not as valuable in itself as we are likely to do today, but only as an opportunity for transformation and personal enrichment, a point de Tocqueville notes as characteristic in *Democracy in America*:

> [L]iving in the wilds, [the pioneer] only prizes the works of man.... In Europe people talk a great deal about the wilds of America, but the Americans themselves never think about them; they are insensible to the wonders of inanimate nature and they may be said not to perceive the mighty forests that surround them till they fall beneath the hatchet. Their eyes are fixed upon another sight...they march across these wilds, draining swamps, turning the course of rivers, peopling soli tudes, and subduing nature.[4]

As Leo Marx, Annette Kolodny, and many others have pointed out, the settled pastoral, not the wild, was the image of the desirable landscape, the other "sight" that the pioneer's eyes were "fixed upon."[5]

That both European women and men were often implacably hostile toward the wilderness in this period and longed for its conversion/ reversion into the pastoral reflected a fairly straightforward eco-ideology, "justifying" the clear-cutting of the Atlantic seaboard, and later the burning of the prairies, the decimation of the buffalo herds, and on and on. My point is not simply to hold up this early view as representative of the "wrong" way of looking at nature, however, but rather to underscore both how we construct nature to reflect our own subjective biases and ideological purposes, and how our belief in those natural constructions as True in turn reifies those subjective biases as Natural. Nature-construction is self-construction and vise versa—a tautological factory for turning "what we want" into "the way it should be," and then into "the way it is." For the settlers to "tame" the wilderness was to own it, and in that act of "taming" not only to reformulate their subjectivity as the conqueror of that wilderness, but to remake the image of human and nonhuman nature. The beaten wild, aka the pastoral, became both a sign of the European settler's power, the corpse of a defeated champion, and the face of nature itself.[6] Rather than finding themselves in the woods, the pioneers found themselves in losing them; rather than losing the woods, the settlers restored them to their pastoral essence.

Since this "desolate" wilderness was, in fact, inhabited by millions of native people who often resisted the colonial expansion fiercely, the link between environmental and racial identity, and environmental and racial violence, was also forged "naturally." Most late eighteenth- and early nineteenth-century views of race (mainly among white Europeans) saw it as at least partially an *effect* of climate and environment, rather than in the uncritically absolute terms of much of Puritan Christianity or the later nineteenth-century essentialist understanding of race as the unchangeable will of God or evolution.[7] This widespread belief in the climatic origin of race made race a result of the intersection between human and natural, an originary permeability between these concepts often obscured by the "harder" scientific racism of the later nineteenth century. The temperate pastoral thus functioned both as the source of white subjectivity and as a reflection of it. Emmerich de Vattell's influential 1797 treatise, *The Law of Nations*, provided the American colonials with an early template for the naturalization of white-might-makes-right/right-might-makes-white:

> The earth, as we have already observed, belongs to mankind in general, and was designed to furnish them with subsistence: if each nation had from the beginning resolved to appropriate to itself a vast country, that the people might live only by hunting, fishing, and wild fruits, our globe would not be sufficient to maintain a tenth part of its present inhabitants. We do not therefore deviate from the views of nature in confining the Indians within narrower limits. However, we cannot help praising the moderation of the English puritans who first settled in new England; who, notwithstanding their being furnished with a charter from their sovereign, purchased of the Indians the land of which they intended to take possession. (qtd. in Saxton, 28)

Vattell's emphasis on the superiority of agricultural societies over hunter/gatherers assumes (in concert with the Eden story) that the "earth belongs to mankind in general," and puts native extermination in a larger evolutionary narrative in which "the views of nature" and not genocidal war is ultimately responsible for "confining the Indians within narrower limits." (And Vattall gets his facts basically wrong too—the New England natives practiced extensive agriculture, a fact that the Puritans enjoyed at the first Thanksgiving and later put to use in the Pequod war by burning Indian crops to induce famine.)

As Alexander Saxton notes, Vattall's threadbare distinction was nevertheless picked up as a central part of the colonial justification for their occupation of native lands, providing a "useful" framework that invited the racialization of the wild/pastoral divide. John Quincy Adams, for example, asked in an 1802 speech at Plymouth commemorating the Puritan's landfall, "shall the fields and valleys which a beneficent God has formed to teem with the life of innumerable multitudes be condemned to everlasting barrenness?" and later declared to Henry Goulburn, the British Commissioner, that "[t]o condemn vast regions of territory to perpetual barrenness and solitude that a few hundred savages might find wild beasts to hunt upon it, was a species of game law that a nation descended from Britons would never endure" (qtd. in Saxton, 36, 38). The Plymouth speech picks up Vattall's notion—that the land's purpose is to support as many humans as possible and that thus cultivation confers title to it—but casts it in a religious frame in which the land must be saved from itself, from its "condemnation to barrenness," by the Puritans' descendants obeying the divine injunction to "be fruitful and multiply" until it is "teeming with the life of innumerable multitudes." These multitudes, it literally goes without saying, are white not red, an interpretation confirmed in the remark to Goulburn in which the "barrenness" of the wild landscape is identified with "a few hundred savages" and the "innumerable multitudes" are explicitly the "nation descended from Britons." Each term slides into the other until the landscape is marked racially and the races are marked by the landscape.[8]

This fluidity between racial and natural identity necessitated constant environmental/racial violence in order to maintain whiteness's alliance with the pastoral; that alliance was simultaneously the source of entitlement and of racial vulnerability. If the landscape at once reflected and produced race, its environmental condition could serve both as a source of racial pride—a pastoral mirror of white "civilization"—and anxiety—a wilderness that tempted whites to, quite literally, "go native." We can see this anxiety in Crèvecoeur's description of the effect of the frontier on the white settler:

> I must tell you that there is something in the proximity of the woods which is very singular. It is with men as it is with the plants and animals that grow and live in the forests; they are entirely different from those that live in the plains.... By living in or near the woods, their actions are regulated by the wildness of neighborhood.... [T]hey soon become professed hunters; this is the progress; once hunters, farewell to the plow. The chase renders them ferocious, gloomy, and unsociable; a hunter wants no neighbor, he rather hates them, because he dreads the competition. In a little time their success in the woods makes them neglect their tillage.... they grow up a mongrel breed, half civilized, half savage, except nature stamps on them some constitutional propensities.... the possession of their freeholds no longer conveys to their mind the same pleasure and pride.
>
> Thus our bad people are those who are half cultivators and half hunters; and the worst of them are those who have degenerated altogether into the hunting state. As old plowmen and new men of the woods, as Europeans and new-made Indians, they contract the vices of

both; they adopt the moroseness and ferocity of the native, without his mildness, or even his industry at home. If manners are not refined, at least they are rendered simple and inoffensive by tilling the earth; all our wants are supplied by it, our time is divided between labor and rest, and leaves none for the commission of great misdeeds. As hunters it is divided between the toil of the chase, the idleness of repose, or the indulgence of inebriation.... After this explanation of the effects which follow by living in the woods, shall we yet vainly flatter ourselves with the hope of converting the Indians? (51–54)

Here Crèvecoeur, writing from the perspective of an "American Farmer" provides a very different portrait of the frontier hunter than that which emerges in Romantic form as Natty Bumpo, Daniel Boone, and Davy Crockett. Intimate contact with the wild in this passage threatens to degenerate the white settler racially, much as later racist writers worried about the effect of "miscegenation." The pastoral conversion, in other words, can work in reverse, taking the white pastoral subject and converting him into a wilderness-identified savage hunter. The result of this fluidity between natural and racial identity is a racially charged validation of the pastoral and a hostile and fearful view of a wilderness with such alchemic power over racial identity; in short, a framework for white supremacy built on ecological destruction and fueled by racial anxiety.[9] The pastoral conversion was the privileged sign of the white settlers' racial superiority and their concomitant right to everything they could clear-cut and plant, dispossess or murder, functioning simultaneously, and contradictorily, as the origin of whiteness and the result of it, much as the Eden myth functioned as both the origin and terminus of wild nature.[10]

Thirty-odd years after Vattall and Crèvecoeur, the European settlement of much of the Atlantic seaboard was complete, the infamous Indian Removal Act had mandated the transfer of native populations west of the Mississippi, and the ideological work of pastoralization had produced a nearly absolute racial division between white and native.[11] As Andrew Jackson said in an 1830 Presidential address to Congress: "What good man would prefer a country covered with forests and ranged by a few thousand savages, to our extensive Republic, studded with towns and prosperous farms...and filled with all the blessings of liberty, civilization and religion?" (qtd. in Saxton, 153). By this point Jackson doesn't need to note that the "good man" is white or "descended from Britons"; the reference to the newly pastoral American landscape in contradistinction to the "few thousand savages" is sufficient. In his speech, whiteness and the pastoral have become the new normative standard; here each "naturally" signifies the other.

TRANSCENDENTALISM, THE WHITE SUBLIME, AND THE TRAUMATIC PASTORAL

However awful their consequences, the ways the twinned binaries of pastoral/wilderness and civilized/savage intersected and reinforced each other in early American history seem straightforward enough. Take the fort building that was inevitably the first act of the colonists upon arrival on this continent as a three-dimensional summary of those binaries— inside the fort, cleared land, the white/normal/civilized; outside, a savage wilderness and savage savages that needed to be tamed and incorporated into a "new world" European identity and an old world global resource economy. Let the fort serve as the sculptural representation of the colonialist pastoral eco-ideology, expanding and multiplying until its walls became the western frontier. The civilized/white versus savage/wild binary was replicated mile by westward mile, a sort of factory that consumed the wild and the native at one end, and extruded gender, the pastoral, and whiteness on the other.[12] While there are certainly exceptions to the short sketch of this intersection in early native/colonial encounters, the pattern generally and brutally held.

While such binaries have been an essential part of American identity from the first colonial encounters, the nearly simultaneous emergence of transcendentalism and the public voice of African Americans in the abolition movement and the slave narratives marks a vitally important shift in the racialization of nature. In this shift, nature becomes represented at once as the degraded site of slavery and environmental destruction and, simultaneously and not coincidentally, as the intensely validated sign of exceptional individuality and absolute freedom. That division marks the United States to this day, and its emergence and development is the focus of the chapters that follow. I want to begin here by offering a reading of how this shift functioned in transcendentalism, a genealogy that makes the avoidance of race part of the white American love of wilderness.

The epicenter of this shift is, importantly, not the West but the New England landscape and the Southern plantation fields, two pastoral landscapes whose man-against-nature struggle had long been resolved and moved on to the West. The celebration of the wilderness and wilderness experience did not occur, in other words, until the wilderness began to recede. As Roderick Nash notes,

> Constant exposure to wilderness gave rise to fear and hatred on the part of those who had to fight it for survival and success. Although there were a few exceptions, American frontiersmen rarely judged wilderness with criteria other than the utilitarian or spoke of their

> relation to it in other than a military metaphor. It was their children
> and grandchildren, removed from a wilderness condition, who began
> to sense its ethical and religious values. (42–43)

The view of the wilderness shifted once the work of the original colonial
eco-ideology had been accomplished—the Native Americans killed, large
(nonhuman) predation eliminated, agriculture established—shifted
from savage Indians to tragic ones, from a hostile nature to a loving
nature, from a reflection of the devil's face to a reflection of the Spirit's.
While I think Nash is right about the fact of the shift, his explanation of
it somewhat uncritically embodies a Romantic or transcendentalist
assumption that the wilderness intrinsically has a preexisting "ethical
and religious" essence, another mythic origin. But, as Nash's own work
demonstrates so well, such an assumption depends on the perspective of
the viewer: the wild must be viewed from the perspective of the non-
wild, the settled, the cleared, in order to be seen as "intrinsically" valuable in the familiar ways it is now. Built into the very definition of the
valorized wilderness is an unacknowledged not-wild perspective from
which that wilderness, as it were, emerged. At the same time this "new"
wild was seen as an origin of the not-wild, reformulating the earlier view
that the newly made pastoral reflected an Edenic source that the
wilderness had departed from, into a sense that the observer's pastoral
viewpoint was itself belated.

   Both the Eden myth and the Romantic wilderness are fundamentally structured by this curious temporal and spatial latency, a longing
for a utopian return to a supposedly originary past that can only be
viewed from—and in that sense originates from—a time and place
outside of it. Immersed in the wilderness, the early settlers violently
"restored" an Edenic pastoral; immersed in the settled pastoral,
the transcendentalists pined for the ever-retreating wild. This
simultaneous assertion of union from a position of separation was
perhaps built into the alienation between human observer and natural scene implied by the very (European) idea of a "landscape," which,
as Leslie Marmon Silko points out, "assumes the viewer is somehow
outside or *separate from* the territory he or she surveys" (265–66).[13]

   Sublimity captures the way this separation from the desired landscape is simultaneously an alliance with it, a careful positioning of the
subject between loss and fulfillment. Neither wholly separate from
nature nor lost in it, oscillating between union and difference, the
sublime subject comes to make nature signify his or her own newly
empowered subjectivity in an experience that from Kant onward
served as an implicit sign of whiteness. Thomas Weiskel offers a useful

structural account of this sequence in his study of the Romantic sublime, understanding it as a three-phase "economic" process, a "series of changes in the distribution of energy within a constant field" that ultimately resolves the ambiguity of the subject's relation to the world into hierarchy and empowerment (25). In Weiskel's first phase, before the sublime strikes, the relationship between self and world is peaceful, a "smooth correspondence of inner and outer" obtains with nothing to interrupt "the automatic, linear rhythm of sensation and reflection" (23). In the second phase this "habitual relation of mind and object suddenly breaks down" and "there is an immediate intuition of a disconcerting disproportion between inner and outer. Either mind or object is suddenly in excess—and then both are, since their relation has become radically indeterminate" (23–24). Finally, the sublime resolves when "the mind recovers the balance of outer and inner by constituting a fresh relation between itself and the object such that the very indeterminacy which erupted in phase two is taken as symbolizing the mind's relation to a transcendent order" (24).

Weiskel's work remains influential more than a quarter century after its publication, in part because he so acutely identifies how sublime experience is built around a series of *transitions*, from quiescence to eruption to resolution, rather than necessarily inhering in any one of the phases. (He is perhaps less insightful on the political "unconscious" of the experience, an issue I will turn to in a moment.) Although his work is explicitly concerned with British Romantic poetry, we can see Weiskel's structure clearly, and how it facilitated a reconstituting of both subject and landscape, in what is perhaps the most well-known passage in American transcendentalism:

Crossing a bare common, in snow puddles, at twilight, under a clouded sky, without having in my thoughts any occurrence of special good fortune, I have enjoyed a perfect exhilaration. I am glad to the brink of fear. In the woods, too, a man casts off his years, as the snake his slough, and at what period soever of life is always a child. In the woods is perpetual youth. Within these plantations of God, a decorum and sanctity reign, a perennial festival is dressed, and the guest sees not how he should tire of them in a thousand years. In the woods, we return to reason and faith. There I feel that nothing can befall me in life—no disgrace, no calamity (leaving me my eyes), which nature cannot repair. Standing on the bare ground—my head bathed in the blithe air and uplifted into infinite space—all mean egotism vanishes. I become a transparent eyeball; I am nothing; I see all; the currents of the Universal Being circulate through me; I am part or parcel of God. The name of the nearest friend sounds then foreign and accidental: to be brothers, to

> be acquaintances, master or servant, is then a trifle and a disturbance.
> I am the lover of uncontained and immortal beauty. In the wilderness,
> I find something more dear and connate than in streets or villages. In
> the tranquil landscape, and especially in the distant line of the horizon,
> man beholds somewhat as beautiful as his own nature. (Emerson, 6)

Corresponding to the first of Weiskel's phases, the prequel in which
subject and natural world are in "smooth correspondence," Emerson
here is "crossing a bare common...without having in [his] thoughts
any occurrence of special good fortune." The setting, importantly, is
not the wild, but cleared land, a "bare common," the embedded, if
unrecognized, historical fruit of the earlier colonial struggle to create the pastoral out of the wilderness, and an explicitly human and
political space. The second phase erupts from that setting, "suddenly
break[ing] down" Emerson's "habitual relation of mind and object,"
so that his relation to the natural world is marked by "disconcerting
disproportion," a simultaneous "excess" of consciousness and land, a
"radical indetermin[acy]" in the relation between subjectivity and
nature. Emerson goes from having "no thoughts of special good
fortune" to the instantaneous experience of "perfect exhilaration."
"[G]lad to the brink of fear," the excess of subject and object is writ
large (to say the least) in his simultaneous transformation into a giant
transparent eyeball, and the ordinary world's transformation into
"infinite space" and the "currents of Universal Being." Finally, in
the third phase, this moment of power-flooded radical ambiguity is
resolved when Emerson reconstitutes himself by taking that "indeterminacy...as symbolizing the mind's relation to a transcendent
order." Hence the final lines, in which Emerson becomes "the lover
of uncontained and immortal beauty," in which the "*wilderness*"
becomes "dear and connate" (as opposed to the "streets or villages,"
where the bare common is presumably located), in which the "tran-
quil landscape, and especially in the distant line of the horizon,"
becomes the sign of something as "beautiful" as "man['s]...own
nature." The politically and eco-historically marked space of the
"bare common" is transformed by the sublime, and Emerson tele-
ports to the ahistorical, indeed timeless, "woods," a natural space
that later is transformed into the "dear and connate" "wilderness." It
would be hard to find a better example of the shift in identification
from pastoral to wild, from settler to Romantic transcendentalist.
Indeed, here the shift in identification itself—the metamorphic transition from the "bare common" to the "dear and connate...wilder-
ness" and from ordinary Emerson to Visionary Emerson—is arguably
the sublime object, rather than a mountain or cataract.[14]

Critics have explained this new validation of the wilderness in a range of ways, from the influence of Deism that saw the wild as closer to the original divine creation, to a recoiling from the beginnings of industrialization in the east, to the influence of Romanticism and theories of the sublime that dovetailed nicely with an attempt to distinguish American identity from Europe on the basis of wilderness where America certainly had the advantage, rather than on cultural production, where it certainly did not.[15] More recently, and perhaps most powerfully, that recoil from the pastoral has been seen in gendered terms, as a masculine panic over the influence of a feminized/tamed nature. While all of these views are important and right, ecocritics haven't generally connected this shift to race or slavery, despite the fact that to see race as flowing from landscape and environmental practice had long been an effective way of justifying the terrible history of early violence against the Native American population and the natural world, and despite the fact that slavery was the overriding political issue for the Romantic transcendentalists and for most everyone else in the culture as well. As the "nature" of the pastoral landscape the early settlers identified with changed and degenerated, so too did the meaning of that identification, and with it the stability and permanence of that "naturally" constituted white identity.

Slavery made the white racial identification with the pastoral landscape dangerously unstable. And it often did so eruptively, "intruding" on the white pastoral in a way that mirrors, though does not simply replicate, white sublime experience. If, as I have argued, the placement of the subject in sublimity also describes a voyeuristic "safe distance" between that subject and a traumatic scene, the "usefulness" of sublime experience as a way of both broaching and repressing the individual and social suffering of slavery starts to become clear. Sublimity allows something terrible to be transformed into something pleasurable, allows the ecocidal drive of the early colonists to become the reestablishment of Eden. More important for my purposes here though, it provided a structure for white subjects to recoil from a pastoral identification that was increasingly contaminated by slavery in favor of an ever-retreating, infinitely available wild. Consider another exemplary passage from Crèvecoeur in which the "smooth correspondence between inner and outer" is interrupted much differently. Its immersive qualities necessitate an extended quotation:

> The following scene will I hope account for these melancholy reflections, and apologize for the gloomy thoughts with which I have filled this letter: my mind is, and always has been, oppressed since I became a witness to it. I was not long since invited to dine with a

planter who lived three miles from ‑‑‑‑‑‑‑‑, where he then resided. In order to avoid the heat of the sun, I resolved to go on foot, sheltered in a small path, leading through a pleasant wood. I was leisurely traveling along, attentively examining some peculiar plants which I had collected, when all at once I felt the air strongly agitated, though the day was perfectly calm and sultry. I immediately cast my eyes toward the cleared ground, from which I was but a small distance, in order to see whether it was not occasioned by a sudden shower; when at that instant a sound resembling a deep rough voice, uttered, as I thought, a few inarticulate monosyllables. Alarmed and surprised, I precipitately looked all round, when I perceived at about six rods distance something resembling a cage, suspended to the limbs of a tree; all the branches of which appeared covered with large birds of prey, fluttering about, and anxiously endeavoring to perch on the cage. Actuated by an involuntary motion of my hands, more than by any design of my mind, I fired at them; they all flew to a short distance, with a most hideous noise: when, horrid to think and painful to repeat, I perceived a Negro, suspended in the cage, and left there to expire! I shudder when I recollect that the birds had already picked out his eyes, his cheek bones were bare; his arms had been attacked in several places, and his body seemed covered with a multitude of wounds. From the edges of the hollow sockets and from the lacerations with which he was disfigured, the blood slowly dropped, and tinged the ground beneath. No sooner were the birds flown, than swarms of insects covered the whole body of this unfortunate wretch, eager to feed on his mangled flesh and to drink his blood. I found myself suddenly arrested by the power of affright and terror; my nerves were convulsed; I trembled, I stood motionless, involuntarily contemplating the fate of this Negro, in all its dismal latitude. The living spectre though deprived of his eyes, could still distinctly hear, and in his uncouth dialect begged me to give him some water to allay his thirst. Humanity herself would have recoiled back with horror; she would have balanced whether to lesson such reliefless distress or mercifully with one blow to end this dreadful scene of agonizing torture! Had I had a ball in my gun, I certainly should have dispatched him; but finding myself unable to perform so kind an office, I sought, though trembling, to relieve him as well as I could. A shell ready fixed to a pole, which had been used by some Negroes, presented itself to me; I filled it with water, and with trembling hands I guided it to the quivering lips of the wretched sufferer. Urged by the irresistible power of thirst, he endeavored to meet it, as he instinctively guessed its approach by the noise it made in passing through the bars of the cage. "Tanke, you white man, tanke you, pute some poison and give me." "How long have you been hanging there?" I asked him. "Two days, and me no die; the birds, the birds; aaah me!" Oppressed with the reflections which this shocking

spectacle afforded me, I mustered strength enough to walk away, and
soon reached the house at which I intended to dine. There I heard
that the reason for this slave being thus punished, was on account of
his having killed the overseer of the plantation. They told me that the
laws of self-preservation rendered such executions necessary; and
supported the doctrine of slavery with the arguments generally made
use of to justify the practice; with the repetition of which I shall not
trouble you at present. (171–73)

Crèvecoeur's traumatic experience begins, like much of his book, in
an embrace of the pastoral. He is walking off to dinner at another
farmer's house, "leisurely traveling" down a "small path" leading
through a "pleasant wood," his attention riveted on some plant spec-
imens he has collected. The description of the scene, his absorption in
the "peculiar" plants he has picked, and his destination all suggest an
anthropocentric landscape, devoid of predation, a non-wild nature
that unproblematically assumes and reflects his central if not dominant subjectivity—the normative and quickly forgotten pastoral
setting for Weiskel's first phase of the sublime.

But if the form of the experience seems to shadow the Romantic
sublime, the content is terribly different. Instead of transporting
Crèvecoeur ecstatically to an ideal wild away from human history
and political and personal relationships, the unbearable vision/
experience that erupts (mirroring Weiskel's second stage) before
Crèvecoeur and his reader manifests the political reality of antebellum America, the truth about the planter he is to visit and the source
of much of the labor that created the pastoral in the first place. In the
place of Emerson's departure from the common to the wild, this
experience renders the pastoral horrific and unnatural in the images
of the inverted predation of the birds and insects, the suspended
cage, the slave's desire for water and then poison. Rather than providing the experience of "pleasurable terror" that marks Burke's
sadomasochistic version of sublimity, the horror of the suffering
before Crèvecoeur seems to exceed the capacity of subjective incor-
poration, his descriptive failure underscored by the repeated immo-
bility of his reaction as he is "arrested by the power of affright and
terror," "convulsed," "trembling," "oppressed." Perhaps most
important, instead of the experience resolving in a new order in
which the eruptive instability becomes a "symbol of the mind's new
relation to a transcendent order," Crèvecoeur experiences what seems
like the clinical definition of psychological trauma, an endless and
helpless recalling of the original traumatic event—his "mind is, and
always has been, oppressed since [he] became a witness to it."

Despite his insistence that the trauma of viewing the slave's suffering was "arresting" and "oppressive," Crèvecoeur's focus on his own reactions and his passivity in the face of the man's grotesque suffering seems reprehensibly narcissistic; he only "muster[s] strength enough to walk away." While he claims he "sought, though trembling, to relieve him as well as [he] could," Crèvecoeur makes no attempt to rescue the man, never asks him what happened, provides no succor save passing him water through the bars via the pole and shell as if he were some sort of biohazard. He is willing to shoot him, of course, but his gun is unloaded, and any form of direct contact with the man's body, violent or otherwise, is apparently out of the question. Indeed, for Crèvecoeur, the trauma of the scene seems to center on his own emotional disturbance rather than the slave's real suffering; the slave is an object of pity, a caged animal, some monstrous part of the landscape, but not a human subject whose agony matters in the same way that a white victim's would. When Crèvecoeur declares that "Humanity herself would have recoiled back in horror," he makes his reaction the reaction of an unmarked/white universal subject.

What shatters the initial pastoral reverie, then, is not Leo Marx's "machine in the garden" but white on black racial trauma, a sudden shift from a racially unmarked identification of the white subject with the "pleasant wood" to the explicitly marked, indeed racially saturated, horror of the slave pastoral. For Marx, writing on Hawthorne's reaction to a locomotive intruding on his pastoral reverie, the train signifies an epistemic break: "the fact is that nothing quite like the event announced by the train in the woods had occurred before. A sense of history as an unpredictable, irreversible sequence of unique events makes itself felt ..." (31). For Crèvecoeur, conversely, the scene does not reveal something disjunctively new, but something that had long been present, the racial ideology half-hidden behind the American pastoral idyll, a racial content "this Negro" names in immediately calling Crèvecoeur "white man" without being able to see him. Despite this replacement of an idyllic pastoral with a "truer" slave pastoral, the conflation of blackness and nature remains: the slave remains in his cage, remains part of the landscape, remains conflated with the natural world in a way that seems to relieve Crèvecoeur from any obligation other than shuddering remembrance and generalized disapproval.

This scene exemplifies, then, the more generalized crisis in the identification of whiteness and the settled pastoral that slavery produced, at least for white viewers like Crèvecoeur with the basic moral sensibility necessary to be appalled by it. And so the "melancholy reflections" that his relation of this traumatic scene "accounts for" at the opening of the passage are reflections on the evil of humanity that, in the immediately preceding paragraph, call into question the fundamental justification of the earlier white/pastoral domination:

> Where do you conceive then that nature intended we should be happy? Would you prefer the state of men in the woods, to that of men in a more improved situation? Evil preponderates in both; in the first they often eat each other for want of food, and in the other they often starve each other for want of room. For my part, I think the vices and miseries to be found in the latter, exceed those of the former; in which real evil is more scarce, more supportable, and less enormous. Yet we wish to see the earth peopled; to accomplish the happiness of king-doms, which is said to consist in numbers. Gracious God! to what end is the introduction of so many beings into a mode of existence in which they must grope amidst as many errors, commit as many crimes, and meet with as many diseases, wants, and sufferings! (171)

Here the central justification for the takeover of the Atlantic seaboard offered elsewhere in Crèvecoeur's writing, and by figures like Emmerick de Vattall, Johns Adams, Andrew Jackson, and many others—that the populous pastoral was the justification of white racial and environmental dominance and the sign of it—is explicitly called into profound question by the slave's literal and figurative asso-ciation with that pastoral landscape. No wonder Emerson found his solitary elevation to the wild sublime so appealing.

Indeed, it's tempting to see Emerson's experience as at least an unconscious recoiling from Crèvecoeur's very well-known earlier pas-sage. Certainly a strange sort of inverted parallelism haunts both (a parallel that might serve as a miniature of this book's argument). Where Emerson is elevated above the landscape, the caged slave is suspended above it. The central image of Emerson's experience is cer-tainly his transformation into a *"transparent* eyeball," a metamor-phosis whose vulnerability paradoxically (and somewhat comically) underscores Emerson's utter security, since he feels "no calamity could befall [him] saving [him] his eyes."[16] Conversely, the drama of Crèvecoeur's passage turns on the *opacity* of the initial scene in which the slave's body is obscured by birds, an opacity that then parts to reveal a yet more calamitous inverse of Emerson's image in the night-marish revelation that the slave's eyeballs have been eaten by the rav-enous birds and insects. Where Emerson becomes "part or parcel of God," the slave's merge with nature is intensely physical and material; where the "currents of Universal Being" circulate through Emerson, the slave's body is pierced. Perhaps most tellingly, while Emerson thrills to the simultaneous marking and erasure of his white privilege in the "plantations of God," where "to be master or servant is a trifle," (and note that "servant" was the "polite" Southern term for "slave"), the slave in the Crèvecoeur passages suffers; he is black, opaque, in a real plantation in which to be white master or black servant consumes identity literally, symbolically, and, in this case, utterly. Rather than being "elevated" to a hyper-individualized extraracial humanism, Crèvecoeur records a scene in which racial difference is marked with absolutist violence, a violence that, however disturbing, Crèvecoeur accepts, "mustering strength enough to walk away," rather than rescuing the man from his unspeakable torments.

If the fort served as the paradigm for the colonialist relation to nature, let Emerson's transformation of politicized (un)natural racial trauma into extrahistorical sublimity represent this new normative form of modern white natural experience and its resolution. In such experiences, moments of instability in the relation between the Romantic or transcendentalist subject and nature are generally understood to empower the subject in a way that makes the subject and the world of politics a "mere trifle and disturbance." This empowering sublime experience of a natural world outside of race and history—of a grand, wild world that is fundamentally identified with the subject and that the subject identifies with in the sublime moment—is, among other things, an idealized version of what it is like to be white. As George Yancy insists in a comment just as tellingly (and coincidentally) relevant to understanding Emerson's experience as Weiskel's analysis,

[W]hiteness sees what it wants to see and thus identifies that which it wants to see with that which is. The power and privilege of whiteness obfuscates its own complicity in seeing a "reality" that it constructs as objective....

Through the process of "white-world-making," the construction of a world with values, regulations, and policies that provide supportive structures to those identified as "white," a world that whiteness then denies having given birth to, a possible slippage between knowing and being is often difficult to encourage. In short, what whiteness *knows* is what there *is*....

Whiteness has the power to create an elaborate social subterfuge, leading both whites and nonwhites to believe that the representations in terms of which they live their lives and understand the world and themselves are naturally given, unchangeable ways of being. (10–11)

I want to suggest that Emerson's sublime is (among other things) just such a "process of 'white-world making,'" part of whiteness's disappearance into the normal or natural positioned just outside slavery's historical and cultural trauma. Whiteness is unmarking in Emerson's experience—at the moment of sublimity "all mean egoism vanishes," and he becomes "transparent," a "nothing," an unraced subject who "sees all," who is a representative of "Universal Being." Uplifted, empowered, distinguished, blessed by this experience, Emerson's natural escape is marked by his unacknowledged racial privilege, making whiteness "transparency." Whatever else it does the natural sublime performs this deracializing operation on a gigantic scale. The wild provided a crucial site for the disarticulation of whiteness from race, a place where empowered white subjectivity is naturalized, "a world that whiteness then denies having given birth to."[17] To pair Emerson's ecstasy with the slave's agony is to begin to see how the color line was formed not simply as a mutually constituting binary relation between whiteness and blackness, but one that was instantiated in and through natural experience. This pairing produces both an irreducible racial marking of the slave and an irreducible racial unmarking of Emerson, an association that whiteness can both produce and escape from through a sublime association with the (supposedly) uncreated wild.

The subterranean link between Crèvecoeur's horror and Emerson's ecstasy doesn't have to be factually true (though I imagine it is) to be representative of my general point that the trauma of slavery catalyzed the disassociation of whiteness from the pastoral and its new identification with the extrahistorical, extrapolitical wilderness. How could it do otherwise, especially for deeply moral and perceptive figures like Emerson and Thoreau, who loved nature as much as they hated slavery?[18] Indeed, I want to argue that their love of the wild sublime was the profoundly entangled inverse of their abolitionist commitments, whether or not they were explicitly aware of the depth of that connection. Understanding this complex relationship requires undoing the division between nature and politics, understanding each term as intimately tied up with the other, no matter where we go or what we do, or what a given writer claims. Under such a green reading, the emphasis throughout transcendentalism on freedom, self-reliance, and self-creation in a natural context, and the corresponding diagnosis of how the social could produce conformity, obedience, and submission, must not be understood as *simply* a retreat from political realities into a green world outside of it. It was that, of course, but not only that; in antebellum America, questions about freedom, self-creation, and bondage inevitably referred, even if implicitly and unconsciously, to slavery. Transcendentalism's love of wilderness and freedom was always contextualized by its horror of slavery's naturalized trauma.

This is not to argue that Emerson's hyper-individualized ecstasy or Thoreau's love of self-creation at Walden necessarily had a conscious abolitionist content, but rather an often unconscious, repressed, abolitionist context. Hence Emerson's "quotation" of Crèvecoeur. The woods *are* a political space, and the flight to them is therefore not simply an escape from politics, at least not one that works. Moreover, given the definitional emphasis in transcendentalism on the role the human observer played in constructing the natural world, Emerson and Thoreau's staunch abolitionism meant that slavery always threatened to intrude on their sublime "white-world making." As Emerson notes in the paragraph that concludes *Nature's* first chapter and that immediately follows his ocular transformation:

> Yet it is certain that the power to produce this delight does not reside in nature, but in man, or in a harmony of both. It is necessary to use these pleasures with great temperance. For nature is not always tricked in holiday attire, but the same scene which yesterday breathed perfume and glittered as for the frolic of the nymphs is overspread with melancholy to-day. Nature always wears the colors of the spirit.... The sky is less grand as it shuts down over less worth in the population. (7)

Emerson's waffle on whether sublimity comes from nature, man, or a "harmony of both" underscores how the imbrication of the discourses of nature and race both instantiates the subject, and threatens to transform subject and nature if either changes radically. The "harmony" between human and nature that produces "delight" can become discordant; an unworthy "population" will produce a landscape degraded aesthetically, spiritually, and materially.

That degradation returns—or anxiety about that degradation returns—as this first chapter, "Nature," ends and the second, "Commodity," begins (a shift that itself mirrors the traumatic operation of slavery itself, as I will argue shortly). Emerson insists in this exceptionally brief chapter (five short paragraphs in all), that the earth's bounty is produced almost effortlessly by natural processes, an enlargement of his earlier repression of the "disturbance" of "master and slave" in the "plantations of God." As he says,

> All the parts [of nature] incessantly work into each other's hands for the profit of man. The wind sows the seed; the sun evaporates the sea; the wind blows the vapor to the field; the ice, on the other side of the planet, condenses rain on this; the rain feeds the plant, the plant feeds the animal; and thus the endless circulations of the divine charity nourish man. (8)

While he's of course right to identify (and appreciate) how the ecosystem works independently of human agency, he seems less eager to acknowledge how much human labor is added to that natural "divine charity" in order to "profit" and "nourish" "man." When he interpolates an epigram a few sentences later, for example, declaring that "More servants wait on man/Than he'll take notice of," the irony is seemingly external to Emerson. "Servants" refers *only* to non-human natural processes, the "beasts, fire, water, stones, and corn [that] serve him"; slave labor is absent here, and for me conspicuously so (7). Indeed, this natural abundance explicitly occludes human suffering: "the misery of man appears like a childish petulance, when we explore the steady and prodigal provision that has been made for his support and delight on this green ball which floats him through the heavens" (7). Such an assertion once again depends on a naturalization of Emerson's racial (and economic) privilege, a position that again (and unconsciously) inverts a slave's likely experience, in which provisions were far from "steady and prodigal" and misery all too real, a condition flowing directly from being used, like nature, for (white) men's "support and delight."[19]

TERRITORY AND THE
FUGITIVE SLAVE LAW

Slavery functioned as a metaphysical toxin in transcendentalist nature writing, always threatening to pollute the supposedly pristine wilderness and the supposedly transparent white identity that produced it and was produced by it, seeping into Emerson's transcendence and, as we will see, even into Thoreau's withdrawal. This threat becomes material and greatly magnified when, in 1850, the Fugitive Slave Law was passed, declaring that slaves who escaped to free states remained chattel, and legally mandating their return to their Southern masters. A green perspective allows us to see how the fury the law provoked in the North was not simply outrage over slavery (most Northern whites were virulently racist and opposed to abolition), but at the way the law deterritorialized it, eliding the division between free and slave states, between territory that was defined *as* slave and territory (imagined) *as* free.

Emerson describes this deterritorialization in his address on the law, claiming, "I have lived all my life without suffering any known inconvenience from American Slavery. I never saw it; I never heard the whip; I never felt the check on my free speech and action, until, the other day, when Mr. Webster, by his personal influence, brought the

Fugitive Slave Law on the country," and a few pages later that "I had never in my life *up to this time* suffered from the Slave institution. Slavery in Virginia or Carolina was like Slavery in Africa or the Feejees, for me" (780, 784, my emphasis).[20] For Emerson the law joined together the previously separate political and natural landscapes of Virginia, Africa, and Massachusetts, perversely uniting the country into a single ecosystem suffering the pollution of slavery. This seepage between the discourses of slavery, race, and nature is embodied in Emerson's description of Webster as both the incarnation of the American landscape and the source of the hated law. Before the law's passage, Webster has "the same quiet and sure feeling of right to his place that an oak or a mountain have to theirs," and is admired by the people as "the representative of the American Continent. He was there in his Adamitic capacity, as if he alone of all men did not disappoint the eye and the ear, but was a fit figure in the landscape" (781). But this resonant merge between the "Adamitic" Webster and the neo-Edenic American landscape is corrupted by its contact with the uncontainable degraded pastoralism of slavery via the medium of the Fugitive Slave Law. Webster's vote for the law is described as a failure to extend his uplifting white sublime identification to black people, a failure that degrades them both:

> Here was the question, Are you for man and for the good of man or are you for the hurt and harm of man? It was the question whether man shall be treated as leather? Whether the negro shall be, as the Indians were in Spanish America, a piece of money? Whether this system, which is a kind of mill or factory for converting men into monkeys, shall be upheld and enlarged? And Mr. Webster and the country went for the application to these poor men of quadruped law. (783–84)

Here the degrading transformation of slavery is seen as operating in the same metaphoric logic—"quadruped law"—as the commodification of the landscape and the fall of Webster from his natural sublimity: in slavery's "mill or factory for converting men into monkeys," "the negro" becomes "leather" or "a piece of money." Webster's degradation was also and simultaneously slavery's and the country's generally. The Fugitive Slave Law threatened to allow slavery to pollute the entire American landscape and all within it, fundamentally undermining the transcendentalist dream of a landscape outside of slavery, of a geography unmarked by race.

The essential geographic resonance of the Fugitive Slave Law becomes sharper still, when viewed from Thoreau's more explicitly

ecocritical perspective. Thoreau sees the law in environmentally apocalyptic terms in his aptly named "Slavery in Massachusetts":

> I have lived for the last month,—and I think that every man in
> Massachusetts capable of the sentiment of patriotism must have had a
> similar experience,—with the sense of having suffered a vast and indefi-
> nite loss. I did not know at first what ailed me. At last it occurred to me
> that what I had lost was a country. I had never respected the Government
> near to which I had lived, but I had foolishly thought that I might man-
> age to live here, minding my private affairs, and forget it. For my part,
> my old and worthiest pursuits have lost I cannot say how much of their
> attraction, and I feel that my investment in life here is worth many per
> cent. less since Massachusetts last deliberately sent back an innocent
> man, Anthony Burns, to slavery. I dwelt before, perhaps, in the illusion
> that my life passed somewhere only *between* heaven and hell, but now I
> cannot persuade myself that I do not dwell *wholly within* hell. The site of
> that political organization called Massachusetts is to me morally covered
> with volcanic *scoriae* and cinders, such as Milton describes in the infer-
> nal regions. If there is any hell more unprincipled than our rulers, and
> we, the ruled, I feel curious to see it. Life itself being worth less, all
> things with it, which minister to it, are worth less....
>
> I walk toward one of our ponds, but what signifies the beauty of
> nature when men are base? We walk to lakes to see our serenity
> reflected in them; when we are not serene, we go not to them. Who
> can be serene in a country where both the rulers and the ruled are
> without principle? The remembrance of my country spoils my walk.
> My thoughts are murder to the State, and involuntarily go plotting
> against her. (344–46)

Under the law, Thoreau loses his ability to escape to the woods, loses
his serenity; and, moreover, the woods themselves in effect change,
become not the Massachusetts he is familiar with, the land he loves,
but, hell, a lava-strewn wasteland. Rather than nature serving simply
as a transcendentalist escape from culture and history, here Thoreau
suggests that slavery rewrites both the New England landscape and
the white New England subject. The formal qualities of the transcendentalist merge of the enlightened individual with his surroundings is
retained, but the content of the surroundings and hence the transcendentalist subject, changes. Rather than a resolution of that merge
according to the template of the Romantic sublime, trauma moves
from its "safe" location in the enslaved black Southern body, and
infects Walden, infects Thoreau.

This scene revisits, in a broader political way, the racialized trauma
Crèvecoeur experienced earlier: the suffering of the anonymous slave

becomes the exemplary Anthony Burns, the "pleasant woods" become Massachusetts, what matters most is the white subject's secondary suffering over the trauma of slavery and not the black subject's primary suffering. But the trajectory is reversed here—Thoreau moves quickly to assert the essential purity of nature, concluding his invective with an image that to me in fact demonstrates how deeply woven slavery and race are into his landscape:

> But it chanced the other day that I secured a white water-lily, and a season I had waited for had arrived. It is the emblem of purity. It bursts up so pure and fair to the eye, and so sweet to the scent, as if to show us what purity and sweetness reside in, and can be extracted from, the slime and muck of earth. I think I have plucked the first one that has opened for a mile. What confirmation of our hopes is in the fragrance of this flower! I shall not so soon despair of the world for it, notwithstanding slavery, and the cowardice and want of principle of Northern men. It suggests what kind of laws have prevailed longest and widest, and still prevail, and that the time may come when man's deeds may smell as sweet. Such is the odor which the plant emits. If Nature can compound this fragrance still annually, I shall believe her still young and full of vigor, her integrity and genius unimpaired, and that there is virtue even in man, too, who is fitted to perceive and love it. It reminds me that Nature has been partner to no Missouri Compromise. I scent no compromise in the fragrance of the water-lily. It is not a *Nymphoea Douglassii*. In it, the sweet, and pure, and innocent, are wholly sundered from the obscene and baleful. (346)

Despite Thoreau's explicit assertion here that in the flower "the sweet, and pure, and innocent, are wholly sundered from the obscene and baleful," it is hard not to see a racially marked unconscious reemerging in the binary between the wild "*white* water-lily," the "emblem of purity...pure and *fair* to the eye" and the "slime and muck of the earth" that stands for slavery, explicitly "the sloth and vice of man, the decay of humanity," (347) in the closing sentence of the paragraph. Rather than being "wholly sundered" from slavery and blackness, the pure flower grows from their conflation. It is only separated from the racial and political context when *Thoreau* "plucks the first one that has opened for a mile," protesting too much that whatever sort of lily it is, it hasn't suffered the essential degradation of being named for a black abolitionist—it's not a "*Nymphoea Douglassi*." While Thoreau is of course right at some noumenal level that "Nature has been partner to no Missouri Compromise," his insistence here that that noumenal level is available to human beings in an extrapolitical and unconstructed way seems to me both poignant and wrong.

My point is not simply to blame Emerson or Thoreau for wanting to align themselves with a wild nature outside of the racist brutality of their historical moment, or for their desire to keep that realm separate from the degraded pastoralism of slavery. Their commitment to abolition and horror at the Fugitive Slave Law underscores both the appeal of that alliance with a definitionally free nature, and the even more fundamental threat that slavery posed to it for both men. But the desire for a pure natural realm outside of race, history, and politics—a realm in which individual freedom unmarked by racial difference and history is attainable—easily devolves into politically escapist fantasy and the naturalization of privilege, especially in the hands of people less ethically rigorous than Thoreau and Emerson. The fundamental truths of ecology—that "everything is connected to everything" and there is no place that is not nature—and of modern genetics—that there is no biological basis for race, that everyone is connected to everyone, that there is no human who is not human—always threaten to undermine these carefully constructed and violently maintained racial and environmental distinctions. In making that transcendentalist sublime realm "pure," the degraded territory outside it becomes impure, polluted, an Other, a different nature that is available for exploitation. It is not simply the escape promised by the sublime that is problematic, but what drawing that line does to the world outside it and the people who live and work there. When those bifurcated landscapes naturalize a similarly bifurcated racial essentialism, environmental exploitation and racial exploitation fuse in a history from which whites can benefit, while simultaneously washing away their historical consciousness and racial identity in the cool mountain stream of the sublime. This "world outside" the sublime is the place of the real plantation, a place where trauma was experienced directly rather than imagined, and the subject of the next chapter.

3

"Behold a Man Transformed into a Brute": Slavery and Antebellum Nature

Far from empowering the black subject, the conflation of blackness and nonhuman nature served as the principal "justification" for chattel slavery in antebellum America, a conflation that persists at the heart of most subsequent American racist ideologies. For antebellum African Americans, moments of instability between self-identity and the natural world were often violently reductive. The trauma inflicted on the caged slave in Crèvecoeur's passage literally reduces him, peck-by-peck, back to the pastoral landscape: caged like an animal, sightless, almost dumb, his face half-eaten, his humanity degraded to suffering meat that wants only the loss of consciousness that death by poison would bring. His body becomes no longer individual but representative, forced to manifest white terrorism to other slaves, and serving as an object of moral and physical horror for Crèvecoeur and presumably his contemporary white readers.[1]

But African-American slaves had much more to say about these issues than "Tanke, you white man, tanke you, pute some poison and give me." Evidence abounds that enslaved people, both in oral and written testimony, were intensely aware of how profoundly slavery depended on a violent and mutually constituting relation between blackness and a degraded pastoral—the reduction of the human to a locus of agricultural productivity, fertility, or a commodified and domesticated animality. As Mia Bay summarizes in her recent study of the early twentieth-century Works Progress Administration (WPA) interviews with former slaves,

> Throughout their oral testimony and their written accounts of bondage as well, former slaves compared the status of slaves to the condition of domestic animals. Rejecting the planter class's ideology of

paternalism, which designated slaves the dependent children of their benevolent masters, ex-slaves found their analogy for the slave-master relationship entirely outside the familial realm. Identifying not with their masters' dependent children but with their masters' four-legged chattel, ex-slaves remembered being fed like pigs, bred like hogs, sold like horses, driven like cattle, worked like dogs, and beaten like mules.

The parallels that ex-slaves drew between their status as slaves and the subordination of domestic animals suggests that enslaved African-Americans confronted racial slavery as an institution that blurred the line between man and beast, while confusing other categories as well. Servitude, subjection, and color, likewise, became overlapping categories in a society where all slaves were black, and most blacks were slaves. Amid this confusion of categories, the slaves highlighted one central fact: chattel slavery gave white people license to treat black people like beasts. The institution itself drew a line between the races that seemed to allow for the humanity of only one race. Hence, slave racial thought began with an assertion of sameness that embraced both blacks and whites: "Us an't hogs or horses," argued the slaves, "Us is human flesh." (119–20)

The narratives provide countless supporting examples in which slaves saw their condition not simply as the reduction to the status of a "thing" or property or capital (nor the "children" imagined by the slaveholder's disingenuous paternalism), but to a domesticated animal—an ox, mule, hog, horse, dog. So Harriet Jacobs declares, "These God-breathing machines are no more, in the sight of their masters, than the cotton they plant, or the horses they tend" (128) and "women are considered of no value, unless they continually increase their owner's stock. They are put on a par with animals" (175); Mary Prince says, "Oh the Buckra people who keep slaves think that black people are like cattle, without natural affection" (9); Henry Bibb asks, "whether a man can...hold his Christian brethren as property, so that they may be sold at any time in market, as sheep or oxen, to pay his debts?" (170–71); and Solomon Northup summarizes his young master's racial understanding: "He looked upon the black man simply as an animal, differing in no respect from any other animal, save in the gift of speech and the possession of somewhat higher instincts, and, therefore, the more valuable. To work like his father's mules—to be whipped and kicked and scourged through life—to address the white man with hat in hand, and eyes bent servilely on the earth, in his mind, was the natural and proper destiny of the slave. Brought up with such ideas—in the notion that we stand without the pale of humanity—no wonder the oppressors of my people are a pitiless and unrelenting race" (371).

The conflation of individual slaves with domestic animals paralleled a larger equation of slaves generally with the Southern landscape. Walter Johnson's important recent work on the history of the slave market underscores how tightly the slave trade was linked to commodity agriculture, particularly cotton production. Johnson notes, for example, that "the price of slaves traced the price of cotton to such a degree that it was a commonplace in the years after 1840 that the price of slaves could be determined by multiplying the price of cotton by ten thousand (seven cents per pound for cotton yielding seven hundred dollars per slave)" (6). Similarly, slaves were commonly used to underwrite mortgages; in one Louisiana parish slaves made up four-fifths of mortgage security.[2] Johnson notes how contemporary Southern agricultural manuals "included rising slave values among the attributes of a good crop" (26). Slaves were literally interchangeable with cotton and land in such calculations, different manifestations of the capitalized pastoral. And as the soil in the upper South became exhausted from erosion and monoculture tobacco farming, more than a million slaves were sold into the lower South to clear-cut and plant the huge cotton fields of the Gulf Coast and Mississippi Delta, a migration that itself ebbed and flowed in direct relation with the seasons of tillage and harvest.[3]

This fundamental discursive and material entanglement between blackness and nature suggests that slavery and racism in part sprang from a preexisting ecological instrumentalism practiced by European Americans. The genealogy of slavery and racism has roots in the exploitation of the African and North American continents and the islands of the Caribbean, the love/hate relation to the natural world that has marked the white attitude toward the land from the first European explorers to the present day. While I do not mean to equate the exploitation of black people and the exploitation of the environment morally, that doesn't mean that what is wrong about the conflation of black people and nature is exhausted by the fact of the conflation itself. That a structurally similar moment of blending between the white Romantic or transcendentalist subject and the natural world resolves so differently in the sublime underscores the determinative importance of the particular environmental assumptions and practices referenced by the nature with which the subject is merged. It was not simply the treatment of black people as if they were part of nature that underpinned slavery, in other words, but in making black people coextensive with a nature that existed solely to be exploited and "improved" by whites. Just as it would be simplistic to invoke a generalized category of "humanity" uninflected by constructions like race, gender, and class, so too it would be a mistake to overlook how different nature was from the perspective of a brutalized slave, as opposed to a white transcendentalist.

Among other things, nature is a human, ideological construction that generally reflects the political, cultural, and economic needs of the viewer. The nature with which the slave was conflated and from which he or she struggled to disassociate was not the untouched white sublime, but a nature valued chiefly for the resources and wealth it promised its human owners, a manifestation of the same exploitive attitude held by the early European settlers toward the wilderness and the possibility of transforming it into the "productive" pastoral that I discussed in the previous chapter. We see this second sort of nature exemplified in the "triangle trade" that peaked in the eighteenth and early nineteenth century, in which more than ten million slaves were purchased in Africa and traded to plantations in the West Indies for the tobacco, indigo, rice, cotton, coffee, and sugar cultivated by other slaves, commodities that were in turn sold in North America and Europe with the proceeds going to purchase more slaves in Africa and continue the cycle.[4] The triangle trade reflected not only the unholy confluence of economics and racism, but a more basic environmental viewpoint. Africans were literally seen as raw materials, an abundant natural resource of the "Dark Continent" that fueled the transformation of the Caribbean islands and the American South from a biodiverse semi-wilderness to clear-cut, farmed-out monoculture plantations. The economic practice of plantation slavery—from the African slave trade, to the internal slave trade, to the localized practices of breeding, beating, and auctioning individual slaves—depended not only on a set of economic practices and racial practices, but environmental ones. Slavery was in part the grotesque extension of a brutal set of preexisting environmental assumptions.

While the fact that slaves were often compared to domestic animals has hardly escaped critical notice, the tendency has often been to conflate that comparison with a comparison to property, capital, a thing, or even, for Houston Baker, a "nothing" from which the slave's "being had to erupt" existentially ("Autobiographical Acts," 245).[5] This largely unconscious tendency to confuse the animal or the pastoral with mere "thingdom," property, or money, reflects not only a widespread critical anthropocentrism, but misses how fundamentally important the specificity of the conflation was to the ways slavery was justified and perpetuated. To conflate the human and the domesticated animal was, in a symbolic sense, to *make a slave*, to retain the "usefulness" of the slave's human intelligence, sexuality, skills, and so forth, while justifying the whole thing by ascribing the slave's vocal and physical resistance to his or her animal status. As Kawash notes, the basic ideological challenge inherent in seeing slaves as property, "is that while the slave might be understood as property, they often refuse to act like property. The danger to slavery of such signs of rebellion is not necessarily all-out revolt…rather, such personal rebellion challenges the institution of slavery to recognize its own contradiction. To recognize the free will of the slave would require a recognition of the rights of the slave—and slavery demands the slave have none" (46). By recognizing the important particularity of the conflation of slaves with domesticated animals, rather than capital or property or "thingdom" generally, we see how the ideological challenge Kawash notes was not so much resolved as subsumed, avoided rather than answered. It becomes, for the slaveowner, a subset of the (non)question of animal rights, whether, for example, a pig's terrified struggle at its slaughter, or the evident suffering of calves and their mothers at their early separation in dairy farming should be a matter of human concern.[6] This is a question that few people worry about very much, particularly on a nineteenth-century farm. And this is why it matters that the slave is part of nature, a "brute" and not a wagon, a domesticated animal and not just capital. The slave's animal status "absorbed" the paradox of how a possession could be actively rebellious far more effectively than mere thing-status would. By making the slave an animal, the bracketing of the question of the rights of nature that had already been so successfully accomplished became available to the slave owner. Rather than confronting the question of rebellious property, the slave holder dodged it, subsuming it under the related, but much less pressing, question of animal rights.

David Walker, in one of the earliest—and perhaps the most vehement—abolitionist tracts authored by an African American, the 1829 *Appeal to the Coloured Citizens of the World*, sees this specific reduction of a human subject to an animal at the traumatic core of slavery's violence. He cries out:

> I call upon the professing Christians, I call upon the philanthropist, I call upon the very tyrant himself, to show me a page of history, either sacred or profane, on which a verse can be found, which maintains, that the Egyptians heaped the *insupportable insult* upon the children of Israel by telling them that they were not of the *human family*. Can the whites deny this charge? Have they not, after having reduced us to

> the deplorable condition of slaves under their feet, held us up as
> descending originally from the tribes of *Monkeys* or *Orang-Outangs*?
> O! my God! I appeal to every man of feeling—is not this insupport-
> able? Is it not heaping the most gross insult upon our miseries, because
> they have got us under their feet and we cannot help ourselves? (12)

Walker's anguished insistence here that slavery's exile of black people
from the "human family" is a "gross insult" of greater than Biblical
proportions, an unbearable, "insupportable" addition to the already
"miserable" and "deplorable" physical suffering of slavery records a
widely experienced trauma that echoes throughout the slave narratives that follow.[7] And for Walker, this reduction is not only extremely
painful, but provides the central ideological underpinnings for slavery
and racism, a conflation Walker traces to Jefferson's infamous racial
speculations in his *Notes on the State of Virginia*:

> I ask you, then, what set of men can you point me to, in all the world,
> who are so abjectly employed by their oppressors, as we are by our
> *natural enemies*? How can, Oh! how can those enemies but say that we
> and our children are not of the HUMAN FAMILY, but were made by
> our Creator to be an inheritance to them and theirs for ever? . . . . How
> could Mr. Jefferson but say, "I advance it therefore as a suspicion only,
> that the blacks, whether originally a distinct race, or made distinct by
> time and circumstances, are *inferior* to the whites in the endowments
> of both body and mind?"—"It," says he, "is not against experience to
> suppose, that different species of the same genius, or varieties of the
> same species, may possess different qualifications." [Here, my breth-
> ren, listen to him.] → "Will not a lover of natural history, then, one
> who views all the gradations in all the races of *animals* with the eye of
> philosophy, excuse an effort to keep those in the department of MAN
> as *distinct* as nature has formed them?"—I hope you will try to find
> out the meaning of this verse—its widest sense and all its bearings:
> whether you do or not, remember the whites do. *This very verse, breth-
> ren, having emanated from Mr. Jefferson, a much greater philosopher the
> world never afforded, has in truth injured us more, and has been as great
> a barrier to our emancipation as any thing that has ever been advanced
> against us.* I hope you will not let it pass unnoticed. (28–29)[8]

In Walker's analysis, the ideological nexus of white supremacy is this
literal naturalization of racism he finds in Jefferson's text. In the
passage Walker quotes, the supposedly neutral "lover of natural
history" first dodges the question of whether blacks were the same
species as whites—the debate in white eugenics between theories of
"monogenesis" and "polygenesis"—subsuming the origin of racial
difference under his broader "suspicion" that "the blacks are *inferior*
to the whites in the endowments of both body and mind." This

"suspicion" then becomes naturalized in a two-part process. First, Jefferson groups "all the races of animals" with "the department of MAN," seeing both as "formed" by "nature." Second, Jefferson's "suspicions" reemerge as empirical fact, when the supposedly neutral and scientific "lover of natural history...with the eye of philosophy" comes to see black inferiority as an intrinsic and readily observable trait—a "different qualification," a "gradation in all the races of animals" that reflects a "distinct[tion]" in the "department of MAN" that is "formed" by "nature"—akin (say) to the difference in size between a Great Dane and a Pekinese. Moreover, the (transparent?) "eye of philosophy" gazes at this (now) natural hierarchy from a place also outside it, another unmarked space of whiteness extruded at the moment of natural observation. While whites are placed at once at the top of the natural hierarchy and outside of it, both "naturally" superior and self-created, blackness remains rooted in its inferior—indeed, its enslaved—position within that natural hierarchy. The violent social construction of blackness and slavery on plantations like Monticello is here greenwashed in a way that absolutely depends on the conflation of African Americans with nature rather than with more explicitly human and artificial constructions like property, a conflation Walker understandably believes "has in truth injured us more, and has been as great a barrier to our emancipation as any thing that has ever been advanced against us."

AUTOBIOGRAPHY AND NATURE'S SILENCE

At the heart of most slave narratives is a simultaneous recoiling from, and return to, this traumatic conflation between African-American subjectivity and the natural world. Indeed, the generic structure of the slave narrative might be understood in terms of the authorial subject's movement along a continuum between "brute" nature and a fully articulate, self-created, generally urban, writer. Along this continuum, moments of greatest trauma occur when enslaved people are violently made consubstantial with nonhuman nature—when they are whipped, auctioned, "bred," raped, and otherwise denied sexual self-possession, when they are sold into the Deep South to farm cotton and sugar cane, when they work in the fields rather than the house, and, worst, when they despair and internalize such naturalized degradation as part of their own self-image. Conversely, moments of liberation occur when the separation from nature and animality is most marked, in physical and psychological resistance to such degrading moments—in assertions of grief over the loss of family and lovers, in religious faith, in escape from the largely pastoral South to the

largely urban North, and perhaps most conspicuously, in the achievement of literacy, the creation of the narrative itself.[9]

Viewed in this way, the slave narrative becomes, literally, *anti-
nature* writing, the enactment of, and proof of, the author's disconnection from nature, from the bestial and the field. To achieve literate
voice, to tell one's story, was to separate oneself categorically from the
South's commodified pastoral.[10] And in this sense, the difficulty many
authors felt in representing the trauma of slavery is in part a function
of this very connection to the definitionally speechless otherness of
nature.[11] When Henry Bibb, for example, claims, "that no tongue, nor
pen ever has or can express the horrors of American Slavery," and
"despair[s] in finding language to express adequately the deep feeling
of my soul, as I contemplate the past history of my life" (65), the problem is not simply that Bibb's suffering is too intense for words, but that
slavery's suffering is in part the denial of the possibility of being a
speaking subject at all, since to be a slave was to be aligned with nature
rather than humanity.[12] Bibb's struggle to describe what it was like to
be degraded to a commodified animality is (perversely) linked to the
difficulty nature writers generally face in reconstructing the definitionally extralinguistic within language, of making nature "speak."
Indeed, to speak the naturalized trauma of slavery is in some sense to
miss the point of what that trauma consisted in. Hence I think in part
the frustration Hortense Spillers notes that "in a very real sense, a full
century or so 'after the fact,' 'slavery' is *primarily* discursive, as we
search vainly for a point of absolute and indisputable origin, for a
moment of plenitude that would restore us to the real, rich 'thing'
itself before discourse touched it" ("Changing the Letter," 29).[13]

Spillers' passage raises several important questions for how critics
should approach the discursive lacuna of slavery's "true nature." Here
she describes (and quickly criticizes) what in effect is a longing for what
we might call the "slave sublime," not the actual "restoration" of the
terrors of "the real rich 'thing' itself before discourse touched it" but
the viewing of that terrible "point of absolute and indisputable origin,"
from a position of relative safety. The desire is not to return to the traumatic experience of human/natural conflation itself, but to peek at the
discursive collapse at the heart of slavery that conflation names from
the critic's textually instantiated position. In her imagined movement
from a fully textualized existence to a glimpsed prediscursive "moment
of plenitude," Spillers underscores, as I noted in the Introduction,
how sublimity might be thought of as a voyeurism of the traumatic, a
careful positioning of the subject just outside of the occurrence's representational and emotional event horizon, a horizon within which the

subject is permanently damaged or annihilated altogether. Our critical imagining of slavery's reduction of the human subject to a silenced animal/nature perhaps inevitably devolves into the sublime at least structurally if not emotionally, the mark of our distance from the inexpressible nature of the event itself. If we think of the naturalized trauma of slavery as the in fact "what happened" real of the history of slavery, then the sublime becomes not only a voyeurism of trauma generally, but in this case a voyeurism of history itself, the establishment of a sort of extrahistorical peephole, a separate place from which to view the others who are caught in the temporal narrative of suffering, and the occasion for the empowered individual to enact a fundamental separation from the traumatic scene of that history. Slavery becomes another representational frontier, a borderland where historical trauma is neither consuming nor unregistered.

I note how the sublime structures the reception of the slave narrative by present-day critics and its contemporary white audience, both to distinguish "our" experience of inexpressibility from the author's experience of it, and to foreground how that very inexpressibility means that the traumatic core of the slave narrative is only approachable in a second-order way, in terms of the structure of its reception and not "in itself." In arguing that a contemporary critical approach to slavery can replicate the structure of the sublime, I am of course not arguing that contemplating it produces Burkean pleasure, just that it poises the critic at the edge of the traumatic. Contemporary critics cannot "restore" the "rich, real 'thing' itself" before the imposition of this sublime structure but we can at least be aware of the distancing such a structure imposes, and avoid mistaking our experience of the "slave sublime" for the failure of representation at the heart of the trauma it encircles. In grappling with this problem, we are returned to ecocriticism's core problematic: how to account for a nature that is simultaneously a linguistic construction and someThing that escapes representation, an extratextual other that erupts into human textuality at the moment of the sublime, and into which the subject falls in the trauma of slavery. One difference between the natural sublime and the naturalized trauma of slavery comes in the sort of nature—sublime or commodified—with which the subject is conflated, and what possibilities for self-recovery the historical situation affords that subject.

In insisting on the eco-historical context as determinative, we might avoid repeating the very pattern I seek to name, in which blackness is subsumed under the sign of nature. This task is made doubly necessary by a larger commitment in ecocriticism, one that I share, that sees the human species generally as inseparably part of the natural world, and that is engaged by a broad critique of the ways discourse and material practice function to create a definitionally extranatural human sphere or to divide nature into "pure" and exploitable places. The difficulty of reconciling the fundamental eco-critical notion that there is one place, one nature, and that we are all expressions of it, with slavery's fundamental conflation of the human and animal is at the heart of the larger, racially marked division in environmentalism that persists to this day. It persists, I would argue, both because of how difficult that reconciliation is, and how easy it has been for white people historically to walk away from such questions—indeed, making that escape from history pleasurable is one of the functions of the natural sublime. But this division exists, and is historically rooted in slavery, despite the fact that environmentalism and ecocriticism have barely acknowledged it thus far.[14]

While Spillers does not connect the difficulty of finding the prediscursive origin of slavery to the related problem in nature writing of rendering in language the extralinguistic, the two issues are definitionally conjoined in the slave narratives. The moment of human/natural conflation that is slavery's trauma is precisely the moment when representation collapses, when human textuality becomes nature's silence. Just as the violence of slavery and racism piggy-backed on a preexisting ecological instrumentalism, so the difficulty of representing what it was like to be degraded to the status of an animal or a crop made the problem of representing slavery's naturalized trauma part of the problem of representing nature generally. Hence, in the slave narratives the traumatic moment of human/natural conflation often emerges suddenly, overwhelming or breaking the flow of the autobiography in a way that cannot be fully integrated into the larger story. The traumatized author is much more precariously located on that continuum between nature and the human/textual, always in danger of violent slippage back to the speechless. The generic movement from the speechless natural to the textual instantiation of the autobiographer that structures the slave narrative is always liable to sudden breakdown, reverse, a return to the originary reductive conflation at the traumatic core of slavery.

Take, for example, the following flashback Frederick Douglass records in the first version of his autobiography. Douglass is recalling the suffering of his early childhood on the Lloyd plantation, before leaving the rural South for Baltimore:

> I was seldom whipped by my old master, and suffered little from any thing else than hunger and cold. I suffered much from hunger, but

much more from cold. In hottest summer and coldest winter, I was kept almost naked—no shoes, no stockings, no jacket, no trousers, nothing on but a coarse tow linen shirt, reaching only to my knees. I had no bed. I must have perished with cold, but that, the coldest nights, I used to steal a bag which was used for carrying corn to the mill. I would crawl into this bag, and there sleep on the cold, damp, clay floor with my head in and feet out. My feet have been so cracked with the frost, that the pen with which I am writing might be laid in the gashes.

We were not regularly allowanced. Our food was coarse corn meal boiled. This was called *mush*. It was put into a large wooden tray or trough, and set down upon the ground. The children were then called, like so many pigs, and like so many pigs they would come and devour the mush; some with oyster-shells, others with pieces of shingle, some with naked hands, and none with spoons. He that ate fastest got most; he that was strongest secured the best place; and few left the trough satisfied. (33)

The passage records a systematic and degrading collapse of Douglass and the children into the commodified natural. In the first paragraph, Douglass's suffering is rendered in terms of his intimate exposure to the environment—he is kept half naked and terribly exposed to cold, sleeps on the dirt rather than in a bed, and in a particularly painful image that grotesquely illustrates the reductive pastoralism of slavery, crawls head first into a corn bag, his frostbitten feet taking the place of his face in the reader's imagination of the scene. This substitution of his wounded feet for his face—perhaps the most generic part of the body for the one most closely associated with speech and individual identity—and Douglass's literal packaging as an agricultural commodity, provides an image of natural degradation almost surreal in its totality. This image of utter conflation with the commodified natural, of a collapse of the human into the world, echoes the subsumption of the present of Douglass's compositional moment by his traumatic memory. The child becomes the naked chattel, lies on the dirt, becomes the agricultural commodity, becomes his feet rather than his head, becomes the wound, the "crack," the "gash," that testifies to the "frost" and that threatens to swallow Douglass's pen, and with it the possibility of language and the autobiographical project itself.[15] This literal gap in Douglass and in his narrative opens at the precise moment Douglass recalls his exposure to the natural, when the traumatic past suddenly threatens to consume the present. The gash is both a physical wound and a temporal one, a combination that recalls precisely the "latency" Caruth finds at the heart of traumatic experience.

Then, in a sort of nightmarish furthering of the first passage's conflation, in the second paragraph the contents of the bag return from the
mill as food for the slave children. Douglass's individual suffering disappears entirely into the herd-like third person plural of the "children," a
syntactic disappearance now coded as a degradation to the animal—
"the children were then called, *like so many pigs,* and *like so many pigs*
they would come and devour the mush." Simple physical survival
entailed a certain amount of participation in natural degradation, as the
starving children competed with each other for the inadequate supply of
food, eating from a trough, desperately scooping up the mush with
shells, shingles, and hands. This substitution of agricultural practice for
child-raising produces slavery and blackness *in and as* that substitution,
both for the children involved and for the whites who controlled and
observed such moments. Douglass encodes this production in the
repetition-with-a-difference of his simple, terrible simile. In the first
iteration, the children are called by the white overseer, "like so many
pigs" a simile that makes the white overseer responsible for the conflation: it is his *calling* that misidentifies the children as pigs. In the second
iteration, however, the simile moves much closer to a form of internalized identity, what Althusser would call "interpellation"—the children
are "like so many pigs" not because they are "called," but because they
answer, because they "come" and "eat" as if they were pigs.[16] And the
simile finds perhaps a third iteration in the reader's own consciousness,
as we make sense of Douglass's simile, seeing both the process of its
construction and the result as his comparison structures our imagination of the children and their degradation, as we recognize them as the
subjects of the slave ideology's hailing. None of which is to blame the
children, Douglass, or even the reader, but to note how the process of
human/animal conflation operates to produce a particular, familiar
image of slavery and blackness. Douglass doesn't say—and doesn't need
to say—anywhere in the passage that the children are black or that they
are slaves for the reader to know both their race and status.

GROWING UP INTO SLAVERY

The interpenetration of subjectivity and nature does not naturalize
either slavery or its associated landscapes in fact—only in practice.
There is, of course, nothing natural about slavery, nor its complex and
intimate historical association with an instrumentalized, violently
objectifying relation to the natural world. This does not mean, however, that there is a preexisting unconstructed "human nature" or pure
landscape that then gets corrupted by slavery. Rather, one construction

is exchanged for another, much worse one; slave childhood becomes a sort of Blakean Song of Innocence, a stereotypical pastoral nature that depends on ignorance of the realities of the commodified historical and economic landscape in which the child has already been emplaced.[17] Maturation is figured as the simultaneous recognition of the constructedness and fragility of that stereotypically pastoral nature with which the child is associated, the transition from a salutary, to a profoundly traumatic intimacy with the constructed landscape, a moment of exposure to the preexisting commodification of the Southern landscape that reflexively produces and is produced by the practice of slavery. Slavery shapes the landscape and the landscape shapes slavery; both the *fact* of this connection, and the fact that is not natural but violently constructed, is another way of stating the thesis of this chapter.

In a few pages at the start of his 1855 autobiography, *My Bondage, My Freedom*, Douglass returns three times to this complex interchange in which the identification with an external nature that mixes salutary and historically traumatic elements in turn produces a similarly conflicted subject. Indeed, Douglass stages the dawning of the traumatic awareness of his slave status as both his passage into adolescence and as a recognition of the commodification of a previously existing bond with his surroundings. In all three passages he moves from the supposedly "innocent" enjoyment of a stereotypical American boyhood spent in the great outdoors to the terrible realization of his coming adult identity as the chattel property of another, a thematic repetition that underscores the clinically traumatic nature of this transformation as Douglass and his narrative keep returning to the originary traumatic event.[18]

The first passage describes the setting of Douglass's childhood as utterly embedded in a larger, terrible context. It is the shock of discovering that context and the consequent shattering of that natural innocence that Douglass returns to again and again at the opening of this autobiography:

> Living here, with my dear old grandmother and grandfather, it was a long time before I knew myself to be *a slave*. I knew many other things before I knew that. Grandmother and grandfather were the greatest people in the world to me; and being with them so snugly in their own little cabin—I supposed it to be their own—knowing no higher authority over me or the other children than the authority of grandmamma, for a time there was nothing to disturb me; but, as I grew larger and older, I learned by degrees the sad fact, that the "little hut," and the lot on which it stood, belonged not to my dear old grandparents, but to some person who lived a great distance off, and who was called, by grandmother, "OLD MASTER." I further learned the sadder fact, that not only the house

and lot, but that grandmother herself (grandfather was free,) and all the little children around her, belonged to this mysterious personage, called by grandmother, with every mark of reverence, "Old Master." Thus early did clouds and shadows begin to fall upon my path. Once on the track— troubles never come singly—I was not long in finding out another fact, still more grievous to my childish heart. I was told that this "old master," whose name seemed ever to be mentioned with fear and shuddering, only allowed the children to live with grandmother for a limited time, and that in fact as soon as they were big enough, they were promptly taken away, to live with the said, "old master."...

The absolute power of this distant "old master" had touched my young spirit with but the point of its cold, cruel iron, and left me something to brood over after the play and in moments of repose. Grandmammy was, indeed, at that time, all the world to me; and the thought of being separated from her, in any considerable time, was more than an unwelcome intruder. It was intolerable. (142–43)

In this passage Douglass counterpoises his early life with his grandparents, "the greatest people in the world," in their "snug little cabin" with a cascading knowledge of the terrible thoroughgoing commodification of everything around him. First he discovers that "the little hut and the lot on which it stood, belonged not to my dear old grandparents, but to some person who lived a great distance off, and who was called, by grandmother, "Old Master." Second, in a by now familiar pattern, he finds that the relationship of the white master to the land extends to include the black people living on it; that the alliance with nature he initially finds salutary, is in fact a source of degradation—he learns "the sadder fact, that not only the house, and lot, but that grandmother herself...and all the little children around her, belong to this mysterious personage." Finally, Douglass learns that the link between owned-him and the owned-land that marks him as a slave is itself fungible, that his reduction to the status of a natural commodity makes him portable, means that his organic relationship to place and relative is to be, inevitably and traumatically, broken. Tellingly, this experience is described as the touch of a made, inorganic thing, "the point of cold, cruel iron." This touch, this commodification, this sundering of Douglass from his identification with place, family, and self, is the essence of his trauma, an ever-returning, "intolerable" thought.

Douglass then switches temporal and authorial perspectives, redescribing the relation of the slave child to the natural world from the position of an adult self with ample experience of how slavery operates:

[F]reed from all restraint, the slave-boy can be, in his life and conduct, a genuine boy, doing whatever his boyish nature suggests; enacting, by turns, all the strange antics and freaks of horses, dogs, pigs and barn-door fowls, without in any manner compromising his dignity, or incurring reproach of any sort. He literally runs wild; has no pretty little verses to learn in the nursery; no nice little speeches to make for aunts, uncles, or cousins, to show how smart he is; and, if he can only manage to keep out of the way of the heavy feet and fists of the older slave boys, he may trot on, in his joyous and roguish tricks, as happy as any little heathen under the palm trees of Africa. To be sure, he is occasionally reminded, when he stumbles in the path of his master—and this he early learns to avoid—that he is earning his "*white bread*," and that he will be made to "*see sights*" by-and-by. The threat is soon forgotten; the shadow soon passes, and our sable boy continues to roll in the dust, or play in the mud, as bests suits him, and in the veriest freedom. If he feels uncomfortable, from mud or from dust, the coast is clear; he can plunge into the river or the pond, without the ceremony of undressing or the fear of wetting his clothes; his little tow-linen shirt—for that is all he has on—is easily dried; and it needed ablution as much as did his skin. His food is of the coarsest kind, consisting for the most part of corn-meal mush, which often finds its way from the wooden tray to his mouth in an oyster shell. His days, when the weather is warm, are spent in the pure, open air, and in the bright sunshine. He always sleeps in airy apartments; he seldom has to take powders, or to be paid to swallow pretty little sugar-coated pills, to cleanse his blood, or to quicken his appetite. He eats no candies; gets no lumps of loaf sugar; always relishes his food; cries but little, for nobody cares for his crying; learns to esteem his bruises but slight, because others so esteem them. In a word he is, for the most part of the first eight years of his life, a spirited, joyous, uproarious, and happy boy, upon whom troubles fall only like water on a duck's back. And such a boy, so far as I can now remember, was the boy whose life in slavery I am now narrating. (144–45)

Douglass here interweaves several narrative levels in an extraordinarily subtle and bittersweet analysis of the ways natural experience and historical context shape the slave's childhood while he is still innocent of his fate. The passage's effect depends on the simultaneous conjunction and incompatibility of a wide range of attitudes toward the natural world. On the one hand, the slave child's relation to nature makes him happy and free, more so than his white counterparts: he is "a genuine boy, doing whatever his boyish nature suggests," "joyous and roguish," spending summer days "in the pure, open air, and in the bright sunshine" and his nights sleeping in "airy apartments," "a spirited, joyous, uproarious, and happy boy, upon whom troubles fall only like water on a duck's back." However compromised, this early experience describes an extraordinarily unmediated bond with the natural world, one of which Daniel Boone and Davy Crockett, Tom Sawyer and Huck Finn, even William Wordsworth, might have been proud. By invoking a stereotypically ideal natural boyhood, "freed from all restraint," in which the young slave is empowered to engage in a "wilder" and much closer relation to the natural world than his white counterparts are permitted, Douglass makes the black child's behavior exemplify a human rather than racial natural—but, of course only temporarily.

At the same time, however, the mature Douglass and the reader bear the "intolerable" knowledge of what is to come, the "touch of iron" that will not "fall only like water," the imminent pollution of this "genuine...boyish nature." The very bond with the natural world that the child enjoys, and that nurtures and sustains him, is simultaneously a form of terrible neglect: Douglass is not taught anything, from table manners, to basic etiquette, to bathing, and his tears and bruises are entirely ignored. It leads him (as a boy) to the unconscious performance of a range of ugly racialized stereotypes, "enacting, by turns, all the strange antics and freaks of horses, dogs, pigs, and barn-door fowls," acting "as happy as any little heathen under the palm trees of Africa," "roll[ing] in the dust, or play[ing] in the mud," and eating, (like a pig), "corn meal mush" from a "wooden tray."

Perhaps more important, in "doing what comes naturally"—acting in the "untamed" manner that the white children might emulate if they weren't tightly controlled/cared for—Douglass's imminent conversion from the "state of nature" to chattel becomes synecdochic for the larger "improvement" of the landscape into a more "useful" capitalized form, for the domestication of the wilderness. The early colonial entwining of ecological and racial practice, in which the wild was coded as the racial other and the controlled pastoral as white, is here transposed onto the slave boy himself, forcing him to signify not simply the wild or the pastoral, but the whole process of conversion from raw material to agricultural commodity. In doing so, Douglass offers us a portrait of the irreducible mix of beauty and trauma that comprises the slave's relation to the natural world and its fundamental links to environmental exploitation.

The last passage in this sequence of repetition-with-a-difference records this process of conversion in Douglass's own personal history, the final and inexorable internalization of the "intolerable" knowledge of the difference between being identified with a "free" nature and a commodified one:

> The fact is, such was my dread of leaving the little cabin, that I wished to remain forever, for I knew the taller I grew the shorter my stay. The

old cabin, with its rail floor and rail bedsteads up stairs, and its clay floor down stairs, and its dirt chimney, and windowless sides, and that most curious piece of workmanship of all the rest, the ladder stairway, and the hole curiously dug in front of the fire-place, beneath which my grandmammy placed the sweet potatoes to keep them from the frost, was MY HOME—the only home I ever had; and I loved it, and all connected with it. The old fences around it, and the stumps in the edge of the woods near it, and the squirrels that ran, skipped, and played upon them, were objects of interest and affection. There, too, right at the side of the hut, stood the old well, with its stately and skyward-pointing beam, so aptly placed between the limbs of what had once been a tree, and so nicely balanced that I could move it up and down with only one hand, and could get a drink myself without calling for help. Where else in the world could such a well be found, and where could such another home be met with? Nor were these all the attractions of the place. Down in a little valley, not far from grand-mammy's cabin, stood Mr. Lee's mill, where the people came often in large numbers to get their corn ground. It was a water-mill; and I never shall be able to tell the many things thought and felt, while I sat on the bank and watched that mill, and the turning of that ponderous wheel. The mill-pond, too, had its charms; and with my pin-hook, and thread line, I could get *nibbles*, if I could catch no fish. But, in all my sports and plays, and in spite of them, there would, occasionally, come the painful foreboding that I was not long to remain there, and that I must soon be called away to the home of old master.

I was A SLAVE—born a slave—and though the fact was incomprehensible to me, it conveyed to my mind a sense of my entire dependence on the will of *somebody* I had never seen; and, from some cause or other, I had been made to fear this somebody above all else on earth. Born for another's benefit, as the *firstling* of the cabin flock I was soon to be selected as a meet offering to the fearful and inexorable *demi-god*, whose huge image on so many occasions haunted my childhood's imagination. (146–47)

Rather than a movement toward adult self-possession that "should" mark an American narrative beginning in such natural auspiciousness, Douglass's physical development becomes only a sign of his increasing commodification—"I knew the taller I grew the shorter my stay." The familiar cry of grandparents, aunts and uncles—"My how you've grown"—and the corresponding pride such growth evokes in the child is perverted by slavery's substitution of an agricultural model of development for a human one. Having established this most intimate anxiety about commodification that pervades even growth, the most basic and natural sign of maturation, Douglass suddenly returns to a salutary portrait of his relation to his natural surroundings, offering his readers another stereotypical—though I think genuinely felt—version of boyish natural delight at the beloved homestead, complete with the be-laddered old cabin, loving grandparents, a root cellar, old fences, skipping squirrels, an old well, a watermill, a pond, the nibble of ever-uncaught fish. But of course, however idyllic, this pastoral nature offers no protection from the violence of the Old Master's ownership, suffusing Douglass's "sports and plays" with "painful foreboding." Douglass's slave identity finally arrives in the metaphoric transformation of his "glad animal spirits" (to borrow Wordsworth's phrase) in the first paragraph to literal animality in the second, as he comes to see himself as the "*firstling* of the cabin *flock*...soon to be selected as a meet offering to the fearful and inexorable *demi-god*." The Romantic pastoral becomes a scene of animal sacrifice. Douglass goes from identifying with the former to *being* the latter, or more precisely, his initial identification of himself with the natural world becomes the conduit for the simultaneous commodification of both at the hands of Old Master. Indeed, that idyllic nature itself becomes the trigger for the traumatic break, a break recorded repeatedly in these passages as the disjunctive move from Douglass's evident bond with the natural setting of his childhood to the terrible adult realities of who owns it, and him.

Whipping and Auctions

The two most traumatic events that recur endlessly throughout the narratives—whipping and auctions—might each be read as a primal scene of human/natural conversion that reinforced the lessons of slave childhood. Both were forms of trauma that not only caused terrible physical and psychic pain, but functioned systematically, as symbolic machines that took human beings and at least attempted to reinscribe them as degraded and racially marked pastoral commodities. And, as many of the narratives point out, this conversion operated on both whites and blacks—to be beaten or sold was to be treated like an animal; to beat, sell, or buy others was to subsume and repress a recognition of their personhood under the white/human dominance over the nonhuman natural.

Descriptions of whipping were governed by metaphors of "taming" or "breaking" the slave's rebellious humanity, and characteristically stressed the stripping and public display of the slave's naked body, the binding of the slave to a tree or the ground, the application of the lash (often referred to as the "cowhide")—a particular form of punishment or discipline otherwise reserved for animals—the substitution of blood and wound for the body's human shape, of cries and moans for speech. The result was a procedure that at every point strove to reduce the humanity of the enslaved person to the bestial, both for the person receiving the beating and for the person administering it. "You are nature" says the whip, "and this is what I do to nature when it resists my will."[19] Take Mary Prince's description as exemplary:

> How can slaves be happy when they have the halter round their neck and the whip upon their back? and are disgraced and thought no more of than beasts?—and are separated from their mothers, and husbands, and children and sisters, just as cattle are sold and separated? Is it happiness for the driver in the field to take down his wife or sister or child, and strip them, and whip them in such a disgraceful manner?—women that have had children exposed in the open field to shame! There is no modesty or decency shown by the owner to his slaves; men, women, and children are exposed alike.... They tie up slaves like hogs—moor them up like cattle, and they lick them, so as hogs or cattle, or horses never were flogged.... (22–23)

Prince's almost frantic compendium of abuses returns again and again to the ways physical punishment is tied to symbolic degradation, how the "halter" and "whip upon their back" are not simply bad because they are painful, or the stripping in the field because immodest, but because such acts signify the conflation of the slave to domesticated animals like "cattle," "hogs," and "horses."[20] Whipping is a form of nature writing, like the tree it inscribes on Sethe's back in Morrison's *Beloved*, both the construction and instantiation of a violent and wholly instrumentalist view of the natural world, and the conflation of black people with that instantiated construction.

Similarly, the terrible drama of the auction that recurs throughout the narratives also functions as a symbolic mechanism for converting human beings into natural capital. For the whites attending the auction—and often for subsequent critics as well—such a transformation was often perceived in strictly commercial terms, as a binary exchange between the slave's identity and his or her cash value.[21] While this fluidity between the slave and money was certainly present, such an analysis can overlook how the experience was perceived by the slaves themselves, making the moment of capitalist exchange the privileged center of the auction's trauma. I want to argue that that moment of exchange depended on, and occurred within, the context of a by-now-familiar set of attitudes toward blackness and the natural world. The slave was not simply converted into money, but first and always already into a commodified natural object.[22] For the slaves involved, the insult and agony of the auction did not necessarily lie only in the fact of being bought and sold, but the assumptions upon which that reduction to a price depended. To stand on the block was not necessarily to feel one's degradation to cash value, but to confront the more primary degradation to animality or natural resource that the secondary degradation of purchase manifested. Hence the bitter protest Bay reports one slave woman made at auction, raising her hands and shouting "Weigh 'em cattle, weigh 'em cattle" (133). Or as Mary Prince describes in more detail:

> At length the vendue master, who was to offer us for sale like sheep or cattle, arrived, and asked my mother which was the eldest. She said nothing, but pointed to me. He took me by the hand, and led me out into the middle of the street, and, turning me slowly round, exposed me to the view of those who attended the vendue. I was soon surrounded by strange men, who examined and handled me in the same manner that a butcher would a calf or a lamb he was about to purchase, and who talked about my shape and size in like words—as if I could no more understand their meaning than the dumb beast. I was then put up to sale. (4)

To see the auction as simply establishing a racially based fungibility between human identity and cash value is, I would argue, a form of the same mistake critics have made in subsuming the particularity of the landscapes and animals with which the slaves were identified under the more general category of "thing-ness," "nothingness," or undifferentiated "property." While the auction undoubtedly performed such alchemic transformations of money and people, that alchemy was not magical but entirely contained within a broader, systemic, and thoroughly commodified relation to nature, a relation that was applied to black people in the very assumptions underlying the auction. The moment of the transaction may have been the center of the auction's meaning for the white seller and buyer, but it wasn't for a writer like Prince.[23] Rather, in her account, it is the material performance of another animal simile like Douglass's that is the primary humiliation—the *manner* of the examination that literally treated her like veal or mutton, the total suppression of her ability to hear and speak.[24] Only then—*after* suffering this degradation—is she "put up to sale." The locus of the auction's meaning was not the transaction—or was only so for the white seller and buyer—but in the assumptions about black people and a commodified nature that underlay the auction, assumptions that were naturalized as the enabling conditions of the sale.

SEXUAL AND ENVIRONMENTAL VIOLENCE

While Prince's "viewing," "handling," and "examination" by the men in the street were forms of humiliation common to both male and female slaves, the endemic rape and other sexual abuse of slave women made Prince's degradation to the animal also a form of sexual commodification.[25] These two forms of degradation or vulnerability should not simply be conflated, however. While slave women were subject to the ungendered racism that broadly "justified" slavery, and often endured the same sort of violence—whipping, auctions, back-breaking field work, and the like—that men did, they were also vulnerable to forms of gendered exploitation and sexual violence in a way that was often in perverse tension with the "transformation" to the "brute" those generically violent practices were meant to produce.[26]

The relation of female slaves to the land and domesticated animality was frequently more complex and contradictory than it was for male slaves, and accordingly their alienation from the natural world was often more acute than for black men. Widely held extraracial gender assumptions about women's particular suitability for domestic labor granted men in general much greater access to natural experience than women. As a result, while male slaves were often purchased for outdoor labor and valued for their health, strength, docility, manual skills, and so forth, slave women were more frequently employed for more domestic tasks than men (which is not to say they weren't used extensively in the fields as well), and were valued for a range of attributes, from suitability for cotton picking and reproductive capacity on the "brute" side of the continuum, to cooking, cleaning, and sewing, and companionship on the other.[27] And for many female slaves, of course, this domestic work included occasional or regular rape by the white men of the house. Indeed, the most valuable female slaves—often light skinned, "delicate" women, called "fancies" by the brokers and selling for three times the price of a male field hand—were sold expressly for concubinage.[28]

In a painful irony, this exposure to sexual predation afforded some slave women temporary "protection" from the complete conflation with the natural that marked slavery for most, though what they were shielded from was often preferable to the treatment they received instead. As Harriet Jacobs declares, "I would rather drudge out my life on a cotton plantation, till the grave opened to give me rest, than to live with an unprincipled master and a jealous mistress.... I had rather toil on the plantation from dawn till dark; I had rather live and die in jail, than drag on, from day to day, through such a living death"

(154, 179). The more a female slave was degraded to the animal through flogging, field work, bad diet, psychological collapse, and so forth, the less sexually attractive she presumably became to her white master, the less "fancy." And yet, the less natural, the more "human"— read white—she seemed, the more the whole justificatory structure of slavery was called into question, as evidenced by the stream of "tragic mulattas" pleading the case of their "race" before expiring in countless antislavery novels.[29]

It was this very contradiction that the fancy embodied. Making the monetary value of the fancy a measure of what sort of black women white men, in general, found particularly sexually attractive does not mean they were desirable simply because they "looked white." The fancy's identity was hybrid; she was attractive for being *both* black and white. That hybridity allowed a wide range of fantasy projections: for some she was undoubtedly a figure that promised the supposed hypersexuality of black women in a white package, whose status as chattel made her a "white" woman who could be legally raped; for others her "whiteness" undoubtedly provided cover for white men who were in fact primarily attracted to darker-skinned women.[30] This contradiction—in which slave women were simultaneously rendered as chattel that could be exploited without qualm or limit, and as sexual objects whose monetary value to their white masters increased in direct proportion to their distance from chattel—turned the slave woman's body and sexuality from the site of self-possession into a racially saturated locus of conflicting definitions, a battleground both semiotic and intimately physical.[31]

This distinction mirrored the familiar bifurcated relation whites had long had with the American landscape itself, a place both of "unspoiled" beauty and limitless exploitation. Jacobs both makes this connection explicit, and reveals how the sexual practices of plantation slavery profoundly interconnected the two landscapes:

> I once saw two beautiful children playing together. One was a fair white child; the other was her slave, and also her sister. When I saw them embracing each other, and heard their joyous laughter, I turned sadly away from the lovely sight. I foresaw the inevitable blight that would fall on the little slave's heart. I knew soon her laughter would be changed to sighs. The fair child grew up to be a still fairer woman. From childhood to womanhood her pathway was blooming with flowers and overarched by a sunny sky. Scarcely one day of her life had been clouded when the sun rose on her happy bridal morning.
>
> How had those years dealt with her slave sister, the little playmate of her childhood? She was also very beautiful; but the flowers and

sunshine of love were not for her. She drank the cup of sin, and shame, and misery, whereof her persecuted race are compelled to drink. (153)

Here the pastoral landscape itself splits along racial and gendered lines. Both sisters start off playing together in a place "blooming with flowers and overarched by a sunny sky." But this originary unity divides at the point of adolescence, when the unhappy sexual history of the plantation that produced their interracial sisterhood reasserts its traumatic pattern. The emergence of sexual maturity bonds the white girl's sexuality to the idyllic pastoral, in ways familiar to anyone who has read the white Southern romance. The sun shines continuously on her, from childhood to her "bridal morning"; the unspoiled pastoral signifies her purity and her purity signifies the unspoiled pastoral in an unbroken reflexive relationship. Conversely, the black girl is quickly exiled from that originary landscape, her sexual maturity taking her out of "the flowers and sunshine of love" to the arms of the master where she "drink[s] the cup of sin, and shame, and misery." As Jacobs says just before this passage, "If God has bestowed beauty on [the slave girl], it will prove her greatest curse. That which commands admiration in the white woman only hastens the degradation of the female slave" (151). From the same starting point—"natural" childhood beauty—two very different, racially marked resolutions obtain: one white, pastoral, fragile, and pure, one black, "cursed," "degraded," and exploitable.[32]

Throughout *Incidents in the Life of a Slave Girl*, Jacobs figures the violently exploitive sexuality of the Southern plantation as a sort of toxin that pollutes the Southern social, familial, racial, and physical landscape, noting a few pages later what a coarsening loss of innocence awaits the white bride:

The poor girls have romantic notions of a sunny clime, and of the flowering vines that all the year round shade a happy home. To what disappointments are they destined! The young wife soon learns that the husband in whose hands she has placed her happiness pays no regard to his marriage vows. Children of every shade of complexion play with her own fair babies, and too well she knows that they are born unto him of his own household. Jealousy and hatred enter the flowery home, and it is ravaged of its loveliness.

Southern women often marry a man knowing that he is the father of many little slaves. They do not trouble themselves about it. They regard such children as property, as marketable as the pigs on the plantation; and it is seldom that they do not make them aware of this by passing them into the slave-trader's hands as soon as possible, and thus getting them out of sight. (159–60)

In Jacobs's analysis, the institutionalized sexual exploitation of black women in slavery corrupts everyone and everything that comes into contact with it, from the innocent Northern white bride whose dreams of a "sunny clime" and "flowery vines" shading a "happy home" are "ravaged," to the already brutalized Southern women, who accept their husbands' systematic infidelity by transferring their "jealousy and hatred" into an enactment of the very human/natural commodification I have argued is at the heart of slavery.[33] Their husbands' children are transformed by the Southern white women's "regard" into "property, as marketable as the pigs on the plantation."[34] While Jacobs explicitly blames white male sexuality for the "all-pervading corruption produced by slavery" (177) and takes great care to avoid invoking racist stereotypes about black women's sexuality, in the white wives' transference (and throughout Jacob's narrative) we can see the larger, tragic, and quite familiar story of female slaves becoming scapegoats for white male crimes, forced to represent the unrestrained sexuality of which they are in fact the victim.[35]

Caught between different, profoundly interconnected and terribly dangerous ways of relating to the natural—a temporary elevation to the white female pastoral that exposed her to rape, or a degradation to the animal that (perhaps) made her less desirable to the master while exposing her to all the generic brutality of slavery—slave women could neither safely identify with the natural world nor safely separate themselves from it. While black men like Douglass could often mark with bitter precision their position on the continuum between "brute" and man (if not, indeed, literate urban autobiographer), black women's position on it was much more ambiguous, a hypermobility on that continuum produced by the shifting desires of their male and female owners, their relation to black men, and their own struggles for autonomy.[36]

It is in the context of this ambiguity and hypermobility on the human/natural continuum that we should read the central image of Jacobs's "escape" from slavery and Mr. Flint's sexual abuse, to what she calls a "loophole of retreat" in her grandmother's tiny attic:

> A small shed had been added to my grandmother's house years ago. Some boards were laid across the joists at the top, and between these boards and the roof was a very small garret, never occupied by any thing but rats and mice. It was a pent roof, covered with nothing but shingles, according to the southern custom for such buildings. The garret was only nine feet long and seven wide. The highest part was three feet high, and sloped down abruptly to the loose board floor. There was no admission for either light or air.... The air was

stifling; the darkness total. A bed had been spread upon the floor.
I could sleep quite comfortably on one side; but the slope was so
sudden that I could not turn on the other without hitting the roof.
The rats and mice ran over my bed; but I was weary, and I slept such a
sleep as the wretched may, when a tempest has passed over them.
Morning came. I knew it only by the noises I heard; for in my small
den day and night were all the same. I suffered for air even more than
for light.... This continued darkness was oppressive. It seemed horrible to sit or lie in a cramped position day after day, without one gleam
of light. Yet I would have chosen this, rather than my lot as a slave,
though white people considered it an easy one; and it was so compared
with the fate of others. I was never cruelly over-worked; I was never
lacerated with the whip from head to foot; I was never so beaten and
bruised that I could not turn from one side to the other; I never had
my heel-strings cut to prevent my running away; I was never chained
to a log and forced to drag it about, while I toiled in the fields from
morning to night; I was never branded with hot iron, or torn by blood-
hounds. On the contrary, I had always been kindly treated, and ten-
derly cared for, until I came into the hands of Dr. Flint. I had never
wished for freedom until then. But though my life in slavery was
comparatively devoid of hardships, God pity the woman who is
compelled to lead such a life! (250–51)

Jacobs does not leave this cramped space for *seven years*, suffering
from biting insects, rats and mice, stifling heat in the summer, frost-
bite in the winter, and nearly losing the use of her limbs entirely; she
means it when she claims that she would prefer any amount of physical suffering to enduring Flint's sexual torment.[37]

Jacobs's loophole of retreat is safe in part because it refuses to
align itself with either pole of the human/natural contradiction; it
is neither a natural space nor a domestic space, but a material and
symbolic hybrid of the two.[38] As she says elsewhere, "...it was the
last place they thought of.... there was no place, where slavery
existed, that could have afforded me so good a place of conceal-
ment" (253). To "retreat" to the loophole, a "no place" extruded
into the midst of slavery, is both to be utterly enfolded into the
indoor domestic and to be outside the house, exposed to the elements. In occupying both places, being both inside and outside,
Jacobs straddles the contradictory poles of female slave identity,
holds them in suspension rather than oscillating between them.[39]
The attic is "the last place they thought of" because it is a "place"
not readily locatable on the continuum that organizes the personal
and physical geography of slavery. In the loophole—and at a terrible
cost—Jacobs is neither a brute nor a kept woman, neither an animal

nor a domestic, but can leave the mental and material landscape "where slavery existed."

THE NATURES OF SLAVERY

Just as whipping, the auction, and sexual exploitation serve as exemplary moments of slavery's traumatic conflation of black people and a commodified pastoralism, so in turn do such practices act reflexively to reinforce the split between an abject "nature" seen as a source of raw materials, profit and as a receptacle for waste, and a pure realm, untouched by the brutality of human history. The narratives display an acute awareness of the distinction between these two natures, a distinction vital to both the rhetorical strategy of the narratives and to the possibility of retrieving some sense of the salutary bond between enslaved African Americans and the natural world that, however conflicted and vulnerable to exploitation, was also an important site of resistance and sustenance. The sharp contrast between a traumatized and a "free" nature is evident, for example, in Henry Bibb's anguish and longing at the sight of the Ohio River:

> Sometime standing on the Ohio River bluff, looking over on a free State, as far north as my eyes could see, I have eagerly gazed upon the blue sky of the free North, which at times constrained me to cry out from the depths of my soul, Oh! Canada, sweet land of rest—Oh! when shall I get there? Oh, that I had the wings of a dove, that I might soar away to where there is no slavery; no clanking of chains, no captives, no lacerating of backs, no parting of husbands and wives; and where man ceases to be the property of his fellow man. These thoughts have revolved in my mind a thousand times. I have stood upon the lofty banks of the river Ohio, gazing upon the splendid steamboats, wafted with all their magnificence up and down the river, and I thought of the fishes of the water, the fowls of the air, the wild beasts of the forest, all appeared to be free, to go just where they pleased, and I was an unhappy slave! (72)

> [W]hile I was permitted to gaze on the beauties of nature, on free soil, as I passed down the river, things looked to me uncommonly pleasant: The green trees and wild flowers of the forest; the ripening harvest fields waving with the gentle breezes of Heaven; and honest farmers tilling their soil and living by their own toil. These things seem to light upon my vision with a peculiar charm. I was conscious of what must be my fate; a wretched victim for Slavery without limit; to be sold like an ox, into hopeless bondage, and to be worked under the flesh-devouring lash during life, without wages. (93)

In Bibb's account the contrast between the emancipatory and enslaving meanings of nature—between the freedom of "the fishes of the water, the fowls of the air, the wild beasts of the forest" and the "chains,...captives,...lacerating of backs,...parting of husbands and wives" that is the lot of the "unhappy slave," between the "beauties of nature, on free soil" and being "sold like an ox, into hopeless bondage"—provides a powerful rhetorical means of underscoring the fundamental violation inherent in the practice of slavery. Each passage invokes some version of a pure and beautiful nature as a sort of common ground shared by the reader and the narrator, only to connect that nature with the degraded landscape of slavery. By connecting these two natures, the slave narrative both marks and unsettles the longstanding eco-ideological division of the natural world into pure landscapes and exploited ones, and does so in the same gesture that both marks and unsettles the binary construction of racial identity associated with those landscapes.

The two sorts of nature are not just contrasted in these passages in other words, they are conjoined; one slides into the other. The fact that we can identify two broadly different sorts of nature in the slave narratives in no way means that the two are not profoundly connected for the enslaved person. Indeed, the trauma of slavery as a form of natural(izing) practice often makes "free" nature a mnemonic trigger for the return of some unbearable moment of degradation to the commodified pastoral of slavery. The possibility of a safely salutary relation to nature depends absolutely on the historical context of the observer—it helps to be a wealthy white male transcendentalist if you're trying for the sublime out in the woods. Take, for example, the total inaccessibility of the sublime template when Henry Bibb and his family confront a pack of ravenous wolves in an attempt to escape (yet) another vicious master, Deacon Whitfield:

We made our bed that night in a pile of dry leaves which had fallen from off the trees. We were much rest-broken, wearied from hunger and traveling through briers, swamps, and cane brakes—consequently we soon fell asleep after lying down. About the dead hour of night I was aroused by the awful howling of a gang of blood-thirsty wolves, which had found us and surrounded us as their prey, there in the dark wilderness many miles from any house or settlement.

My dear little child was so dreadfully alarmed that she screamed loudly with fear—my wife trembling like a leaf on a tree, at the thought of being devoured there in the wilderness by ferocious wolves.

The wolves kept howling, and were near enough for us to see their glaring eyes, and hear their chattering teeth. I then thought that the hour of death was at hand; that we should not live to see the light of

another day; for there was no way for our escape. My little family was
looking up to me for protection, but I could afford them none. And
while I was offering up my prayers to that God who never forsakes
those in the hour of danger who trust in him, I thought of Deacon
Whitfield; I thought of his profession and doubted his piety. I thought
of his hand-cuffs, of his whips, of his chains, of his stocks, of his
thumb-screws, of his slave driver and overseer, and of his religion; I
also thought of his opposition to prayer meetings, and of his five hundred lashes promised me for attending a prayer meeting. I thought of
God, I thought of the devil, I thought of hell; and I thought of heaven,
and wondered whether I should ever see the Deacon there. And I
calculated that if heaven was made up of such Deacons, or such per-
sons, it could not be filled with love to all mankind, and with glory
and eternal happiness, as we know it is from the truth of the Bible.

The reader may perhaps think me tedious on this topic, but indeed
it is one of so much interest to me, that I find myself entirely unable to
describe what my own feelings were at that time. I was so much excited
by the fierce howling of the savage wolves, and the frightful screams of
my little family, that I thought of the future; I thought of the past;
I thought the time of my departure had come at last. (126–27)

Bibb curiously seems to think of *everything*, in fact, *except* the immediate and very pressing situation that is confronting him, in the
form of a pack of hungry wolves. At the moment an almost clichéd
opportunity for forging a new sublime identity according to the
"(white)-man-against-savage-nature-in-defense-of-self-and-helpless-
wife-and-child" template presents itself in the narrative, Bibb instead
flashes back to the traumatic scene of slavery, its instruments of torture and degradation, the religious hypocrisy of his sadistic master.
He can't help doing so; the intense confrontation with the natural
world, a confrontation in which he is "supposed" to discover a new,
empowered identity, instead triggers what is an almost textbook
example of posttraumatic stress.[40] Despite knowing he is disap-
pointing the reader's narrative expectations and in danger of repeating himself ("the reader may...think me tedious on this topic"),
Bibb is "entirely unable to describe what [his] own feelings were at
that time"; unable to do so precisely because the traumatic memories of slavery—the memories that are "of so much interest to
[Bibb]"—intervene on "that time," on the sublime confrontation.
Rather than providing an escape from history, the sublime moment
thrusts Bibb back into history, swerving from the present into
"thought[s] of the future" and "thought[s] of the past," a heaven to
come and a human hell in hot pursuit, a future and past utterly
defined by their relation to slavery.

Indeed, the work of Melvin Dixon on the symbolic and religious liberation promised by the images of the wilderness notwithstanding, for many slaves the real wilderness between themselves and the North was the site of suspended cages more often than transparent eyeballs, a barrier as much as a refuge.[41] Jacobs, for example, first attempts to flee to the aptly named "Snaky Swamp" before retreating to her loophole, a marsh so infested with mosquitoes her "flesh is poisoned," within an hour of her arrival, and so overrun with snakes she and her companion "were continually obliged to thrash them with sticks to keep them from crawling over us" (249). And yet even this fiercely wild space is not, in Jacobs's narrative, outside of slavery; the captain of the vessel Jacobs ultimately escapes on describes it as " 'a slave territory that defies all the laws,' " its wilderness not the definitionally extrahuman, but a point of defiance enmeshed within the "slave territory" (300). Compare this with Thoreau's encomium to swamps in "Walking":

> Yes, though you may think me perverse, if it were proposed to me to dwell in the neighborhood of the most beautiful garden that ever human art contrived, or else of a dismal swamp, I should certainly decide for the swamp....
>
> When I would recreate myself, I seek the darkest wood, the thickest and most interminable, and, to the citizen, most dismal swamp. I enter the swamp as a sacred place,—a *sanctum sanctorum*. There is the strength, the marrow of Nature. The wild-wood covers the virgin mould,—and the same soil is good for men and for trees.... A town is saved, not more by the righteous men in it than by the woods and swamps that surround it. A township where one primitive forest waves above, while another primitive forest rots below,—such a town is fitted to raise not only corn and potatoes, but poets and philosophers for the coming ages. In such a soil grew Homer and Confucius and the rest, and out of such a wilderness comes the Reformer eating locusts and wild honey. (241–42)

A sharper contrast with Jacobs's experience would be difficult to imagine.

For the slave, the former slave, and for a very wide range of African Americans subsequently, the American landscape is inescapably and explicitly political.[42] Frederick Douglass makes clear how profoundly the wild was interpenetrated by the all-too-human in his description of the anxiety he and his fellow conspirators felt at the prospect of running north:

> The case sometimes stood thus: At every gate through which we were to pass, we saw a watchman—at every ferry a guard—on every bridge

a sentinel—and in every wood a patrol. We were hemmed in upon every side. Here were the difficulties, real or imagined—the good to be sought, and the evil to be shunned. On the one hand, there stood slavery, a stern reality, glaring frightfully upon us;—its robes already crimsoned with the blood of millions, and even now feasting itself greedily upon our own flesh. On the other hand, away back in the dim distance, under the flickering light of the north star, behind some craggy hill or snow-covered mountain, stood a doubtful freedom—half frozen—beckoning us to come and share its hospitality. This in itself was sometimes enough to stagger us; but when we permitted ourselves to survey the road, we were frequently appalled. Upon either side we saw grim death, assuming the most horrid shapes. Now it was starvation, causing us to eat our own flesh;—now we were contending with the waves, and were drowned;—now we were overtaken, and torn to pieces by the fangs of the terrible bloodhound. We were stung by scorpions, chased by wild beasts, bitten by snakes, and finally, after having nearly reached the desired spot,—after swimming rivers, encountering wild beasts, sleeping in the woods, suffering hunger and nakedness,—we were overtaken by our pursuers, and in our resistance, we were shot dead upon the spot! (73–74)

While it is the case, as Walter Johnson and others have noted, that slaves often left the plantation and hid themselves in the surrounding countryside, frequently negotiating the terms of their return through intermediaries, such places were more liminal than wild, precarious and temporary refuges akin to Jacob's "loophole of retreat," natural spaces that were always already saturated with the authority of slavery and the possibility of violent punishment.[43] Examples of that saturation are visible in Jacobs and Douglass's descriptions, which shift rapidly back and forth between human and natural terrors, offering a portrait of a wild thoroughly interpenetrated with the violence of slavery, a marked counterpart to the (largely) white experience of the wilderness as Thoreau's *sanctum sanctorum*, an opportunity to "get away from it all." Nowhere, in my reading of the slave narratives, is a sublime embrace of the wild found.[44]

4

Trauma, Postbellum Nostalgia, and the Lost Pastoral

The Last Chattel

In the front cover image from the January 6, 1866 *Harper's Weekly*, published just a few months after the end of the Civil War, we see the logical terminus of the slave boy's childhood, a lifetime spent conflated with the degraded pastoral of the Southern plantation.[1] The Last Chattel is an aged man, dressed in rags, his hands folded in supplication over his walking stick, his eyes looking upward, presumably in humble prayer. Around him extends a blasted landscape, the ground denuded, the ruined chimney of a destroyed home rising among bare and broken trees, the sky a sunless gray. The man seems lost, abandoned; rather than celebrating his emancipation, he prays, grieves, awaits instruction. Despite his newfound freedom, he's stuck in a wasteland extending as far as the eye can see, an environmental representation of the historical trauma of slavery and the war. As the land goes, so goes the man.

At his feet lies an abandoned whip, a complex synecdoche for the historical moment the landscape and the man both incarnate. While the whip's abandonment underscores that slavery has just ended, it remains intact, still signifing both the land and the (ex)slave, still performing its symbolic/material function of domesticating the human into chattel. While the date and the ruined expanse might suggest radical change, the racist sentimentality of the portrait functions in a far more ideologically conservative way. The old man's identity still collapses into the pastoral landscape; regardless of his putative freedom, he is still chattel. The image makes the man a helpless object of pity, reassures the white readers of *Harper's* that, for a while at least, everything and nothing has changed: despite the victory of the Union, black people remained rooted to the Southern land, their identities still encompassed by the familiar agricultural metaphors of slavery. At the same time, he is the *last* chattel; other, younger African Americans won't necessarily be imprisoned in the same "natural" identity.

Figure 2 The Last Chattel.
Source: Cover Image, *Harper's Weekly: A Journal of Civilization*, January 6, 1866.

Let this image, then, serve both as the conclusion of slavery's institutionalized conflation of human and pastoral, and the harbinger of an
environmental and racial crisis just over the horizon, the start of a violent struggle to reconfigure the relation of blackness, whiteness, and the
postbellum environment. This iconic image of an old black figure who
straddles slavery and Reconstruction, squatting in a blasted landscape,
signifies not just the end of the war, but the beginning of what James
Berger calls the "language of post-apocalypse" (xx). The Last Chattel in
the wasteland marks one of the most fiercely contested sites in postbellum
culture, indeed the place where the very content of antebellum Southern

history was defined—and with it, of course, the meaning of the contemporary political and racial struggles that wracked the South.

The challenge for naturalized white supremacy after the war was (at least) two-fold. First, it needed to renovate the divided association of race and nature that had "justified" slavery and that underpinned the reified construction of both black and white racial identity. Newly freed African Americans could no longer be treated as chattel. They "suddenly" demanded wages for their labor, were (legally) free to move when and where they wanted, were no longer bred, whipped, or auctioned, and could at least attempt to acquire their own land and start their own farms. Emancipation not only ended the legal conflation of black subjects and domesticated animals, it challenged a whiteness that had long "found" its ahistorical normative identity in an association with a "pure" nature that was absolutely (and overdeterminedly) the opposite of the slave pastoral.[2] This challenge was heightened by the fact that the war had largely destroyed Southern agriculture as it had been traditionally practiced, and had placed the entire ecosystem of the South under great pressure—hence the wasteland surrounding the Last Chattel. Fields were farmed out, badly eroded, and overgrown. Cotton, one of the few crops that could earn hard currency abroad, had been planted in the place of grains and vegetables, and as a result, the once fertile South actually had to import food during and after the war.[3] Deforestation was rampant. Most livestock had been slaughtered to feed the starving Confederacy and most edible species had been hunted to near extinction. There was little "pure" nature to associate with in the postbellum South and not much of the commodified pastoral either; rather, a general—and rapidly racialized—sense of devolution prevailed.

Second, not only did white supremacy need to reconstruct the essential association of blackness and whiteness with particular forms of natural experience, it needed to do so while inoculating itself from the trauma of the antebellum racial history it had produced. With the victory of the Union came a broad national consensus that slavery had been wrong (though anti-black racism certainly remained virulent). And with that consensus, Southern whites found themselves, at least temporarily, explicitly guilty, publicly implicated in the sorts of trauma writers like Douglass and Jacobs had laid bare in their narratives. The content of the Last Chattel's memories—the traumatic truth of antebellum Southern history—threatened to unravel the core white antebellum fantasy of the Southern plantation as an aristocratic racial Eden, rewriting what was perhaps the foundational myth of Southern whiteness according to a traumatic template.

The danger posed by those memories was in part what Cathy Caruth calls trauma's "contagion," its tendency to spread from narrator to listener in a chain of transmission that was no longer blocked by slavery's censor. Caruth asks: "How does one listen to what is impossible? Certainly, one challenge of this listening is that it may no longer be simply a choice, to be able to listen to the impossible, that is, is also to have been *chosen* by it, *before* the possibility of mastering it with knowledge. This is its danger—the danger, as some have put it, of trauma's 'contagion,' of the traumatization of those who listen" (*Trauma*, 10). Trauma's ability to transmit itself as a sort of viral representation to even an unwilling listener, repositioning his or her subjectivity in reference to the original unassimilable event, was particularly acute in a postbellum moment in which racial identity and the landscapes that had grounded that identity for so long were both in a state of radical transition. This chapter focuses on how this antebellum trauma saturated postbellum white cultural production, specifically forming the heart of the postbellum nostalgic fantasy of so-called Lost Cause writers like George Bagby, Thomas Nelson Page, and Joel Chandler Harris who attempted to rewrite the history of slavery on the antebellum plantation according to an Arcadian model.

Before turning to them, however, I want to note explicitly how a focus on the possibility of such contagion risks collapsing the primary horror into its secondary reception, substituting the listener's narcissism for the irreducible otherness of the trauma victim's experience, as Crèvecoeur does in his recollection of the caged slave. While there is a clear difference between remembering an experience one has had and identifying with another's experience, the line between the two is not nearly as bright as one might wish. Trauma's resistance to cure, its stubborn persistence, comes in part from how it combines both the particular materiality of the original event and, in its latency, an intensely literal form of transmission that evades strict limitation within the traumatized individual's particular experience. It might be argued that the flashbacks that afflict trauma victims are themselves forms of representation and accordingly subject to the sorts of slippage that mark language generally; that there isn't an important difference between trauma transmitted via the "representation" of memory and trauma transmitted through external forms of representation.[4] At some level, of course, it is impossible to "argue" that the traumatic memories recorded in the slave narratives refer to something real, material, and historically true in a way that, say, Disney's *Song of the South* doesn't. Linguistic assertions of the extralinguistic are always poised on the brink of collapse into what constitutes them; indeed I have argued from the start that that poising might serve as another definition of the sublime. We should be wary, though, of confusing the sublime's representational valorization of the unassimilable—where the particularity of the object or event finally doesn't matter except in, or as, the way it provides a sign or trace of the general possibility of an escape from representation—with the traumatic in which, definitionally, *all* that matters is the mute, absolute, entirely specific, particularity of the object or event. While there is no response to this familiar postmodern claim of universal representation that is not itself a "response" (except perhaps to yawn, itself a sort of linguistically liminal deixis), the impossibility of, as A.R. Ammons says, "giving up words with words" is not at all the same thing as declaring that language constitutes the limit of our experience, most especially our agony (116). For my purposes here it literally goes without saying that there are experiences of traumatic individual and collective history that are, if not "Real," at least "more real" than others, and that constitutively resist full or satisfactory representation. In what follows, then, I want to claim *both* an historical authority for the traumatic memories of slavery over and against their postbellum white recovery, *and* to claim that the former threatens "contagion" to the latter who are "chosen," however unwillingly, to listen to its "impossible" history.

TRAUMA, NOSTALGIA, AND THE POSTBELLUM ANTEBELLUM PLANTATION PASTORAL

From John Pendleton Kennedy's 1832 *Swallow Barn* that, as Jean Yellin and others have noted, started the tradition of the white plantation pastoral, to postwar works like Thomas Nelson Page's *In Ole Virginia*, George Bagby's *Old Virginia Gentleman* and Joel Chandler Harris's *Uncle Remus*, to twentieth-century incarnations like Margaret Mitchell's *Gone with the Wind* and Disney's *Song of the South*, the Arcadian fantasy of the antebellum South has circulated so widely among Northern and Southern whites it has become itself a clichéd aesthetic.[5] The depressingly familiar and depressingly persistent fantasy of a lost racial Eden where everyone knew their place and was happy in it, where the magnolia- and rose-scented land around the gracious big house produced bountiful harvests, wise masters, beautiful mistresses, and contented and childlike "sarvents" is a readily familiar, continuously reproduced form of commodity-history.[6]

This lost pastoral imaginary depended on two profoundly intertwined distortions of history: that the lands around the plantation were preternaturally lush and fertile, and that slaves liked being slaves. For the former, take the following example from George Bagby whom Page called Virginia's "best interpreter" and whose 1883 *Old Virginia*

Gentleman he deemed "perhaps the best sketch yet written in the South":

> A scene not of enchantment, though contrast often made it seem so, met the eye. Wide, very wide fields of waving grain, billowy seas of green or gold as the season chanced to be, over which the scudding shadows chased and played, gladdened the heart with wealth far spread. Upon lowlands level as the floor the plumed and tasselled corn stood tall and dense, rank behind rank in military alignment—a serried army lush and strong. The rich, dark soil of the gently swelling knolls could scarcely be seen under the broad lapping leaves of the mottled tobacco. The hills were carpeted with clover. Beneath the tree-clumps fat cattle chewed the cud, or peaceful sheep reposed, grateful for the shade. In the midst of this plenty, half hidden in foliage, over which the graceful shafts of the Lombard poplar towered, with its bounteous garden and its orchards heavy with fruit near at hand, peered the old mansion, white, or dusky red, or mellow gray by the storm and shine of years.
>
> Seen by the tired horseman halting at the woodland's edge, this picture, steeped in the intense quivering summer moonlight, filled the soul with unspeakable emotions of beauty, tenderness, peace, home.[7]

Here the devastating erosion, soil exhaustion, and monoculture planting that in fact dominated the Southern landscape are "enchanted" by Bagby's nostalgic vision of a hyperfertile pastoral. "Billowy seas" of "waving grain," emptied of the slave labor that created them, transmute effortlessly—from agricultural abundance, to a "gladdened...heart," to "wealth far spread."[8] The army of "tasselled corn" that stands "tall and dense, rank behind rank in military alignment" both underscores how utterly tamed this landscape is, and neatly inverts the real starvation that beset the ragged Confederate army, and the women, children, and slaves they left behind. Here the red clay of Virginia becomes "rich and dark," and able to support the toll that tobacco planting in fact took on the soil. Even the cattle and sheep are "fat," "peaceful," and "grateful." The ultimate product of this scene, of course, is the plantation house itself, emerging in a sort of vegetative climax—"in the midst of this plenty," surrounded by "foliage," and "the graceful shafts of the Lombard poplar," flanked by a "bounteous garden" and "orchards heavy with fruit near at hand"—the total organic culmination of the pastoral scene that surrounds it.

And then, against this backdrop, Bagby suddenly shifts both the temporal and spatial perspective of the viewer. In the place of the image of sunny daylight abundance where "scudding shadows chase[ ] and play[]," and sheep "repose[], grateful for the shade," in the second paragraph, night has instantaneously fallen, and the fields are "steeped in the intense quivering summer moonlight." And rather than observing the landscape as yet another racially unmarked/white "eye" that the enchantment of the daylight scene "meets," this second moonlit landscape is viewed from a singular perspective, that of a "tired horseman" "halted" at the edge of the woods, gazing at a promised land that literally incarnates "beauty, tenderness, peace, home." Poised perpetually on the edge of the wild, forever longing for the absolute satisfaction promised by the pastoral scene before him, the horseman's temporal and spatial position marks the substitution of postbellum nostalgia for antebellum trauma, an "unspeakable" satisfaction that signifies the moment when the "impossible" of trauma is transmuted into the bathos of the Lost Cause.

In adopting the horseman's perspective, we are implicitly led to accept his experience as a natural response to a beautiful setting, rather than one embedded in a quite specific political and racial context.[9] It is unlikely, for example, that a slave in the real "Old Virginia"—whose labor in fact produced such abundance, who endured the endemic violence and degradation the narratives record, who, if he or she was riding in the woods at night would probably be trying to escape from "home"—would see these fields in the same way. While the scene might trigger "unspeakable emotions" in both the white horseman and the slave, and might produce a structurally similar temporal displacement in which the present was taken over by the past, the emotional content of each experience would be quite precisely inverted: "beauty, tenderness, peace, and home" would reveal their inverted traumatic source in the "degradation, cruelty, violence, and escape" that so conspicuously mark the relation between African-American slaves and the commodified natural in the narratives.

What drops out of view here, however, is not only the slave's perspective, but the very history of the landscape itself, its political content. In identifying with the horseman's perspective, the reader is taught to identify with a natural experience that functions to unmark and dehistorize (or "re/faux-historicize") whiteness in ways related to Emerson's sublime transport from the "bare commons" to the "dear and connate wilderness," discussed in the second chapter, and that gets writ very large in the Western sublime I discuss in chapter seven. In this passage, the ability to join unconsciously in a nostalgic and uncritical appreciation of this landscape becomes a measure of a given subject's racial normativity, an index directly associated with the ability of whiteness to manifest race unconsciously and uncritically.

NOSTALGIA, TRAUMA, AND THE
RACIALIZED AUTHENTIC

Despite their inverted content, nostalgia and trauma are curiously aligned in the way they structure the relation between history and the contemporary moment. Both fundamentally entail loss, and both are built on a domination of the subject's—or culture's—present by the past, a temporal displacement in which a form of memory floods the subject's experience, contextualizing the current reality and the possibilities for experience and action it affords. It is this parallel structure that makes the racialized nostalgic pastoral of nineteenth-century white Southerners like Bagby such an effective intervention on the traumatic history of the South. It would be easy to dismiss the postbellum antebellum plantation pastoral as the lie it was. But to see it simply as a lie, a divergence from the "truth" of the black experience of slavery as recorded in the narratives, is to permit writers like Bagby, Page, and Thomas Dixon a greater separation from the historical trauma of slavery than the temporal structure of Lost Cause nostalgia and the specific sorts of pastoral and racial metaphors it deployed reveals. To see them as simply lying about the truth of antebellum black experience risks permitting them a space wholly outside of the trauma of that experience, risks understanding their fantasies as emanating from some position removed from the terrible history they obscure. Such a white escape from trauma and blood guilt was precisely what Lost Cause fiction strove to provide its authors and readers. But the sorts of trauma recorded in the last chapter were, in fact, contagious to whites as well as blacks, and the struggle to avoid or deny that contagion profoundly shaped the ways whites constructed their cultural, racial, and naturalized identities.

Which is not to say, of course, that the fantasy did not obscure that history, did not substitute a false dream for a true nightmare, did not in fact lie about what happened on the plantation before the war. It did all these things, but did so in a way that manifested how infected that fantasy was with the antebellum trauma of slavery's degraded pastoral, that underscored how imbricated that fantasy was with the racial and environmental trauma it so reflexively pretended had never occurred. The postbellum antebellum plantation pastoral was not simply wrong about the traumatic truth, it was the intimately connected inverse of it. Rather than simply denying antebellum trauma, it rewrote it, accepted, as it were, the fundamental structure of latency that trauma imposed—and then troped on that latency. The intense literality of the traumatic flashback became the totalizing fictionality of the Lost Cause.[10] The discontinuity that such flashbacks impose on the continuity of the contemporary was flipped in Southern nostalgia: the present became discontinuous and the past a seamless narrative.[11] Rather than an unbearable past shattering the present, an unbearable present shattered the past. The exploitive and commodifying conflation of slaves, animals, and the land became a lost green pastoral.

The impossibly fertile antebellum pastoral as imagined by writers like Bagby simultaneously represented absolute accession to the will of the planter (even the corn submits to military discipline!) and "home" itself, the authentic, originary essence of the (imaginary) antebellum South. And it is precisely this combination of submission and authenticity that also forms the core racial fantasy of the white-generated plantation pastoral: the aged ex-slave, rooted in the landscape, whose nostalgic "memories" of slavery couldn't be more different from the traumatic truth recorded in the slave narratives. The iconic image of a black figure like the Last Chattel, who straddles slavery and Reconstruction, marks one of the most fiercely contested sites in postbellum culture. Indeed the very content of antebellum Southern history—and with it the meaning of the contemporary political and racial struggles that wracked the South—was defined at least in part in the struggle over the contents of such a figure's memory. The point on which the traumatic/nostalgia inversion pivoted, what lent verisimilitude to fantasy, was the black(face) faithful old retainer, speaking in a heavy dialect that underscored his authentic blackness and marked his total racial separation from the suddenly drawl-free upper-class white Southerner.[12] Such characters served simultaneously to transmit and authenticate the white author's version of antebellum Southern history, retaining the temporal structure of the slave narrative while converting its traumatic content into nostalgia on the fly. In the places of authors like Jacobs, Douglass, Bibb, and Prince whose narratives brought the traumatic memory of past enslavement into the reader's present, who told the truth about what slavery was like, we find, in the nostalgic inversion of trauma, submissive ex-chattel who reassured their white audience that slavery was beneficent and the antebellum South was "beautiful, tender, peaceful, and home."

Both white apologists for slavery and African-American activists agreed, then, that black memory was the central site for producing the truth of slavery. In both the slave narratives and the plantation pastoral, blackness was the necessary authenticating sign of the historical narrative.[13] That Douglass was a real black man who bore vigorous witness before and after the war to the atrocities of the Southern plantation, and Sam and Uncle Billy (for example) were the fictional creations of an aging white racist named Thomas Nelson Page, hardly decided the struggle over whose memories had authority—indeed, quite the opposite.[14] Here's Sam (for whom read "Page-in-blackface"), for example, in "Mars Chan," the first story in Page's *In Ole Virginia*, reminiscing about antebellum life to the nameless white narrator he has just met:

> "Dem wuz good ole times, marster—de bes' Sam uver see! Dey wuz, in fac'! Niggers didn' hed nothin' '*t all* to do—jes' hed to 'ten' to de feedin' an' cleanin' de hawses, an' doin' what de marster tell 'em to do; an' when dey wuz sick, dey had things sont 'em out de house, an' de same doctor come to see 'em whar 'ten' to de white folks when dey wuz po'ly, an' all. Dyar warn' no trouble nor nuttin." (10)

Sam's reassurance here to the narrator/reader in the tale's postbellum frame serves as a sort of trauma-inoculation for the white reader on his or her way back into the Southern past. A past too awful to bear when it happened, becomes "good ole times...de bes' Sam uver see!" The endless labor and abjection that constituted slavery becomes the contradictory assertion that slaves had "nothin' '*t all* to do"—nothing, that is, except "doin' what de marster tell 'em to do." The pervasive commodification of the interaction between slaves and masters is reconceived here as paternalism; the master's economic interest in keeping his slaves healthy is displaced by Sam's gratitude for his master's beneficent charity—an equality of treatment that, of course, only obtains in extremis, though Sam's certainly not complaining. Indeed, the very notion of any slave discontent is dismissed by this putative ex-slave—we are assured that "dyar warn' no trouble nor nuttin'"—at least until the war loomed.

Perhaps the most egregious example of this nostalgic inversion of the historical trauma of slavery—and certainly, to my eye, the most quietly vicious in the *In Ole Virginia* collection—is Page's story "Ole' 'Stracted." Ole 'Stracted is a mentally ill ex-slave squatting in a broken down cabin on a postbellum plantation, waiting for his old master to come back and fulfill the promise he made forty years earlier to redeem him and reunite his family after he was sold to pay debts. At the point of his antebellum sale and his master's promise, 'Stracted ceased recording anything else in memory, forgetting even his own name. He is emptied of everything except for the antebellum order that he carries, supposedly unalloyed, into the postbellum moment. This terrifying psychological evisceration is, according to Page, a beautiful example of "the sublime devotion of this poor old creature to his love and his trust, holding steadfast beyond memory, beyond reason, after the knowledge even of his own identity and of his very name was lost" (151). History ends for 'Stracted at the point of his sale, an event that produces a sort of totalized pathological nostalgia for Sam's "good ole days":

> He was unable to give any account of himself, except that he always declared that he had been sold by some one other than his master from that plantation, that his wife and boy had been sold to some other person at the same time for twelve hundred dollars (he was particular as to the amount), and that his master was coming in the summer to buy him back and take him home, and would bring him his wife and child when he came. Everything since that day was a blank to him, and as he could not tell the name of his master or wife, or even his own name, and as no one was left old enough to remember him, the neighborhood having been entirely deserted after the war, he simply passed as a harmless old lunatic laboring under a delusion. He was devoted to children, and Ephraim's small brood were his chief delight. They were not at all afraid of him, and whenever they got a chance they would slip off and steal down to his house, where they might be found any time squatting about his feet, listening to his accounts of his expected visit from his master, and what he was going to do afterward. It was all of a great plantation, and fine carriages and horses, and a house with his wife and the boy. (153–54)

'Stracted's trauma is figured as the *loss* of the (imaginary) antebellum South, an intensification and blackface-ing of the loss Page and the other white Lost Cause writers felt. The parallel between trauma and nostalgia couldn't be closer than it is here. 'Stracted's antebellum memories have entirely taken over his present moment, and have done so for almost a half a century. He cannot remember his name, his wife's name, his master's name, not anything, indeed, except for the glories of the old plantation and the authority relation that apparently provided the essential structural element in his psyche. Rather than merely flashing back like a PTSD sufferer might, the real trauma of slavery has been vacuumed out and replaced by an endlessly running loop of Page's own nostalgic fantasy in which it is not slavery, but the *loss* of slavery that proves unbearable to the old man.

Indeed, by the end of the story, 'Stracted's mental illness itself gets retroped as religious devotion—trauma becomes nostalgia becomes apotheosis, a series that ends, unsurprisingly, in 'Stracted's death: "The evening sun, dropping on the instant to his setting, flooded the room with light; but as Ephraim gently eased him down and drew his arm from around him, it was the light of the unending morning that was on his face. His Master had at last come for him, and after his long waiting, Ole 'Stracted had indeed gone home" (160–61). The traumatic hierarchies of slavery get washed in the bath(os) of nostalgia and emerge with a blasphemous, if not uncommon, equation of the master with God-the-Master and the antebellum plantation with heaven. The sentimentalized violence of this fantasy is meant to obliterate antebellum trauma, substituting a blind faith that is, literally and figuratively a "blank" to history itself.

Worse still, 'Stracted has saved his price—$1,200—and has been waiting to give it to his master in triumph when he finally returns. Ephraim, a black sharecropper on the land who, along with his wife, is present in the cabin for 'Stracted's demise, discovers he is in fact 'Stracted's long-lost son at the moment of his death, and inherits/is bought for the $1200, which, coincidently, is just the amount he needs to buy the land he is currently renting from an exploitive lower-class white landlord. Ephraim and his wife have only managed to save a few dollars in several years of work, and are in danger of being turned off the land. The message is clear: the only way a black person can achieve the iconic mark of American independence and get a farm of his own is through a return to the blind devotional hierarchy of the "good ole days."

However effective this nostalgic inversion was in inoculating postbellum white Americans from the contagious trauma of slavery's unimaginable brutality, granting (putative) black people the authority to relate the "true" history of the South risked undermining the fundamental post-Reconstruction white supremacist project of radically disempowering black people through practices like Jim Crow segregation, lynching, and the discourses of scientific racism.[15] If blacks were the "true" voice of the Southern past—however distorted that past was—then where did that leave white authority over the present?[16] How was it possible to make the character of slavery the central issue in Southern history without being infected by the traumatic core that the nostalgia of the postbellum antebellum plantation pastoral encircled? How could the narrator's racially marked voice be both the site of authenticity *and* the site of his disempowerment?

The answers to these questions turn, once again, on an updated version of slavery's association between black people and the commodified pastoral. What marks these iconic figures is not only the continuation of a literally slavish adherence to their prewar status, but a continuation of their prewar association with the pastoral landscape. It is in the way these stories perpetuate and develop the link, first forged in slavery, between blackness, a total internalization of a subservient identity, and the Southern landscape itself, that the seeming contradiction between submission and authenticity is suppressed. Extended and romanticized descriptions of the landscape like Bagby's were rare in dialect tales, largely because such descriptions were themselves marks of white refinement, requiring a separation from the scene that allowed for its aestheticization—and as we have seen, such separation was precisely what was denied to black people in the conflation with the natural world that "justified" their oppression. Black people were considered *part* of the pastoral Southern landscape produced and consumed so avidly by Northern and Southern whites alike after the war, not themselves producers or consumers of it. And so when the blackface narrator spoke, the lost landscape itself, a place of organic hierarchy and limitless abundance, spoke with him or her; in the union of blackness and the land, a traumatic legacy of unconscionable brutality and environmental devastation became their forever-receding nostalgic opposite, a racially harmonious garden.

Accordingly, the "history" recalled by characters like Sam, 'Stracted, and Page's other narrators is entirely focused on the affairs of the white people on the plantation; like the plantation grounds, these narrators exist only to provide an utterly self-effacing and endlessly nurturing setting in which whites are the only actors. These characters' absolute inability to produce the sublime or the beautiful themselves is part of a systematic repression of even the possibility of a independent interior black life, of an observational perspective that isn't under white control. The result of this systematic repression is that these stories are not only not about black people, they don't have any black characters in them.[17] Instead they proffer stereotypes whose racial disguise is donned to lend authenticity to the fantastic ideology of pastoralized white supremacy that emerges in this period and region, an emergence accomplished precisely in the postbellum emplacement of an antebellum racial Eden, a mythic origin created and lost in the same gesture that displaces the actual traumatic origin of the postbellum South. That gesture is another name for this blackface narrative perspective, a locus of frictionless racial and temporal displacement that permits the author to forget his role in the wholesale creation of the lost South he mourns. It is also another name for nostalgia itself. The ideological operation of this substitution of nostalgia for trauma requires the elimination of black interiority, the sort of vacuuming out of subjectivity that reaches its terminus in 'Stracted's lobotomized fealty. When these blackface characters channel that white nostalgia, speak as the compliant, authenticating pastoral landscape (and only to say, "I love you marster and need your firm hand"), they in fact function more as an infinitely loving and forgiving *context* than as characters, as a fantasized natural environment that provides the setting, the narratological ecosystem, for the only—white—lives that mattered.

We can hear this mutually constructing nostalgic relation between a lost Edenic landscape and an "authentic" blackness that exists only to preserve and transmit the "history" of that lost time in the concluding ruminations of Uncle Billy, the narrator of Page's "Meh Lady," as he overhears his mistress talking with her new husband ("the Cun'l") on the porch:

> An' dat night...I wuz settin' in de do' wid meh pipe, an' I heah 'em settin' dyah on de front steps, dee voices soun'in' low like bees, an' de moon sort o' meltin' over de yard, an' I sort o' got to studyin', an' hit 'pear like de plantation 'live once mo', an' de ain' no mo' scufflin', an' de ole times done come back ag'in, an' I heah meh kerridge-horses stompin' in de stalls, an' de place all cleared up ag'in, an' fence all roun' de pahsture, an' I smell de wet clover-blossoms right good, an' Marse Phil an' Meh Lady done come back, an' runnin' all roun' me, climbin' up on meh knees, callin' me 'Unc' Billy,' an' pesterin' me to go fishin', while somehow Meh Lady an' de Cun'l, settin' dyah on de steps wid dee voice hummin' low like water runnin' in de' dark— (138)

When "de plantation 'live once mo', an' de ain' no mo' scufflin', an' ole times done come back ag'in," that means, for Billy, he's returned home: a return defined by the reestablishment of the supposedly original racial and environmental hierarchies. The plantation land has been cleared and refenced, the clover that fodders the cattle is growing once again in the pasture, the fish are biting, just like the old days. And just like the old days, Billy can resume the "naturally" subservient position the war and its aftermath interrupted, once again taking care of the carriage horses, driving the white folks around, and entertaining the white children. In a single gesture, this passage rewrites the past in an almost dizzying series of self-serving falsehoods and inversions: a white supremacist author becomes a black ex-slave supposedly longing for the restoration of a time that in fact never occurred, longing for the restoration of a natural racial hegemony that in fact required constant brutality to maintain, longing for the return of a lush ever-fertile pastoral landscape in the place of the clear-cut, farmed out, eroded soil that was the legacy of antebellum agricultural practice.[18]

The same bracketing of the wild by an Edenic origin and neo-Edenic telos that "justified" the first European settlers' racially marked conversion of the wilderness into the pastoral that I discussed at the beginning of the second chapter, here returns in perhaps an even uglier form in which the traumatic real is coated with layer upon layer of magnolia-scented fiction. The postbellum moment in which Page is writing and in which Billy is sitting becomes a temporary wilderness, a degeneration from the earlier pastoral order, and (Page/Billy hopes) the promise of that order's restoration. But if the identification with the pastoral empowered those colonial white Europeans, serving as a sign of their *ownership* of the landscape, the pastoral fantasy Billy channels collapses him back into the natural scene, a collapse that, of course, recalls the particular symbolic operation of slavery itself. Rather than serving as a sign of ownership, Billy's relation to the land serves as a sign of his status as property, subsumes him once again under the broader eco/racial white hegemony. And the mark of this subsumption comes in Billy's inability to describe the landscape's beauty in his own voice. While Page grants Billy's language some measure of poetry here, perhaps because the story is about to end, most of his description (under the same transformative moonlight Bagby invokes) involves a resuscitation of the old commodified pastoral of the slave plantations. The *beauty* of the landscape is heard only through the voices, "soun'in' low like bees," and "hummin' low like water runnin' in de' dark"—of the white couple. The black narrator, in other words, channels that nostalgia-ridden natural beauty to the postbellum white audience, but doesn't himself produce it. He gives it voice—Page's voice—speaks *as* the ever-authentic, ever-compliant pastoral, not *for* it.[19]

TALKING ANIMALS/UNCLE REMUS

"In dem days," continued the old man, "de creeturs kyar'd on marters same ez folks. Dey went inter fahmin', en I speck ef de troof wuz ter come out, dey kep' sto', en had der camp-meetin' times en der bobbycues w'en de wedder wuz 'gree'ble." (69)

Page's systematic collapse of the black narrator's subjectivity into the nostalgia-saturated pastoral landscape depended on a total repression of the terrors the slave narratives record, particularly the systematic degradation to a bestial nature that formed the core of the experience of bondage for many slaves. Indeed, his narrators conspicuously refuse black interiority altogether. They're as open as the landscape itself. When we "overhear" Billy's thoughts, it turns out he's just channeling white voices. But even the most blinkered contemporary white apologist hardly believed that black people only thought about white people. A complete transformation of antebellum trauma into Lost Cause nostalgia required addressing the specific content of slave experience, colonizing slave culture for white audiences to immunize them from their profound implication in that original trauma.

Joel Chandler Harris's hugely popular series of fables, first published just fifteen years after the war ended, addressed the issue of African-American culture and experience directly, providing what was certainly the most influential postbellum renegotiation of the human/animal conflation at the heart of slavery's trauma. A number of critics have defended aspects of Harris's project as a generally sympathetic treatment of an aged African-American storyteller and as an effort to preserve characteristic African-American speech patterns and folklore. I have no quarrel with either point, considered in its particularity.[20] But looking at these tales in the context of the fraught intersection between slaves and animals, and of the postbellum traumatic contagion that threatened guilty white Southerners, leads to a much more disturbing reading of the tales' structure and effect. For if the pervasive conflation of human beings and domesticated animals was central to how whites "justified" slavery, to how it functioned ideologically, and to the literally unspeakable trauma it inflicted on people it marked as black, Harris's decision to write (or record) hundreds of pages of stories in which animals living in the antebellum South speak in black dialect in ways that clearly align them with slaves inevitably resonates far beyond Harris's own conscious intentions and the tales' putative purpose of children's entertainment. Put simply, Harris's fundamental conceit—talking animals—is also slavery's fundamental conceit. Perhaps more important, his work bridges slavery with the hardening racism of Reconstruction and its aftermath, an amalgamation of pseudoscience, sexuality, and terrorism that rendered the connection between African Americans and the natural world perhaps even more demeaning and dangerous than it had been.

The tales make the connection between slaves and animals explicit throughout the various collections. For example, in addition to this section's epigraph, Brer Tarrypin is described as "es proud ez a nigger wid a cook 'possum" (34), Brer Fox comes through the woods "singing like a nigger at a frolic" (49) and is terrified on a number of occasions when Brer Rabbit tells him the "patter-rollers"[21] are coming for him. Brer Rabbit even does a minstrel act at one point:

> Bimeby, w'ile he wuz a settin' dar, up he jump en crack his heels tergedder en sing out:
>   Make a bow ter de Buzzard en
>   den ter de Crow,
>   Takes a limber-toe gemmum fer
>   ter jump Jim Crow. (98–99)

This association between the fables and antebellum slave life is not Harris's own invention, of course, but in fact reflects their "authentic" source in African-American folk culture under slavery and, especially in trickster figures like Brer Rabbit, the influence of African religion and storytelling, as Eric Sundquist and others have documented. Certainly the way Brer Rabbit consistently outsmarts the rapacious Brer Fox, often by appealing to his greed or ego, encodes a more generally useful strategy for resisting the master's power. And the violence of Brer Rabbit's revenge—Brer Fox is, variously, boiled, burnt, diced, and decapitated—underscores in a grimly satisfying way the murderous fury that underlay the slave's subservient mask. In this sense, these tales—retold from generation to generation, built around a conflation of human and animal, and incorporating countless variations on an endless violence—themselves suggest a trauma narrative, the animalization and brutality at the core of slavery's unspeakable scene. Indeed, to the extent they were authentic, how could they not?

Despite these traces of an originary trauma and a genuine African and African-American folk tradition, Harris's work isn't cultural anthropology, or at least not the sort we should admire. In Uncle Remus's version, *all* the talking animals, including Brer Fox, are clearly marked as black. Accordingly, their violent struggles and the potential resistance they encode are repackaged by Harris's tales as intraracial, "black-on-black" conflicts. Since animals that don't talk are also present in the tales but are not given race or quasi-human status, the (white) reader is "naturally" invited to view antebellum black figures according to the template of postbellum ethnographic "science," as not white/human, but as a different species, a higher sort of animal. Harris underscores this natural difference by including human characters—"Mr. Man," and "Little Gal," for example—who take their supposedly rightful place at the top of the pastoral hierarchy, dominating and domesticating the talking animals, possessing the landscape, and violently enforcing their position and ownership. That Mr. Man is white literally goes without saying (though it is also clear from the story's original illustrations). When Brer Rabbit, for example, talks Little Gal into giving him greens from Mr. Man's garden, the punishment for talking to a white girl and "stealing" produce echoes with brutality all-too familiar to Harris's contemporary audience:

Sho nuff, nex' mawnin' dar wuz de Little Gal playin' 'roun', en yer come Brer Rabbit atter he 'lowance er greens. He wuz ready wid de same tale, end den de Little Gal, she tu'n 'im in, she did, en den she run up ter de house en holler:

"O pa! pa! O pa! Yer Brer Rabbit in de gyardin now! Yer he is, pa!"

Den Mr. Man, he rush out, en grab up a fishin'-line w'at bin hangin' in de back po'ch, en make fer de gyardin, en w'en he git dar, dar wuz Brer Rabbit tromplin' 'roun' on de straw-be'y-bed en mashin' down de termartusses. W'en Brer Rabbit see Mr. Man, he squar behime a collud leaf, but 'twa'n't no use. Mr. Man done seed him, en 'fo' you kin count 'lev'm, he done got ole Brer Rabbit tie hard en fas' wid de fishin'-line. Atter he got him tie good, Mr. Man step back, he did, en say, sezee:

"You done bin fool me lots er time, but dis time you er mine. I'm gwine ter take you en gin you a larrupin',' sezee, 'en din I'm gwine ter

skin you en nail yo' hinde on de stable do',' sezee; 'en den ter make
shod at you git de right kinder larrupin', I'll des step up ter de house,'
sezee, 'en fetch de little red cowhide, en den I'll take en gin you brin-
jer," sezee. (128)

While Brer Rabbit ultimately escapes his fate, convincing Little Gal
to untie him by promising to dance and sing for her—more
minstrelsy—Mr. Man's threat redraws the color line across the natural
world in a disturbingly familiar way. The overflowing violence here—
Mr. Man promises to beat Brer Rabbit, skin him, and nail his hide to
the stable door, all before the real whipping begins—while presumably
comic in its misordering, clearly resonates with the systematically violent
practices of slavery and lynching, with punishments meted out to black
men for talking with white females or for agricultural trespass.

The addition of this white human figure atop and outside of the
black animal world creates a naturalized mythology of white supremacy breathtaking in its totality. The white-on-black violence Mr. Man
threatens is put on the same moral level as defending one's garden
against a pest in a postbellum version of the subsumption of slave
rights under animal rights that I discussed in the previous chapter.
Mr. Man's absolute racial dominance is rendered coextensive with his
absolute dominance of the natural world; rather than something brutally, traumatically, and endlessly constructed through a set of specific material and psychological practices, Mr. Man's authority is
written onto the landscape, as natural as the pastoral itself.

We can see the profound intermingling between white racial and
white environmental dominance that I have traced throughout this
project crystallize in Harris's tale, "Mr. Lion Hunts for Mr. Man." This
fable features none of the familiar animal characters from the previous
tales—the "Brer" creatures that stand for individual antebellum black
men and women in a particular locality. Instead, Harris substitutes
generally representative animals—Mr. Lion, Mr. Steer, Mr. Hoss, and
Mr. Jack Sparrer—whose shifted honorific signifies how they, like
Mr. Man, stand for a broader categories in the natural hierarchy. The
story turns on Mr. Lion's "biggity" decision to challenge Mr. Man's
dominance—"I'm gwine ter show 'im who de boss er deze neighbor-
hoods,' sezee, en wid dat Mr. Lion, he shake he mane, en switch he tail,
en strut up en down wuss'n one er deze yer town niggers"—despite the
warning of the other creatures "dat he better let Mr. Man 'lone" (142).
The lion's status as "king of the jungle," his popular identification both
with Africa and wilderness, here is brought into direct conflict with the
white dominated Southern pastoral, a juxtaposition whose unlikeliness

is explicable only in the context of slavery's global context. Under its benign exterior, this is an allegory of large-scale racial struggle and a particular sort of environmental history as well.

Mr. Man's inevitable victory over Mr. Lion is characteristically transmuted into a broader pattern of environmental dominance, as stressed by each of the three creatures Mr. Lion meets in his search for Mr. Man. Mr. Steer, Mr. Hoss, and Mr. Jack Sparrer warn him, respectively:

> "You see me stan'in' yer front er yo eyes, en you see how big I is, en w'at long, sharp hawns I got. Well, big ez my hett is, en sharp dough my hawns be, yit Mr. Man, he come out yer en he ketch me, en he put me und' a yoke, en he hitch me up in a kyart, en he make me haul he wood, en he drive me anywar he min' ter. He do dat. Better let Mr. man 'lone," sezee. "If you fool 'long wid 'im, watch out dat he don't hitch you up en have you prancin' 'roun' yer pullin' he kyart," sezee. (143)

> "I speck you better let Mr. Man 'lone," sezee. "You see how big I is, en how much strenk w'at I got, en how tough my foots is," sezee; "well, dish yer Mr. Man, he kin tak'n take me en hitch me up in he buggy, en make me haul 'im all 'round', en den he kin tak'n fassen me ter de plow en make me break up all his new groun'," sezee. "You better go 'long back home. Fus' news you know, Mr. Mann'll have you breakin' up his new groun'," sezee. (143)

> "You better let Mr. Man 'lone. You see how little I is, en likewise how high I kin fly; yit, 'spite er dat, Mr. Man, he kin fetch me down w'en he git good an' ready," sezzee. "You better tuck yo tail en put out home," sez Mr. Jack Sparrer, sezee, "kaze bimeby Mr. Man'll fetch you donw," sezee. (144)

All that the slave narratives taught us about the traumatic conjunction of blackness and a commodified, domesticated animality, the literal naturalization of white racial dominance as a subset of white environmental dominance, here returns. The steer and the horse speak only to warn the lion about their enslavement, how their superior size and strength have become rendered into merely a source of agricultural productivity for Mr. Man—pulling carts and carriages, hauling wood, and breaking ground—and a sign of his unlimited power over the "animal" kingdom. Similarly, the sparrow's warning testifies to the scope and extent of man's power over nature—even the skies aren't free.

Unsurprisingly—since, after all, the point of the story is to dramatize the foolishnesses of Mr. Lion's resistance to Mr. Man's dominance—the symbol of the wild/black/African doesn't listen to these warnings. Mr. Lion eventually finds Mr. Man engaged in the Lincolnesque task of splitting rails to make a fence, the quintessential symbol of the wild/pastoral conversion. But Mr. Lion doesn't know what a man looks like, and so serio-comically asks his enemy if he knows where he can find this Mr. Man. Mr. Man offers to go find him for Mr. Lion, but asks in the meantime if the lion will hold open the split with his paw. Mr. Lion does so, Mr. Man knocks out the wedge, and the split closes on the paw, trapping the Lion. The end of this story is all-too-familiar: Mr. Man "sa'nter out in the bushes en cut 'im a hick'ry, en he let in on Mr. Lion, en he frail en frail 'im twel frailn' un 'im wuz a sin" (144). The Lion is turned from a symbol of wild Africa to a fool, "one er deze yer town niggers," a creature compounded of stupidity and false pride whose punishment at the master's hands is deservedly severe, part of the natural order.

While these tales evoke the trauma of slavery and the postbellum South and structure themselves around contemporary racist ethnography, the point of Harris's evocation was, like Page's nostalgic pastoralism, *inversion* rather than celebration or denial. The fundamentally traumatic conflation of human and natural at the heart of slavery is retroped by the tales' frame into a supposedly celebratory preservation of black folk culture related in authentic dialect by the friendly and submissive old black narrator for the entertainment of a young white child, the son of his (former) mistress. As it was in Page's fantasy pastoral, the traumatic historical memory of antebellum black life is changed in and by Harris's stories from a recurring terror characteristic of PTSD, into an endless nostalgia. Harris admits to as much in his introduction:

> I am advised by my publishers that this book is to be included in their catalogue of humorous publications, and this friendly warning gives me the opportunity to say that however humorous it may be in effect, its intention is perfectly serious; and, even if it were otherwise, it seems to me that a volume written wholly in dialect must have its solemn, not to say melancholy features. With respect to the Folk-Lore series, my purpose has been to preserve the legends in their original simplicity, and to wed them permanently to the quaint dialect—if, indeed, it can be called a dialect—through the medium of which they have become a part of the domestic history of every Southern family; and I have endeavored to give the whole a genuine flavor of the old plantation. (xxi)

Though his intention is certainly not confessional, Harris here reveals the complex sequence by which the historically unspeakable is transformed into the pastoral/nostalgic in the stories that follow. The first of these transformations is straightforward and total: antebellum history is included on the list of "humorous publications." But even the racist white audience of the time could hardly believe, at least for long, that antebellum black "Folk Lore" was simply a series of light-hearted stories. So Harris backs off, distinguishing between a "humorous…effect" and a "perfectly serious" "intention," linking the stories' black origin—marked by being "written wholly in dialect"—to an inevitably "solemn, not to say melancholy" subtext.

But this hint at a traumatic subtext gets, in turn, subsumed by a cascading series of white observational frames, each of which enforces a racist and nostalgic reading of that melancholy. Rather than an eruptive trauma that perpetually escapes representation, this "melancholy" content is kept at a safe distance, "preserved" as a "legend" in its readily comprehensible "original simplicity." The face of this legendary original simplicity is, of course, Harris's iconic blackface narrator Uncle Remus. Remus is the point of transmission, the black "medium" through which the tales cross the color line into the unmarked whiteness of "the domestic history of every Southern family." Like Page's Sam or Uncle Billy, Uncle Remus serves as a sort of filter who both guarantees the stories' racial authenticity and strictly quarantines the terrors of the real history of the antebellum plantation. What the reader gets instead is the fantasy of the Lost Cause, a wholesale nostalgic falsehood repackaged as a product suffused with "the genuine flavor of the old plantation."

The pleasure of the stories—underscored by their immense popularity—came in part from the relief they promised their white readers from historical guilt over practices that had only been legally stopped fifteen years earlier, and from the "justification" of violent postbellum racial oppression they afforded whites in the name of restoring a lost racial Eden and punishing blacks for "devolving," like the untilled fields of the South, back to an originary savage wilderness. The tales, in short, offered their white readers the childlike natural purity exemplified by the young white boy who serves as Uncle Remus's audience (and thus, by extension, the reader's own representative) in the framing narrative. The boy represents a set of implicit instructions for the reader's reception of the stories—we are to listen to them as if we were entirely innocent of the history they signify, as if we knew nothing of what had happened before the war, as if Uncle Remus's amiable submission sprang entirely from his freely chosen devotion to "his white folks." This fantasy of purity, historical innocence, and voluntary enslavement is captured at the beginning of "How Mr. Rabbit Saved His Meat":

> "Well, Uncle Remus, you know you said the Rabbit poured hot water on the Wolf and killed him," said the little boy.
>
> The old man pretended not to hear. He was engaged in searching among some scraps of leather under his chair, and kept on talking to the imaginary person. Finally, he found and drew forth a nicely plaited whip-thong with a red snapper all waxed and knotted.

> "I wuz fixin' up a whip fer a little chap," he continued, with a sigh, "but, bless gracious! 'fo' I kin git 'er done, de little chap done grow'd up twel he know mo'n I duz."
>
> The child's eyes filled with tears and his lips began to quiver, but he said nothing; whereupon Uncle Remus immediately melted.
>
> "I 'clar' to gooness," he said, reaching out and talking the little boy tenderly by the hand, "ef you ain't de ve'y spit en image er ole Miss w'en I brung 'er de las' news er de war. Hit's des like skeerin' up a ghos' w'at you ain't feard un."
>
> Then there was a pause, the old man patting the little child's hand caressingly.
>
> "You ain't mad, is you, honey?" Uncle Remus asked finally, "kaze ef you is, I'm gwine out yere en butt my head 'gin de do' jam'."
>
> But the little boy wasn't mad. Uncle Remus had conquered him and he had conquered Uncle Remus in pretty much the same way before. (66)

The passage's sequence provides a remarkable summary of the ideological comforts Harris's stories afforded. The white child is initially admonished for his rational insistence on historical accuracy and consistency—Brer Wolf, had, indeed, been boiled alive by Brer Rabbit in an earlier tale. But Uncle Remus is the historical authority over what happened back then, no matter what the facts are. Uncle Remus asserts that authority over the content of antebellum history, however, only by threatening to stop submitting so utterly to the white child—he may not give him the whip he was making. All the child has to do is cry, though, and Remus's devotion immediately overwhelms him again; the child's tears cause him to flash back to his grief at telling his white mistress the war was over. Rather than remembering the whip as a resonant symbol of black antebellum trauma, a principle instrument for treating African-American subjects as animals, Remus's flashback is produced by the memory of *white* grief over the loss of the war, substituting nostalgia—the "skeerin' up [of] a ghos' w'at you ain't feard un"—for that traumatic content. Then, as if his submission wasn't sufficiently total, he offers to go beat his head against the door jamb to assuage the boy's possible anger at Remus's momentary reluctance to give him the whip Remus himself made. It is difficult to imagine greater abjection—though as we know all too well, "Uncle Remus had conquered him and he had conquered Uncle Remus in pretty much the same way before." Needless to say, Uncle Remus presents the whip to the boy at the end of the tale, and the stories of black/animal life keep flowing for decades to come.

5

TRAUMA AND METAMORPHOSIS IN CHARLES CHESNUTT'S CONJURE TALES

INTRODUCTION: AFTER THE WAR

Writers like Page and Harris construct the plantation pastoral by transforming the temporal structure and experiential content of slavery's trauma into the nostalgia of the Lost Cause, the always-receding fantasy-history of an antebellum Southern Garden where white authority over black slaves was literally natural—coextensive with white stewardship of a pastoral landscape that both entirely subsumed black identity and was symbolized by it. The transformation was never complete, however, never permanent. It required constant repetition, largely because it was, in fact, a secondary effect of slavery's antebellum trauma and not the pastoral origin it claimed to be. That repetition was an echo of the latency that structures all traumatic experience, a nostalgic landscape always at risk of being overrun by the terrible history it so strenuously attempted to keep at bay.

The danger of what Cathy Caruth calls trauma's "contagion" was even more acute for postbellum African-American cultural production. Ron Eyerman has argued recently that slavery formed a "cultural trauma" that has profoundly shaped African-American culture and identity from the antebellum period to our own time.[1] Central to Eyerman's argument—and mine, especially in the postbellum half of this book—is the general claim that trauma can be transmitted and experienced through widely disseminated forms of representation as well as individual memory. As Eyerman writes,

> The notion of cultural trauma implies that direct experience of an event is not a necessary condition for its inclusion in the trauma process. It is through time-delayed and negotiated recollection that

cultural trauma is experienced, a process which places representation
in a key role. How an event is remembered is intimately entwined with
how it is represented. Here the means and media of representation is
crucial, for they bridge the gap between individuals and between
occurrence and its recollection. (12)

Eyerman's work invites us to locate slavery's trauma, especially after
the war, as not adhering only within individuals, but as a problematic
within postbellum representation itself, a terrible historical truth that
always threatens to rise from its shallow grave and overwhelm the late
nineteenth-century cultural productions of white and black writers
and artists alike.

This combination of a virulent traumatic history systematically
repressed by a nostalgic white pastoralism found perhaps its most
powerful and subtle critique in the conjure tales of Charles Chesnutt,
the first commercially successful fiction written by an African
American. Like the literature of the Lost Cause, Chesnutt's stories
are structured around a temporal dislocation produced by the antebellum memories of an elderly black narrator, Uncle Julius, memories
that are, in Chesnutt's trope of "conjuration," centrally concerned
with the conflation of racialized subjects and the nonhuman natural.
But what Uncle Julius remembers about that conflation is awful,
utterly different from Page's Sam or Harris's Uncle Remus. Despite
the fact that the tales are framed as light entertainment for the tales'
white auditors John and Annie, the memories of Julius that overwhelm the present and that constitute the stories' narrative core
almost always incorporate unbearable cruelty inflicted on the central
characters: slaves are sold away from their loved ones, brutal and
humiliating punishments are enacted, work loads are impossibly
increased while rations are cut in an attempt to extract greater value
from the workers and the land.

By wrapping a traumatic core in a white supremacist genre,
Chesnutt's work serves both as a resonant testimony to the traumatic
truth of antebellum Southern history, and as a devastating intervention on the white fantasy of a plantation pastoral.[2]

What makes this insertion of slavery's real history into the format
of Lost Cause nostalgia particularly complex is that Chesnutt's work
points to a traumatic origin for the plantation pastoral from a belated
position—he published his first conjure story in 1887, seven years
after Harris's first collection (the wildly popular *Uncle Remus: His
Songs and Sayings*) and the same year that Page's *In Ole Virginia*
was first published. Chesnutt is intervening on an intervention; his

slave narrative takes the place of another (white) slave narrative itself written to supplant the "original" memories of writers like Douglass and Jacobs. And Chesnutt himself—light-skinned enough to pass (though he didn't), a Southerner transplanted to Ohio, a successful lawyer and businessman whose fame was built on the fictional voice of an uneducated ex-slave, a profoundly engaged critic of race writing in a hyper-racialized genre who longed for acceptance by the white literary establishment—was hardly an authentic source for the real history of the antebellum South. He wasn't a real black person, wasn't a real Southerner—Page would say.

This temporal, geographic, and cultural complexity in Chesnutt's authorial position reflects how trauma itself renders both periodization and authenticity contradictory. In performing periodization, we assert that a given moment supposedly includes everyone at some abstract "democratic" level, and then proceed to look at what was the latest thing at that moment. But the latest thing, however, is precisely what trauma isn't.[3] What this means is that to live in the present is a mark of a certain sort of historical privilege, of a past that doesn't recur. One hidden locus of the hegemony in periodization is its refusal to take trauma into account—since trauma is structured around an historical latency between physical event and emotional experience, to talk about slavery as a strict matter of the antebellum period, or ask uncritically "what happened after it was over?" is to naturalize a privileged temporal and psychological position. Trauma, conversely, denaturalizes the present. In the traumatized subject's or community's helpless return to a past that won't stay in its place, the historically constructed nature of the "now" is revealed. To this extent, Chesnutt's work *is* an authentic slave narrative; he is not only, as he put it, "post-bellum, pre-Harlem," but *antebellum* as well.

Similarly, the authenticity of Chesnutt's tales does not stem from the presentation of slavery's horror as simply a series of terrible events, as an essence, a word standing for some historically delimited occurrence, preserved and contained in Julius's memory and available to the reader's (via John's) full comprehension. Rather than revealing slavery as a set of past-tense practices a white reader like John can readily grasp and comfortably judge, Julius's stories return obsessively to an impossibility, to a primal scene of conjuration in which a subjugated African American is transformed magically into part of the nonhuman natural world. At the center of Julius's memories is a seeming avoidance of a direct or "realistic" description of the brutality of slavery, the same collapse of representation into the natural we saw at the core of the slave narratives. This again underscores the curious authenticity of Chesnutt's narratives—he knows the inexpressible thing that lies beneath the "facts"; his stories repeatedly stage the distinction between a sublime voyeurism of slavery and an unrecoverable descent into the literally speechless trauma of its degradation.

As we will see, Julius's stories consistently swerve away from representing an essential cruelty, substituting conjuration for a "straight" narrative of the consequences of being worked nearly to death, or having children sold, or enduring awful physical and psychological punishment. At the moment Julius's stories become unbearable, they become magical, metamorphic, fictive, impossible. The question that arises for a traumatic reading of *The Conjure Woman*, then, is how to understand these moment of conjuration—are they points of healing, in which the traumatic event finally becomes appropriated symbolically? Or do they somehow remain literal, retain the absolute materiality of the original traumatic experience of slavery? Why does Chesnutt make conjuration the center of Julius's tales, rather than the scenes of whipping, incarceration, or the auction that mark the traumatic center of earlier slave narratives? Put another way, how is slavery a form of conjuration?

To answer these questions successfully we need to explore the particularity of these moments of metamorphosis from human to non-human natural in Chesnutt's text, a task I will turn to shortly. First though, I want to note how reading *The Conjure Woman* as a trauma narrative, and understanding conjuration as an expression of slavery rather than simply a form of resistance to it, distinguishes my reading from contemporary critical interpretations of conjuration that see it as less ambiguously resistant.[4] I do not mean to imply by this that recent critics like Sundquist, who reads conjuration in part as a return of traditional African cultural and spiritual practice, or McWilliams, who stresses conjuration's deconstructive antiessentialist fictivity, or Myers and Mondie, who see it as embodying an Afrocentric environmentalism, are somehow misguided.[5] The intrinsic fluidity of Chesnutt's central metaphor allows his stories to accommodate a wide range of readings. Yet the reluctance of critics thus far to recognize *The Conjure Woman* as a trauma narrative—despite its temporal organization as a series of flashbacks to a time of terrible suffering—reflects, I think, a larger critical tendency to romanticize conjuration, to stress its resistant aspects at the expense of its much less happy ones.[6] Such a tendency can obscure the danger, vulnerability, and degradation that moments of conjuration in the tales often produce. Conjuration can, in stories like "Sis' Becky's Pickaninny," and "Mars Jeems's Nightmare," mark a limited source of African-American resistance to white supremacy, just as Julius's superior knowledge of the landscape occasionally affords him a minor advantage over John. But while conjuration is not simply coextensive with slavery, neither is it separable from it. The metamorphic quality of slavery saturates Julius's tales. Even more deeply than it represents black environmental knowledge and power, conjuration also marks slavery's alchemic reduction of the black subject to an animal, the metamorphosis of a racially marked person into a natural commodity.[7] Rather than representing a too-sweeping notion of black exile from the natural world, or worse, a natural unity between African Americans and environmentalism, that, however well-meant, risks what George Fredrickson calls "romantic racialism," conjuration names the fundamentally *conflicted* quality of the nineteenth-century relationship between African Americans and nature. It is this moment of unity between the racialized subject and the natural object, the salutary and brutal intersection between identity, nature, and race, that forms the traumatic kernel at the heart of *The Conjure Woman*.

In what follows I trace the emergence of that kernel in the first four conjure tales Chesnutt wrote: "The Goophered Grapevine," "Po' Sandy," "The Conjurer's Revenge," and "Dave's Neckliss."[8] This first sequence of tales was composed between 1887 and 1889, more than a decade before the 1899 publication of *The Conjure Woman* collection. They represent Chesnutt's initial vision for the project, unalloyed by the later commercial demands of his white editor that, as Richard Brodhead notes, inserted "an element of disciplinary control" that arguably blunted the critical force of the final collection (17).[9]

Julius's relation to nature embodies the deeply conflicted relation between subjectivity and the natural world at the heart of the stories. Born and raised in slavery, he is, for better and worse, profoundly connected to the rural Southern landscape. John offers the following description of him a description in which I think Chesnutt means us to hear both the patronizing, racist assumptions about the alliance between Julius and nature that John holds, and a glimpse of the deep bond, nevertheless, between rural African Americans and the land:

> We found old Julius very useful when we moved to our new residence. He had a thorough knowledge of the neighborhood, was familiar with the roads and the watercourses, knew the qualities of the various soils and what they would produce, and where the best hunting and fishing were to be had. He was a marvelous hand in the management

of horses and dogs, with whose mental processes he manifested a greater familiarity than mere use would seem to account for, though it was doubtless due to the simplicity of a life that had kept him close to nature. Toward my tract of land and the things that were on it—the creeks, the swamps, the hills, the meadows, the stones, the trees—he maintained a peculiar personal attitude, what might be called predial rather than proprietary. He had been accustomed, until long after middle life, to look upon himself as the property of another. When this relation was no longer possible, owing to the war, and to his master's death and the dispersion of the family, he had been unable to break off entirely the mental habits of a lifetime, but had attached himself to the old plantation, of which he seemed to consider himself an appurtenance. (55)

This passage might serve as a summary of the troubling mix of attitudes toward nature, race, and identity that I've been discussing thus far. John's racist assumptions depend on, in part, his linking of Julius and nature. Julius may know the land thoroughly and John may utterly depend on this expertise, but Julius's knowledge comes to be a sign of his semi-human slave status, rather than a mark of a Thorovian authority and independence. John demeans Julius's ecological literacy, hinting that Julius's mind resembles the canine or equine more than the human, viewing Julius as part of the farm, as "predial" rather than an owner. He declares not only that Julius internalized his earlier slavery—that he had long "been accustomed . . . to look upon himself as the property of another"—but that Julius's ongoing connection to the landscape marks his ongoing mental slavery, makes him an "appurtenance" of the "old plantation." In turning Julius's intimate knowledge of the environment and his hard-earned, well-established residency into a mark of his racial inferiority, John "justifies" both his exploitation of Julius and of the land he has just purchased in a way that crystallizes how the intersection of nature and African-American subjectivity functions ideologically. Julius is "useful," because he knows the soil's productive possibilities, where to hunt, where to fish. What John *doesn't* say—indeed, what he represses—is that if Julius's postbellum relation to the land is a traumatic echo of his antebellum relation, John's position as owner of the "old plantation" presumably makes him the owner of the appurtenance Julius as well. John can keep this recognition from consciousness only by making Julius's association with the land natural, an internalized principle of subjection that John can't do anything about—except, of course, profit from. By defining slavery in part as a white naturalization of black people's supposed closeness to nature—understanding Julius and the landscape as parts of the same exploitable natural resource—and by demonstrating how that traumatic conflation continues in the post-bellum period, Chesnutt illustrates the complexity of the relation between African Americans and the nonhuman environment from slavery onward. Nature is both the site of Julius's power, experience, and expertise, and the source of his degradation, a relation Chesnutt makes us see as *un*natural through John's seeming unconsciousness of the logical implications of his patronizing, dehistoricizing, self-aggrandizing conflation of the two.

Chesnutt makes the conflation of slavery and nature, and the consequent fusion of environmental and racial violence, the primary theme in his first conjure tale, "The Goophered Grapevine," published in 1887 in *The Atlantic Monthly*. The story's framing narrative introduces John and Annie, who have moved to North Carolina where "labor was cheap and land could be bought for a mere song," according to John's cousin who had moved there to start a turpentine business (31).[10] John meets Julius when he comes to scout the overgrown plantation vineyard where (unbeknownst to John), Julius was a slave and where he still lives and earns his livelihood by cultivating grapes.

The antebellum tale that Julius tells John at their meeting serves two purposes. First, it is an unsuccessful attempt by Julius to maintain his relation to the land, to convince John that the vineyard is cursed and that John shouldn't buy it. But, second, the tale that follows is not simply manipulative, just as it is not merely lighthearted entertainment. While John's position as auditor invites us to see Julius's history as little more than a con or as a way of passing the time, viewing *The Conjure Woman* as a trauma narrative allows us the possibility of reclaiming from John's narrative frame the history that Julius channels. Take, for example, the supposedly "neutral" way John describes how the memories of slavery consume Julius at the start of the first tale:

> At first the current of his memory—or imagination—seemed somewhat sluggish; but as his embarrassment wore off, his language flowed more freely, and the story acquired perspective and coherence. As he became more and more absorbed in the narrative, his eyes assumed a dreamy expression, and he seemed to lose sight of his auditors, and to be living over again in monologue his life on the old plantation. (35)

To be "living over again in monologue his life on the old plantation" presumably means something quite different for Julius than for John, a gap into which the reader's own narrative position falls, and that becomes deeper as the memories and the stories become increasingly disturbing.

The "monologue" that follows this first mnemonic return outlines the pattern of environmental commodification that links antebellum slavery and postbellum racism, historicizing Julius's fragile agrarian independence and his vulnerability to John's proprietary plans, and putting their relation into a larger pattern of black vulnerability to white capital. In Julius's tale, the vineyard becomes the site of a struggle between slaves and their master over the meaning of the slaves' connection to the vineyard. At first, that connection is positive—Julius identifies the plantation's scuppernong grapes directly with the black community in terms that, while they resonate with minstrel stereotypes, suggest an intimate appreciation for grape culti-vation and an interweaving of the fruit into antebellum slave culture:

> Now, ef dey's an'thing a nigger lub, nex' ter 'possum, en chick'n, en watermillyums, it's scuppernon's. Dey ain' nuffin dat kin stan' up side'n de scuppernon' fer sweetness; sugar ain't a suckumstance ter scuppernon'. W'en de season is nigh 'bout ober, an de grapes begin ter swivel up des a little wid de wrinkles er ole age,—w'en de skin git sof' en brown,—den de scuppernon' make you smak yo'lip and roll yo' eye en wush fer mo'; so I recon it ain' ver 'stonishin' dat niggers lub scuppernon'. (35–36)

As Julius goes on to relate, the scuppernongs were a favorite food of the black community in the area, so much so that they would walk ten miles to eat them despite the threats, spring guns, and steel traps "Mars Dugal'" deploys to protect his crop (36).[11] Unable to keep his slaves from helping themselves, Dugal' pays Aunt Peggy, the local conjure woman, ten dollars to conjure ("goopher") the vineyard to make it poisonous to black people. Several slaves subsequently die after eating the grapes. Dugal' sees the fruit in strikingly different terms from Julius, as property rather than food; he is "laffin' wid the oberseah fit ter kill" when his wine production the following season rises from a thousand gallons to fifteen hundred (37), transforming the slave's loss into five hundred additional gallons of wine.

These first natural forms of conjuration are fairly straightforward: the vineyard metamorphoses from a place of abundance to a killing field; the black community's relation to this part of the environment goes from sustaining to poisonous; the grapes are turned from Julius's gustatory delight into Dugal''s profit. And the suggestion that the grapes are still dangerously under the influence of the goopher is enough for Julius's purpose, if that purpose is simply to discourage John from buying the land. But these initial, straightforward conjurations function as a sort of précis for a more disturbing conjuration, one that reveals more clearly the impossible traumatic scene of slavery that Chesnutt, via Julius, will return to obsessively throughout *The Conjure Woman*. The story in effect restarts and plays out yet another, inverted, version of the salutary/traumatic intersection between race and nature.

In the next growing season the goopher is still on the field. Dugal' buys an older slave named Henry and forgets to tell him about the goopher. Henry promptly takes some grapes, and Dugal' brings him to Aunt Peggy to see if she can save him. Peggy's new conjure does so in part by linking his health to the grapevines themselves, literally blending him with nature and, in some sense, turning him into food in a way that recalls Prince's and Douglass's fear of becoming cattle in their narratives, and that foreshadows the horrors of Chesnutt's later story, "Dave's Neckliss," that I will turn to shortly. In the spring and summer, when the grapes sprout and grow, Henry's age reverses, his hair grows thick and curly, his arthritis is cured; in the winter, when the vines die, the process reverses itself and Henry is bedridden:

> But de beatenes' thing you eber see happen ter Henry. Up ter dat time he wuz ez ball ez a sweeten' 'tater, but des ez soon ez de young leaves begun ter come out on de grapevimes, de ha'r begun ter grow out on Henry's head, en by de middle er de summer he had de bigges' head er ha'r on de plantation. Befo' dat, Henry had tol'able good ha'r 'roun' de aidges, but soon ez de young grapes begun to come, Henry's ha'r begun to quirl all up in little balls, des like dis yer reg'lar grapy ha'r, an by de time de grapes got ripe his head look des like a bunch er grapes....
>
> But dat wa'n't de quares' thing 'bout de goopher. When Henry come ter de plantation, he wuz gittin' a little ole an stiff in de j'ints. But dat summer he got des ez spry en libely ez any young nigger on de plantation; fac', he got so biggity dat mars Jackson, de oberseah, ha' ter th'eaten ter whip 'im, ef he didn't stop cuttin' up his didos en behave hisse'f. But de mos' cur'ouses' thing happen' in de fall, when de sap begin ter go down in de grapevimes. Fus', when de graps 'uz gathered, de knots begun ter straighten out'n Henry's ha'r en w'en de leaves begin ter fall, Henry's ha'r 'mence' ter drap out; en w'en de vimes 'uz bar', Henry's head wuz baller 'n it wuz in de spring, en he begin ter git ole en stiff in de j'ints ag'in, en paid no mo' 'tention ter de gals dyoin' er de whole winter. En nex' spring, w'en he rub de sap on ag'in, he got young ag'in, en so soopl en libely dat none er de young niggers on de plantation couldn' jump, ner dance, ner hoe ez

much cotton ez Henry. But in de fall er de year his grapes 'mence' ter
straighten out, en his j'ints ter git stiff, en his ha'r drap off, en de
rheumatiz begin ter wrastle wid 'im. (39)

Here the initial merge between the African-American subject and the
natural world is the opposite of traumatic—indeed Henry's transformation is miraculous, Dionysian, an intensification of the delight that
the vineyard originally provided the slaves and that it provides to
Julius before John's capital intervenes.

But the same traumatic pattern manifests itself almost immediately;
the larger context of slavery makes the link between Henry and the
natural world also a source of vulnerability and degradation. Rather
than marveling at Henry's metamorphosis, Dugal' immediately exploits
it, selling Henry to an unsuspecting neighbor for fifteen hundred dollars at the beginning of the summer when he is young and strong, and
buying him back for five hundred in the winter when Henry "inexpli-
cably" loses his vitality. (And note too how Henry's price itself mirrors
Dugal' profit and loss on the scuppernongs.) Rather than making him
the god of the vineyard, under slavery Henry's connection to the land
makes him literally a crop, an agricultural commodity.

This conjunction of human and natural commodification reaches its
depressingly familiar ecological terminus when Dugal' takes the advice
of a Yankee speculator on how to increase his yield dramatically:

He promus Mars Dugal' he c'd make de grapevimes b'ar twice't ez
many grapes, en dat de noo winepress he wuz a-sellin' would make
mo' d'n twice't ez many gallons er wine. En ole Mars Dugal' des drunk
it all in, des 'peared ter be bewitch' wid dat Yankee. W'en de darkies
see dat Yankee runnin' 'roun' de vimya'd en diggin' under de grapevimes, dey shuk dere heads, en 'lowed dat dey feared Mars Dugal' losin'
his min'. Mars Dugal' had all de dirt dug away from under de roots er
all de scuppernon' vimes, an' let 'em stan' dat away for a week er mo'.
Den dat Yankee made de niggers fix up a mixtry er lime en ashes en
amnyo, en po' it 'roun' de roots er de grapevimes. Den he 'vise Mars
Dugal' fer ter trim de vimes close't, en mars Dugal' tuck 'n done
eve'ything de Yankee tole him ter do. (41)

Chesnutt offers us a different, capitalist, conjurer here, one who
"bewitch'[es]" Dugal', and leads him to the environmental insanity
("Mars Dugal' losin' his min'") of chemical farming. In a strangely
violent procedure, Dugal' first severs the vines' roots from the soil,
letting them stand that way for a week, then replaces that soil with the
"mixtry er lime en ashes en amnyo," and finally severely crops the

vines. The results are predictable: the overfertilized vines at first grow extremely fast, and then burn out and wither. Henry, bound to the land, at first becomes unnaturally vital and then dies midsummer when the vines do. Dugal"'s response is to bewail his misfortune at losing two of his most profitable "crops" in a single season.

"The Goophered Grapevine" sets the traumatic pattern that organizes *The Conjure Woman* as a whole, but it does so from a distance. While it is awful to imagine oneself in Henry's place, the story does not require a reader to do so; Julius does not appear in the story and we are given no glimpse into Henry's interiority. In the stories composed after "The Goophered Grapevine," Chesnutt systematically closes this emotional distance, connecting the reader more and more intimately to the traumatic heart of conjuration, making increasingly plain the horror of Julius's memories and the suffering of the other slaves in the tale. His second conjure story, the 1888 "Po' Sandy," for example, presents the flashback moment that initiates the antebellum tale in a much more explicitly traumatic form. The story opens with John looking for lumber to build a new kitchen. He decides to reclaim some wood from an abandoned schoolhouse on the plantation and goes with Julius and Annie to the mill to get the rest.

> We remained seated in the carriage, a few rods from the mill, and watched the leisurely movements of the mill-hands. We had not waited long before a huge pine log was placed in position, the machinery of the mill was set in motion, and the circular saw began to eat its way through the log, with a loud whir which resounded through the vicinity of the mill. The sound rose and fell in a sort of rhythmic cadence, which, heard from where we sat, was not unpleasing, and not loud enough to prevent conversation. When the saw started on its second journey through the log, Julius observed, in a lugubrious tone, and with a perceptible shudder:—
> "Ugh! but dat des do cuddle my blood!"
> "What's the matter, Uncle Julius?" inquired my wife, who is of a very sympathetic turn of mind. "Does the noise affect your nerves?"
> "No, Mis' Annie," replied the old man, with emotion, "I ain' nervous; but dat saw, a-cuttin' en grindin' thoo dat stick er timber, en moanin', en groanin', en sweekin', kyars my 'memb'ance back ter ole times, and 'min's me er po' Sandy." (45)

Julius's tale begins at the moment when the sight of environmental violence at the mill triggers a memory of violent antebellum racial trauma, a return that overwhelms the narrative present of the story, that "cuddles [his] blood" and "kyars [his] 'memb'ance back ter ole times." While this sudden temporal dislocation clearly parallels the moment at the start of the first story when, in John's words, Julius seems "to be living over again in monologue his life on the old plantation," here both the environmental trigger in the narrative present and the intruding narrative that follows demonstrate how intimately natural and racial violence are linked in Julius's imagination and in Chesnutt's own.

Sandy's story is similarly a sharp intensification of the pattern established in "The Goophered Grapevine." He is an unusually productive plantation slave, who is rewarded for his hard work by his master lending him out to his family and neighbors to labor for them as well, and by selling his wife when Sandy is out working himself to exhaustion. When Sandy complains, the master buys him another wife, Tenie. Sandy and Tenie fall in love, and when the master again sends Sandy out to work on another plantation forty miles from home, Sandy despairs, lamenting to Tenie:

> I'm gittin' monst'us ti'ed er dish yer gwine roun' so much. Here I is lent ter Mars Jeems dis mont', en I got ter do so-en-so; en ter Mars Archie de nex' mont', en I got to do so-en-so; den I got ter go ter Miss Jinnie's: en hit's Sandy dis en Sandy dat, en Sandy yer and en Sandy dere, tel it 'pears ter me I an' got no home, ner no marster, ner no mistiss, ner no nuffin. I can't eben keep a wife: my yother ole 'oman wuz sol' away widout my gittin' a chance fer ter tell her good-by; en now I got ter go off an leab you, Tenie, en I dunno whe'r I'm eber gwine ter see you ag'in er no. I wisht I wuz a tree, er a stump, er a rock, er sump'n w'at could stay on de plantation for a w'ile. (47)

In his extremity, Sandy here sees the possibility of merging with the natural world as a kind of freedom—to be a tree, a stump, or a rock would at least offer him some substantive, material, enduring identity, would literally root him in the landscape. Where the link to the grapevine renews Henry, natural metamorphosis only promises Sandy a static escape from slavery. It's better for him, he feels, to give up his human identity when that identity only leads to his limitless exploitation.

As it turns out, Tenie is a conjure woman who had given up her practice when she converted to Christianity. She secretly changes Sandy into a huge pine tree during the day, and back to a man at night so that they can be together. But, despite Tenie's power, the story ends terribly; Sandy's conversion to a natural object doesn't get him out of the slave system, just changes him into a different sort of exploitable natural resource. A few days before Tenie has determined to change the two of them into foxes so they can escape north, she is called away suddenly to nurse a sick white woman. While she is gone, the master, like John, decides to build a kitchen, and with an unusual degree of difficulty, cuts down the Sandy/tree for lumber. Tenie arrives back just in time to see the log being hauled off to the mill. She tries to stop the wagon, and then throws herself on the log as it is being fed into the saw. The mill workers tie her to a post and, with great difficulty, cut Sandy into lumber while she watches. The scene is nightmarish, resonant with lynching's horror:

> De han's at de sawmill had des got de big log on de kerridge, en wuz startin' up de saw, w'en dey seed a 'oman runnin' up de hill, all out er bref, cryin' en gwine on des lick she wuz plumb 'stracted. It wuz Tenie; she cume right inter de mill, en th'owed herse'f on de log, right in front er de saw, a-hollerin' en cryin' ter her Sandy ter fergib her, en not ter think hard er her, fer it wa'n't no fault er hern. Den Tenie 'membered de tree didn' hab no years, en she wuz gittin' ready fer ter wuk her gopher mixtry so ez ter turn Sandy back, w'en de mill-hands kotch holt er her en tied her arms wid a rope, an fasten' her to one er de posts in de sawmill; en den dey started de saw up ag'in, en cut de log up inter bo'ds en scantlin's right befo' her eyes. But it wuz mighty hard wuk; fer of all de sweekin', and moanin', en groanin', dat log done it w'iles de saw wuz a-cuttin' thoo it. De saw wuz one er dese yer ole-timey, up-en-down saws, en hit tuk longer dem days ter saw a log 'en it do now. Dey greased de saw, but dat didn' stop de fuss; hit kep' right on, tel fin'ly dey got de log all sawed up. (51)

Tenie loses her sanity and eventually dies of exposure one night in the building constructed out of the lumber cut from Sandy, the same abandoned structure whose lumber John proposes to reuse for his kitchen.

As in the "Goophered Grapevine," the problem for Sandy and Tenie comes not in their alliance with the natural world, but in the white master's linked understanding of his slaves and the landscape as a limitless resource awaiting transformation into a commodity—Sandy becomes labor, Sandy becomes the tree, the tree becomes lumber, lumber becomes a kitchen. Chesnutt's repetition of this pattern underscores how conjuration should neither be simply conflated with trauma nor romanticized as the sign of a "deeper" originary or inherent green alliance between antebellum African-American culture and the natural world. Conjuration is much more elusive, more neutral, serving as a metaphor for the fluid boundary created between nature and African-American identity in a racist culture, both as a fantasized possibility of escape from an unbearable situation and as a conduit for brutality and degradation. It is not (simply) magic power, religious practice, or deconstructive textuality, but a way for Chesnutt to signify an ongoing, mutually constituting, material instability in the relation between black subjects and world that persisted after slavery, one that has historically exposed African Americans to the same violent commodification that white capitalism has imposed on the natural environment. To see conjuration as linking racial and environmental violence makes Julius's fantastic memories more than a facile ex-post-facto escape from slavery's terrors; rather, stories like "Po' Sandy" offer an extraordinarily subtle analysis of how those terrors continue to function on the individual and ecosystemic levels.

Chesnutt makes explicit how conjuration signifies the interchangeability of African Americans and the commodified nonhuman natural in his third conjure tale, "The Conjurer's Revenge." The story opens by foregrounding the very inversion of human form and animal status that slavery depends upon. John has decided to buy a mule and Julius objects, saying " 'Fac' is . . . I doan lack ter dribe a mule. I's alluz afeared I mought be imposin' on some human creetur; eve'y time I cuts a mule wid a hick'ry, 'pears ter me mos' lackly I's cuttin' some er my own relations, er somebody e'se w'at can't he'p deyse'ves' " (71). John, of course, doesn't get it, calling Julius's notion an "absurd idea," and reducing Julius to "a short silence, during which [he] seemed engaged in a mental struggle" (71). Julius tries again, insisting that an African-American man with a clubfoot they had seen earlier was once a mule, a statement that the literal-minded John and Annie again greet with derision:

> "You en Mis Annie wouldn' wanter b'lieve me, ef I wuz ter 'low dat dat man was oncet a mule?"
>
> "No," I replied, "I don't think it very likely that you could make us believe it."
>
> "Why, Uncle Julius!" said Annie severely, "what ridiculous nonsense!"
>
> This reception of the old man's statement reduced him to silence, and it required some diplomacy on my part to induce him to vouchsafe an explanation. (72)

At the literal level, of course, John and Annie are right. But Julius's assertion is much more complex. It encompasses on one side the most elaborate conning of John that Julius undertakes in the stories—the tale leads John to buy a deceptively poor quality horse rather than a mule, for which Julius receives a payoff from the horse's owner.[12] On the other side, Julius's assertion resonates with the history of slavery: the clubfooted man, Primus, was once a slave, "a man transformed into a brute." The dire questions that slavery poses about identity and commodification are present from the start of the story, and are its central concerns throughout.

In Julius's semi-comic story, Primus is transformed into a mule and sold back to his unwitting master as a black-on-black punishment for stealing the shoat of a powerful conjurer. The story's bitter humor arises from how human the Primus/mule remains after his transformation. No one but the conjurer and Primus know of his "real" identity, a secret that ironically renders Primus the mule more free than Primus the human slave. While doing field work similar to what he performed while a slave, he manages on various occasions to eat two planted rows of chewing tobacco, drink three gallons of wine and spend the afternoon sleeping it off, bite and kick when driven too hard, and to terrify the rival for his former sweetheart's affections. The conjurer ends up converting to Christianity, repents of his conjuration of Primus, and changes him back on his deathbed, expiring just before finishing the job so Primus is left with his clubfoot.

Despite what might seem the obvious meaning of the story as an allegory of slavery, both Annie and John don't understand:

> My wife had listened to Julius's recital with only a mild interest. When the old man had finished it she remarked:—
>
> "That story does not appeal to me, Uncle Julius, and is not up to your usual mark. It isn't pathetic, it has no moral that I can discover, and I can't see why you should tell it. In fact, it seems to me like nonsense."
>
> The old man looked puzzled as well as pained. He had not pleased the lady, and he did not seem to understand why. (79)

But Julius, of course, understands all too well. What Annie misses is the disturbing parallel between conjuration and slavery that the tale exposes, the fluidity between human appearance and animal identity that is slavery's conjure. At the heart of the tale is an indictment of the racist misjudgment inherent in Annie and John's overconfident white gaze. In responding to Annie's shallow assertion, Julius makes this complex point in a way that resonates on multiple levels:

> "I'm sorry, ma'm," he said reproachfully, "ef you doan lack dat tale. I can't make out w'at you means by some er dem wo'ds you uses, but I'm tellin' nuffin but de truf. Co'se I didn' see de conjuh man tu'n 'im back, fer I wuzn' dere; but I be'n hearin' de tale fer twenty-five yeahs, en I an' got no 'casion fer ter 'spute it. Dey's so many things a body knows is lies, dat dey ain' no use gwine roun' findin' fault wid tales dat mought des ez well be so ez not. F' instance, dey's a young nigger

gwine ter school in town, en he come out heah de yuther day en 'lowed
dat de sun stood still en de yeath turnt roun' eve'y day on a kinder
axletree. I tol' dat young nigger ef he didn' take hisse'f 'way wid dem
lies, I'd take a buggy-trace ter 'im; fer I sees de yeath stan'in' still all de
time, en I sees de sun gwine roun' it, en ef a man can't b'lieve w'at 'e
sees, I can't see no use in libbin'—mought 's well die en be whar we
can't see nuffin." (79)

Julius here invites John and Annie to misjudge him, to see him as a
comically overconfident uneducated black. In doing so, they miss the
subtle instructions for reading the tales inherent in the statement that
"[d]ey's so many things a body knows is lies, dat dey ain' no use
gwine roun' findin' fault wid tales dat mought des ez well be so ez
not," and the resonant anguish of his assertion that "ef a man can't
b'lieve w'at 'e sees, I can't see no use in libbin'—mought 's well die en
be whar we can't see nuffin." Annie's demand (and perhaps the white
reader's as well) for a story with predigested racial pathos or a clear
moral rather than "nonsense" is a demand for a story that produces
the same sort of epistemological stability as the "seeing is believing"
model upon which racism depends. It is this model, of course, that
Julius is critiquing here. Julius's example proves that you *can't* believe
what you see; after all, the visual evidence clearly indicates the earth
is flat, just as for Annie, Julius's black skin clearly indicates his
ignorance and inferiority. And in missing this fairly straightforward
"nonsense," Annie protects herself from the despair hinted of in
Julius's conclusion: since he in fact lives in a world where he can't
believe what he sees, he can see no use in living, would prefer to be a
sightless corpse.

Annie's failure is duplicated in John's racist underestimation of
Julius in the story's close. The horse that John buys at Julius's urging
in place of the mule turns out to be different than it appears:

Early the next morning the man brought the horse up to the vineyard. At that time I was not a very good judge of horseflesh. The
horse appeared sound and gentle, and, as the owner assured me, had
no bad habits. The man wanted a large price for the horse, but finally
agreed to accept a much smaller sum, upon payment of which I
became possessed of a very fine-looking animal. But alas for the
deceitfulness of appearances! I soon ascertained that the horse was
blind in one eye, and that the sight of the other was very defective;
and not a month elapsed before my purchase developed most of the
diseases that horse-flesh is heir to, and a more worthless, broken-
winded, spavined quadruped never disgraced the noble name of

horse. After worrying through two or three months of life, he expired one night in a fit of colic. I replaced him with a mule, and Julius henceforth had to take his chances of driving some metamorphosed unfortunate. (80)

Julius appears next Sunday in a new suit of clothes, the apparent payment from the horse's previous owner for manipulating John into the purchase. Julius deftly turns an allegory of slavery's trauma into a test of his white auditors' interpretive powers, a test they both fail, and a failure for which John pays a literal price. If we read Julius's storytelling as itself a form of conjuration, the story's title becomes Julius's own somewhat muted revenge for John and Annie's racist ignorance.[13]

Chesnutt's fourth conjure tale, and the last he was to write for several years, horribly inverts the emphasis on appearance and identity central to "The Conjurer's Revenge." The conjuration at the heart of "Dave's Neckliss" is not magical, but the result of psychic torture by Dugal' of his slave Dave, and Dave's resulting insanity. By removing the magical moment at the center of his previous work, Chesnutt removes the protective fantasy he slipcovers over the traumatic inter-section between antebellum slave identity and the natural world in the other stories. The result is the most emotionally intense and radically critical of Chesnutt's stories, one barred from the 1899 collection of conjure tales, *The Conjure Woman*, by his editor at Houghton Mifflin for "lack[ing] the recourse to conjure" (Brodhead, 17). This is the first of many such censoring misreadings that literalize the fantastic element in the tales and thereby miss the referent of Chesnutt's central, potent, and dangerous metaphor.

"Dave's Neckliss" follows the same broad structure as the other tales: Julius is overwhelmed by a traumatic antebellum memory in which a slave's identity is merged with the commodified environ-ment, narrates that memory to the bored John and Annie, and receives a minor material benefit in return. Chesnutt clearly means to identify the tale with the others. Rather than seeing it as a variation on the magic conjure formula, however, the removal of the fantastic makes "Dave's Neckliss" as direct an account of the traumatic origin of Julius's memories as Chesnutt provides. The story that was excluded from the collection as extrageneric is in fact the clearest statement of the psychological nexus at the heart of *The Conjure Woman*. "Dave's Neckliss" incorporates the formulaic elements of the other tales, but closes the psychological and physical distance between Julius and the events of the story entirely, intensifies the story's emotional charge, and throws into sharper relief the persistence of naturalized racial hierarchy from the antebellum period through the late nineteenth century.

The tale opens with Annie inviting Julius to help himself to slices of a ham on which she and John have just dined. Julius goes inside to eat, and John spies on him in order to count how many slices he consumes. Julius begins crying part way through his meal, as eating the ham triggers another traumatic antebellum memory. What changes here is the intensity of Julius's response—this is the first and only time he weeps in the tales—and the fact that he is apparently unaware that John is watching. Julius's grief here is presumably unalloyed by a desire to manipulate John in the minor ways he does in other stories. For his part, John seems oblivoius to the inappropriateness of his secret observation of Julius's eating, noting how "slice after slice . . . disappeared in the spacious cavity of his mouth," keeping "count of them from a lazy curiosity to see how much he *could* eat," and first assuming Julius's tears are the result of too-strong mustard rather than grief (123–24).

Chesnutt's voyeuristic frame for this tale highlights the implicit racial voyeurism that structures the whole project, for both John and the white reader. John's patronizing objectification/conjuration of Julius as some*thing* rather than some*one*, the "lazy curiosity" that sees Julius as a racialized object of strictly historical interest rather than as a grieving and hungry old man, is almost immediately naturalized in a by-now characteristic move:

> The conditions were all favorable to story-telling. There was an autumnal languor in the air, and a dreamy haze softened the dark green of the distant pines and the deep blue of the Southern sky. The generous meal he had made had put the old man in a very good humor. He was not always so, for his curiously undeveloped nature was subject to moods which were almost childish in their variableness. It was only now and then that we were able to study, through the medium of his recollection, the simple but intensely human inner life of slavery. His way of looking at the past seemed very strange to us; his view of certain sides of life was essentially different from ours. He never indulged in any regrets for the Arcadian joyousness and irresponsibility which was a somewhat popular conception of slavery; his had not been the lot of the petted house-servant, but that of the toiling field-hand. While he mentioned with a warm appreciation the acts of kindness which those in authority had shown to him and his people, he would speak of a cruel deed, not with the indignation of one accustomed to quick feeling and spontaneous expression, but with a furtive disapproval which

suggested to us a doubt in his own mind as to whether he had a right to think or to feel, and presented to us the curious psychological spectacle of a mind enslaved long after the shackles had been struck off from the limbs of its possessor. Whether the sacred name of liberty ever set his soul aglow with a generous fire; whether he had more than the most elementary ideas of love, friendship, patriotism, religion,— these things which are half, and the better half, of life to us; whether he even realized, except in a vague, uncertain way, his own degradation, I do not know. I fear not; and if not, then centuries of repression had borne their legitimate fruit. But in the simple human feeling, and still more in the undertone of sadness, which pervaded his stories, I thought I could see a spark which, fanned by favoring breezes and fed by the memories of the past, might become in his children's children a glowing flame of sensibility, alive to every thrill of human happiness or human woe. (124–25)

John's trying here, or rather he thinks he is, thinks he is seeing Julius with a sympathetic, liberal eye. But John's professions of doubt over how fully he understands Julius's psychic damage in fact mask how strictly that doubt is delimited so that it doesn't extend to granting Julius the possibility of full personhood in the present or, certainly, to seeing the connections between Julius's slavery and his postbellum oppression by John. Instead, Julius's inner life (as John understands it) is as natural, available, and clichéd as the setting itself, with its "autumnal languor in the air," and "dream[y] haze soften[ing] the dark green of the distant pines and the deep blue of the Southern sky," a setting that seems deliberately to quote the sort of purple descriptions offered by Bagby and other white writers in the tradition.

The hermetic imperviousness of John's "sympathetic" racism is manifest in his ability to fold the immediacy of Julius's suffering into what Žižek names as ideology, "a fantasy-construction which serves as support for…'reality' itself: an 'illusion' which structures our effective real social relations and thereby masks some insupportable, real, impossible kernel" (45). The passage exposes the strategies by which John and the white reader inoculate themselves against the contagion of trauma, naturalizing oppression and banishing it to another person, place, and time, the very strategies we have already seen employed by Page, Bagby, Harris, and others. Rather than Julius's trauma establishing continuity between the past and present, it is, for John, what makes Julius a natural slave, the "curious psychological spectacle of a mind enslaved long after the shackles had been struck off from the limbs of its possessor," the "legitimate fruit" that "centuries of oppression" have conjured and that John consumes for his own entertainment.

Julius's trauma is not eruptive, but bound within him; his "way of looking at the past seemed very strange...his view of certain sides of life was essentially different." Despite the fact that he has just seen Julius spontaneously weeping during dinner, John declares with inexplicable certainty that Julius "doubt[s] in his own mind as to whether he had a right to think or to feel," that the "undertone of sadness which pervaded his stories," was only the *possibility* of a "spark which, fanned by favoring breezes and fed by the memories of the past, might become in his children's children a glowing flame of sensibility, alive to every thrill of human happiness or human woe." Julius's eruptive grief is carefully cordoned off from John's own present moment, rendered as strictly an antebellum legacy that jumps safely from the past to Julius's grandchildren without stopping on the porch.

But that trauma does stop on the porch in the form of Julius's disturbing tale. The story takes the form of a perversely inverted version of the classic slave narrative. The enslaved protagonist, Dave, is an exceptional figure, strong, very hardworking and deeply religious, who, at great hardship and against the will of his master, teaches himself to read so that he can become more familiar with the Bible. In narratives like Douglass's, the achievement of literacy is connected to the achievement of full personhood, of freedom from the degrading consubstantiality with the physical that marks slavery. This familiar moment in the slave narrative, however, does not follow the same generic movement toward liberation in Dave's story. When Dugal' discovers Dave can read, he makes his ability an instrument of oppression to the other slaves, co-opting Dave to preach to them that they have a religious duty to work hard, not steal, and obey Dugal'.

Dave is rewarded for his sincere, if misguided, efforts in part by being allowed to get engaged to his sweetheart Dilsey. Unfortunately for Dave, another enslaved man, the appropriately named Wiley, is also in love with Dilsey, and plots to destroy their relationship. He does so by stealing ham from Dugal''s smokehouse and hiding it under the floorboards of Dave's cabin. When the theft is discovered, despite his adamant denial of guilt, Dave is blamed and his literacy held accountable: "Mars Walker [the plantation overseer] say it wuz des ez he 'spected: he didn' b'lieve in dese yer readin' en prayin' niggers; it wuz all 'pocrisy, en sarve' Mars Dugal' right fer 'lowin' Dave ter be readin' books w'en it wuz 'g'in' de law" (128). Dave is given forty lashes, and then, in what Richard Brodhead aptly describes as "the intentional manufacture...of a punitively damaged identity," (18) Walker encloses a ham in a steel mesh, shackles one end of a chain to the ham and the other end around Dave's neck, and sentences him to wear this "neckliss" for six months. Dave immediately goes from the position of leadership in the slave community he enjoyed, thanks to his literacy and preaching, to an entirely humiliated and degraded one, becoming an object of ridicule for the other slaves and losing Dilsey to Wiley.

In shackling Dave to a ham, Dugal' is shackling Dave to a virulent symbol of bondage itself. The Old Testament enslavement of Ham was an oft-cited antebellum justification for the enslavement of black people, Ham's supposed descendents.[14] Not only does his literacy lead to degradation rather than freedom, Dave's "neckliss" brutally demonstrates once again how slavery aims to reduce a human subject to a commodified natural object. Slavery, blackness, and natural commodification collide in a traumatic conflation of the material and the symbolic, a multiply invested symbol that stands between Dave and world:

> But all er Dave's yuther troubles wa'n't nuffin side er dat ham. He had wrap' de chain roun' wid a rag, so it didn' hurt his neck; but w'eneber he went ter wuk, dat ham would be in his way; he had ter do his task, howsomedever, des de same ez ef he didn' hab de ham. W'eneber he went ter lay down, dat ham would be in de way. Ef he turn ober in his sleep, dat ham would be tuggin' at his neck. It wuz de las' thing he seed at night, en de fuss' thing he seed in de mawnin'. W'eneber he met a stranger, de ham would be de fus' thing de stranger would see. (130)

Like a physical precursor of DuBois's veil, the necklace signifies "how it feels to be a problem," how blackness is produced both from the "outside," in the gaze of others, and how that gaze is internalized, how that process of attaching meaning to pigment is, like the chain, both a constructed connection and a very strong one. And the ham itself, as an image of an animal that has been domesticated, slaughtered, and repackaged as a product, grotesquely parallels slavery's reduction of black people to animate meat, as we have seen both Prince and Douglass suggest.

Dave's punishment exemplifies how slavery is a form of conjuration, a spell that in excruciatingly slow motion turns Dave from an unusually self-possessed individual into a thing entirely possessed by another. It requires no magic to realize the transformation, only the gradual breakdown of Dave's sanity under the relentless humiliation imposed by the necklace:

> Fus' Dave didn' mine it so much, caze he knowed he hadn't done nuffin. But bimeby he got so he couldn't stan' it no longer, en he'd hide

hisse'f in de bushes w'eneber he seed anybody comin', en alluz kep'
hisse'f shet up in his cabin atter he come in fum wuk.

It wuz monst'us hard on Dave, en bemeby, w'at wid dat ham
eberlastin' en etarnally draggin' roun' his neck, he 'mence' fer ter do
en say quare things, en make de niggers wonder ef he wa'n't gittin'
out'n his mine. He got ter gwine roun' talkin' ter hisse'f, en singin'
corn-shuckin' songs, en laffin' fit ter kill 'bout nuffin. En one day he
tole one er de niggers he had 'skivered a noo way fer ter raise hams,—
gwine ter pick 'em off'n trees, en save de expense er smoke-'ouses by
kyoin' 'em in de sun. En one day he up'n tole Mars Walker he got
sump'n pertickler fer ter say ter 'im; en he tuk Mars Walker off ter one
side, en tole 'im he wuz gwine ter show 'im a place in de swamp whar
dey wuz of whole trac' er lan' covered wid ham-trees. (131)

Dave's poignant fantasy of hams growing naturally from trees represents a last-ditch psychological strategy to identify himself with wild
nature rather than the agricultural slave economy of the plantation.
If, as Dave dreams, trees in the swamp can produce hams and hams
can be cured in the sun rather than the smokehouse, then hams might
come to signify the wild rather than slavery's exploited pastoral.
Dave's own association with the ham would not be severed, but
rewritten in the context of a sudden natural abundance produced
without labor or exploitation. At the same time, such a fantasy image
is also poised on the edge of the racial trauma of Chesnutt's own
postbellum moment; Dave's dream of natural abundance is also a
nightmare of mass lynching, "a place in de swamp whar dey wuz of
whole trac' er lan' covered wid ham-trees."[15]

Dave's ravings worry Walker, and the necklace is removed, though
not before the meat has cured in the sun like Dave's imaginary ham
so that "de sun had melt all de fat, en de lean had all swivel' up, so day
wa'n't but th'ee er fo' poun's lef' " (131). But Walker acts too late; the
"conjure" has taken effect and Dave's identity has begun to collapse.
He starts secretly hanging a large knot on a string around his neck
when he sleeps at night to mimic the ham, again underscoring the
link between the antebellum trauma of slavery and the postbellum
trauma of lynching. And then, in the story's conclusion—the only
place in the antebellum narration in which Julius directly appears—
Dave reveals to Julius how deeply he has internalized the symbol of
his degradation:

One day...me'n Dave wuz choppin' cotton tergedder, w'en Dave lean'
on his hoe, en motion' fer me ter come ober close ter 'im; en den he
retch' ober en w'ispered ter me.

"Julius's, sezee, 'did yer knowed yer wuz wukkin' long yer wid a ham?"

I couldn' 'magine w'at he meant. "G'way fum yer, Dave." says I. "Yer ain' wearin' no ham no mo'; try en fergit 'bout dat; 't ain' gwine ter do yer no good fer ter 'member it."

"Look a-yer, Julius,' sezee, 'kin yer keep a secret?"

"Co'se I kin, Dave." says I. "I doan go roun' tellin' people w'at yuther folks says ter me."

"Kin I trus' yer, Julius? Will yer cross yo' heart?"

I cross' my heart. "Wush I may die ef I tells a soul," says I.

Dave look' at me des lack he wuz lookin' thoo me en 'way on de yuther side er me, en sezee:—

"Did yer knowed I wuz turnin' ter a ham, Julius?" (132)

The memory of Dave's madness pulls Julius's directly into this antebellum memory, closing the third-personal narrational distance Julius maintains in the other tales, a raw intimacy similar to the story's substitution of psychosis for magical conjuration. Chesnutt signals us here that the antebellum memory of Dave's madness—or what it signifies—is at the heart of Julius's traumatic repetition in all the tales, that the traumatic conflation between human and natural exploitation is central to slavery's horror, not only because of the externalized violence such a conflation permits, but because of how that fluid boundary can collapse inward. Dave's madness is less a delusion than a terrifying exaggeration of the reality of his condition; he is telling the truth as much as he is raving.

Dave's psychological disappearance leads to his physical disappearance, in a suicide that is also a self-lynching, and that renders material his inner transformation. Wiley's plot is discovered, and Dugal' calls all the slaves together to announce Dave's rehabilitation. But Dave is nowhere to be found. Julius reappears in the narrative when Dugal' sends him to fetch Dave. After searching for him around the plantation grounds, he finally tracks Dave's footprints up to the smokehouse:

So I follered dat track 'cross de fiel' fum de quarters 'tel I got ter de smoke-'house. De fus' thing I notice' wuz smoke comin' out'n de cracks: it wuz cu'ous, caze dey hadn' be'n no hogs kill' on de plantation fer six mont' er so, en all de bacon in de smoke-'ouse wuz done kyoed. I couldn' 'magine fer ter sabe my life w'at Dave wuz doin' in dat smoke-'ouse. I went up ter de do' en hollered:—

"Dave!"

Dey didn' nobody answer. I didn' wanter open de do', fer w'ite folks is monst'us pertickler 'bout dey smoke-'ouses; en ef de oberseah had a-come up en cotch me in dere, he mou't not wanter b'lieve

I wuz des lookin' fer Dave. So I sorter knock at de do' en call' out
ag'in:—

"O Dave, hit's me—Julius! Doan be skeered. Mars Dugal' wants
yer ter come up ter de big house,—he done 'skivered who stole de
ham."

But Dave didn' answer. En w'en I look' roun' ag'in en didn' seed
none er his tracks gwine way fum de smoke-'ouse, I knowed he wuz in
dere yit, en I wuz 'termine' fer ter fetch 'im out; so I push de do' open
en look in.

Dey wuz a pile er bark burnin' in de middle er de flo', en right ober
de fier, hangin' fum one er de rafters, wuz Dave; dey wuz a rope roun'
his neck, en I didn' haf ter look at his face mo' d'n once fer ter see he
wuz dead.

Den I knowed how it all happen'. Dave had kep' on gittin' wusser
en wusser in his mine, 'tel he des got ter b'lievin' he wuz all done turnt
ter a ham; en den he had gone en built a fier, en tied a rope roun' his
neck, des lack de hams wuz tied, en had hung hisse'f up in de smoke-
'ouse fer ter kyo. (134)

It is tempting to make this the primal scene of Julius's trauma, the
awful moment of real transformation that the previous three tales have
only approached metaphorically. But despite its utter materiality, such a
total violation is also at some level unrepresentable, in that it is the very
subjective ground for imagining such suffering that is disappearing
under the force of the traumatic event. This conjunction of literality
and a failure of representation is the impossible, unbearable experience
at the heart of trauma, a conjunction Chesnutt insists is also at the
heart of the postbellum antebellum plantation pastoral. Rather than a
symbolic appropriation of slavery's trauma, the image of Dave's self-
slaughtered ham/body dutifully hung over the fire to cure itself serves
as a kind of final metaphor for slavery's threat to subjectivity, the
possibility of losing the ability to propagate narrative altogether, of
internalizing racism deeply and finally. And it resonates with the similarly unrepresentable horrors of lynching. It is a metaphor that represents the end of the possibility of making metaphors, a traumatic echo
that threatens to drown out even Chesnutt's ambitious voice, if not the
reproductions of sentimental nostalgic pastoralism flowing endlessly
from the pens of postbellum white apologists. *The Conjure Woman* in
part serves to contain and present this final and most terrible conjuration, to reveal Dave's body in the midst of the plantation pastoral.

6

STRANGE FRUIT

[T]here is something...that one cannot "get over," one cannot "work through," which is the deliberate act of violence against a collectivity, humans who have been rendered anonymous for violence and whose death recapitulates an anonymity for memory. Such violence cannot be "thought," constitutes an assault on thinking, negates thinking in the mode of recollection and recovery. (486)
—Judith Butler, "After Loss, What Then?"

Nostalgia turns away from a contemporary scene it defines largely through negation, constructing the present moment in terms of its departure from a fantasy of lost individual and collective harmony. As chapter four argued and as Chesnutt insisted, the hyper-racialized pastoral of the Lost Cause—a nostalgia that was the intimately connected inverse of slavery's traumatic collapse of subjectivity into various forms of the commodified natural—offered a way for whites to retreat from the blood guilt of their history, the risk of "contagion" posed by that traumatic antebellum history in which they were enmeshed.

But the white fantasy of a lost natural hierarchy served as more than an anodyne for an awful past. The negation of the present inherent in nostalgia also afforded whites a terrible resource for action in that present. Against the background of a lost imaginary rural landscape of magnolia-scented Southern belles, courageous masters, and flowery plantation homes surrounded by fertile fields filled with happy darkies—a place most fundamentally constituted by everyone "knowing their place"—the figure of the newly liberated African American loomed large. Black people, emancipated from slavery's fundamental conflation of their subjectivity and the agricultural landscape, could (putatively) quit, talk back, vote, move, read, farm, and have romantic relationships with whomever they wanted.[1] For many Southern whites, however, such modest assertions of independence served as the most prominent reminder that not only the good

Figure 3 What Is It?

Source: © Shelburne Museum, Shelburne, Vermont.

old times were gone, but that they never existed. And as a result, what they brutally negated were black people who refused to perform the role of Uncle Remus, who didn't blend into the pastoral background as they "always" had, whose mere and evident humanity had no place in the rigid racial epistemology that so profoundly organized the landscape of postbellum white Southern nostalgia.[2]

If, as I have argued, slavery fundamentally depended on whites conflating black people with the commodified pastoral, particularly domesticated animals—a contagious traumatic scene that, from transcendentalism onward, much of white racial and cultural identity formed itself in repressing—the decades following the war just as fundamentally involved an often violent struggle to reconstruct black and white racial identity in relation to the natural world. This struggle took a wide variety of forms, from the micro- and macro-racial geographies of Jim Crow segregation, to sharecropping, "scientific" racism, and the grotesque violence of spectacle lynching in the South. This chapter and the next will take up these fraught topics, and just as important, will argue for their *interconnection*, for the fundamental imbrication between the formation of the color line in the South and the valorization of the West, between the scientific racism and lynching discussed in this chapter, and the supposedly ahistorical, extrasocial ecstasy of the natural sublime that so many elite white men embraced at the end of the nineteenth century that I examine in the chapter that follows.

What Is It?

In March of 1860—as the country was breaking in half along the racial and territorial fault line of slavery, and hard on the heels of the sensational publication of Darwin's *The Origin of Species: The Preservation of Favoured Races in the Struggle for Life*—Barnum's Museum of Wonders in New York City announced the arrival of its newest "wonder." Called variously the "What Is It?," the "Nondescript," and the "Man Monkey" in Barnum's advertisements and in contemporary newspaper reviews, the supposedly hybrid creature (for most of the exhibition performed by a costumed mentally retarded African American named William Henry Johnson) provided a material representation of contemporary white American anxieties about evolution and racial identity.[3] Such anxieties had been intensified by the looming war and Darwin's book, and only got more intense in the postbellum period. That the What Is It? condensed those anxieties in a particularly resonant and ongoing way is underscored by the exhibit's enormous popularity over a *sixty-seven* year run. Unlike the stable epistemological certainty of predigested sentimental images of African Americans like The Last Chattel, or practices within slavery like whipping, rape, and the auction that brutally defined black people as nothing more than domesticated animals, Barnum's wonder promised its white viewers *both* an exploration of the profound instability of racial definitions of identity, and a strict limitation of the possibilities of those unstable identities within a thoroughly racist set of assumptions.[4]

As I discussed in the third chapter, the justification for slavery depended in part on aligning black people with nature, thereby making them subject to the preexisting exploitive relationship with the environment that European white/humans understood as natural. The profound uncertainty in postbellum racial definition produced by the end of slavery, the impact of evolutionary theory, and the cascading evidence of nature's profound vulnerability in the nineteenth century—including the first mass extinctions in the Northeast and Midwest, the South's devastated agricultural lands, and hydraulic mining in the West—put significant adaptive stress on those antebellum assumptions. The Nondescript's categorical difference from the white viewer functioned as a sort of racial container for the deeper contemporary instability in the relation between the category of the human and its definitional separation from the environment, at once providing a natural and absolute abjection based on the Nondescript's partial collapse into the landscape, while at the same time preserving a fundamental ambiguity about the degree of that collapse. It is this intensely racialized buffer between human and natural that the Nondescript occupies, a site that marks the emergent renegotiation of the postbellum relation between racial definition and natural experience.[5]

The exhibit made blackness, literally and figuratively, the missing link, a sign of something/one neither fully animal nor fully human. Advertisements for the exhibit asked the same sort of questions that would occupy "scientific" racists in the coming decades: "Is it a lower order of man? or is it a higher development of the monkey? or Is it both in combination?"[6] Barnum's pitch was taken up in contemporary newspaper reviews that accepted unquestioningly the museum's spurious backstory of the Man Monkey's African capture in a "PERFECTLY NUDE STATE, roving about among the trees and branches, in the manner common to the monkey and orang outang,"—despite the fact that the Nondescript was, in fact, a costumed black man to whose humanity the racist white audience was blind. The exhibit rewrote the horrors of the slave trade and middle passage—"after considerable exertion the hunters succeeded in capturing three of these oddities—two males and a female. All of them were forwarded to this country, but, unfortunately, two of them sickened and died on the voyage across. The present one is the only survivor"—from the "objective" distance of a scientific expedition, and in an absolutely material way trained whites to see a "real" black person as definitively, if indeterminatively, less than fully human. These contemporary newspaper accounts accepted that the Nondescript was a bridge between the simian and "the negro" and endorsed the invitation to white viewers to see black people themselves occupying a developmental level as close to the Nondescript as to them. So, for example, the *New York Herald* wrote: "He has been examined by some of the most scientific men we have, and pronounced by them to be a connecting link between the wild native African and the brute creation," the *New York Tribune* declared, "It seems to be a sort of cross between the ape species and the negro," and the *New York Sun* called him, "a connecting link in the chain of animal life between the brute and the human ape species," and went on to note, "the ears are far too high and too much back for a negro; the arms are several inches too long in proportion and the jaw and teeth are entirely animal. Its eyes are bright and intelligent but the brain is quite small, and Dan Rice in his palmiest days never could produce a heartier 'Jim Crow' laugh than this creature gets off on the slightest occasion." [7]

In these reviews the Nondescript is not positioned between the animal and the fully (white) human, but between the "wild native African and the brute creation," the "ape species and the negro," the "brute and the [curiously named] human ape species"; he signifies an evolutionary tie between *blackness* and the natural world, not between the unmarked whiteness of "humanity" and that world. Indeed, he serves to quarantine whiteness from its link to that "brute creation," and in doing so, to quarantine whiteness from blackness as well. This dual separation was made visually manifest in a second advertisement for the exhibition, What Is It? or Man Monkey.

Here pictured out of his "native" African habitat and garb, the What Is It? is hardly distinguishable from contemporary racist images of black people—indefatigably happy, helpless, entirely out of place, and sharply different from the white viewer's "civilized" dress and physiognomy.[8] And this slippage in the identity of the What Is It? from "brute creation" to "the negro" finds its logical terminus in a third representation, What Is It? An Heir to the Throne or the Next Republican Candidate, where the political unconscious of this "curiosity" is made explicit.

Figure 4 What Is It? or Man Monkey.

Source: Collection of the New-York Historical Society, Negative #67612.

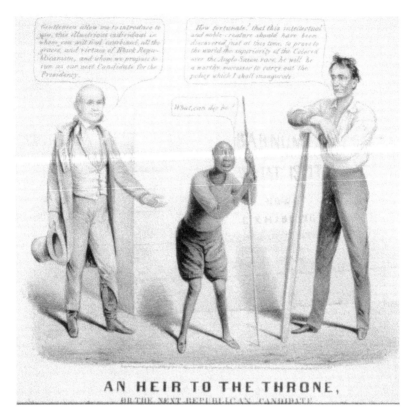

Figure 5   What Is It? An Heir to the Throne or the Next Republican Candidate.
Source: Currier and Ives, 1860. LC-USZC2–2564.

Here the answer to What Is It? comes clearer, and with it the
political energy contained by the representation. The What Is It? is,
in part, independent, enfranchised African Americans, the "danger"
of their disconnection from the landscape underscored by the shift
from a wild "African" background in the first image, to some vague
garden setting signified by the fountain and the whites' outdoor
clothing in the second, to the explicitly urban setting in the third in
which the What Is It? has left the exhibition and, flanked by the abolitionist Horace Greeley and Abraham Lincoln, is heading for the
White House to assert the "virtues of Black Republicanism" and
manifest the "superiority of the Colored Race to the Anglo Saxon."[9]
   It is this instability in the identity and cultural position of the
Nondescript, figured simultaneously as an instability in the precise

nature of his racialized identification with the environment, that
marks the postbellum shift from slavery and the postbellum antebellum plantation pastoral. If "it" wasn't a slave anymore, or a loyal
ex-slave who lived in the past, then what was "it?" And where, among
these eroded, farmed-out, overgrown fields, was the Edenic plantation pastoral "it" used to signify? White certainty about the nature of
black people under slavery—as domesticated animals or the dusky
face of the lost Southern pastoral—gave way after the war to innumerable white-authored "ethnological" studies (and several black-
authored ones) that instantiated race and racial hierarchy in relation
to the natural world in a bewildering variety of ways. Writers like
Joseph A. Tillinghast continued antebellum claims that whiteness
and blackness were formed as a result of climate, and, following the
lead of Louis Agassiz and Samuel Howe, hoped that black people
would, as a result, die out in the North, decline in the South, and
eventually move back to their natural habitat in the jungles of Africa,
the Caribbean, and South America, a doctrine George Fredrickson
aptly calls "a defense of emancipation as a step toward genocide by
natural causes" (159). Scientists working in the tradition of George
Morton and Josiah Nott spent their days measuring angles on people's heads, estimating the cranial volume of collections of skulls, and
comparing the results to gorillas to produce some "objective" taxon-
omy of race. Social Darwinists like Frederick Hoffman shed crocodile
tears over the inevitable extinction of "the negro" in competition
with the "vital, fatal, arrogant, dominant" "Anglo-Saxon," while
others like Edward Gilliam feared that natural "negro fecundity" and
"miscegenation" would overwhelm the breeding capacity of "pure
whites" and lead America itself into either an apocalyptic race war or
a devolution into a semi-savagery. Perhaps the nadir of this genre
came in the peculiarly American combination of tortured fundamen-
talism and virulent racism in the "polygenist" or "pre-Adamite"
theories of, among others, Samuel Cartwright, Jefferson Davis,
Benjamin F. Perry (the governor of South Carolina), Buckner Payne,
and most notoriously, Charles Carroll, author of the 1900 bestseller
The Negro a Beast, a foundational document for modern hate groups
like Christian Identity and the Aryan Nations.[10] Carroll and the other
polygenists argued that black people were not human at all, but had
been created before Adam and Eve as the "beasts of the field" over
which Adam was given "dominion"—at least until one of "them"
tempted Eve and was changed into a serpent for her illicit contact
with a white/human woman.[11] In Carroll's pathological exegesis,
"miscegenation"—for him a form of bestiality—was, in addition to

the Fall, the reason for Cain's punishment, the Flood, the curse of Ham, the crucifixion of Jesus, the destruction of every previous civilization, the South's loss of the Civil War, and the coming day of judgment; as he says conclusively, "the Bible is simply a history of the long conflict which has raged between God and man, as the result of man's criminal relations with the negro" (221).

For Carroll, *any* admixture of "black blood," no matter how distant, meant that a given person was not a person at all, but categorically and absolutely a "beast" without a soul that, like any other animal or "natural resource," was the God-given property of white/humans and could be exploited, slaughtered, commodified, developed, and so forth with His blessing.[12] Accordingly, in Carroll's ravings, environmental and racial exploitation were identical and the religious *duty* of whites:

> As a matter of fact, the Negro was never a slave. To conceive the design of enslaving an individual we must presuppose that he is free; the first act of enslavement is to deprive him of his liberty. This the Negro never had since the creation of man. The Negro is an ape; hence, his status in the universe, his relation to Man, like that of every other animal, was fixed irrevocably by God in the Creation, and no act upon man's part, whether legislative, executive, or judicial, can change it. The will of God upon this most important subject, as expressed in those original statutes given man in the Creation, "Have dominion over the fish of the sea, and over the fowl of the air, and over every living thing that moveth upon the earth," is the supreme law of the universe; and in the eyes of this great law there is not today, there never was and there can never be on this earth, such a thing as a free Negro.... [U]nder the law of God the Negro, like every other animal, is the property of man, without reference to whether he is ever brought into contact with him or not. The mere fact that man in his blind, criminal folly, declines to exert that control over the Negro, in common with the rest of the animals, which God designed him to have and commanded him to exercise, does not free the Negro, it can only damn man, for his shameless contempt for God's plan of Creation, and for his wanton violation of Divine law.
>
> Man was created free. His personal liberty was implied in his assignment to dominion over all the earth, and over the animals. Hence, man can be enslaved; but since you cannot enslave the horse or the dog, how can you enslave the ape? They all belong to "one kind of flesh," and were placed under man's dominion in the Creation. This absurd idea that it is optional with man to enslave, or to emancipate the Negro, is another result of placing man and the ape in the same family. (288–90)

While Carroll's views were extreme, even by the standards of late nineteenth-century race theory,[13] I would argue that in that extremity they reflected the views that in fact produced the traumatic practices of slavery, the endless humiliation of Jim Crow, and the psychopathic brutality of lynching more accurately than other "moderate" or "mainstream" writers seeking to rationalize the unconscionable. Carroll, apparently untroubled by either rationality or a conscience, proves a perversely astute critic of the traumatic intersection of the construction of racial identity and natural experience in nineteenth-century America. The passage first confirms the total collapse of black people into the animal at the heart of slavery; indeed makes that collapse so absolute that slavery disappears altogether along with the very notion of black *people*, subsumed entirely under an originary relation of white dominion of the natural world. Racial and environmental violence become the same thing here, just as they were in the African slave trade and in the colonial embrace of the pastoral at the expense of the wilderness as a sign of white right to the land. The racialized environmental attitudes that underwrote the practices of the Middle Passage and the early "development" of the Atlantic Coast were more alive and virulent than ever in 1900.

THE BLACK BEAST, RAPIST

The figure of the Beast is formed by Carroll's text as the locus of a viciously overdetermined effort to collapse black identity into the natural and establish a categorical alliance between whiteness and humanity, and a concomitant dominion of white people over every living thing.[14] The brittleness of this absolute distinction between white/human and black/animal was evident in the obsessional relation Carroll had with the Beast, a creature at once possessed of apocalyptic sexual and genetic power but that remained, somehow, categorically inferior as well.[15] The Beast was not only Carroll's obsession, however; the figure was nearly omnipresent in the white racist imagination for at least a century after the war, perhaps the primary template for how whites (mis)understood blacks. Like the Nondescript, the Beast was deployed both to negate the manifest humanity of "black" people *and* to "purify" whiteness/humanity of any identity with blackness/nature. And like the Nondescript, the Beast both instantiated and threatened to undermine this supposedly absolute distinction, occupying some shifting location "beneath" white humanity but above or atop the animal kingdom, always threatening to forget the supposedly natural place slavery enforced.

Unlike the 1860 Nondescript, however, the Black Beast wasn't "playful as a kitten," but generically savage. Just as whites used black people to signify the supposedly harmonious antebellum Southern pastoral, the Black Beast represented a "devolution" from both the happy darky of the plantation and the limitless fertility of Bagby's vision of the fields under cultivation.[16] The racist stereotypes of black people that emerge after the war and reach their nadir around the end of the century almost always incorporate a narrative of racial decline from slavery to Reconstruction, a reversion to a supposedly original primitive state that quite precisely and deliberately mirrors the devastation of southern agriculture and industry after the war, the return of croplands to the sort of semi-wilderness over which Uncle Julius and John struggle in tales like the "Goopher'd Grapevine." As George Fredrickson notes, this view of an essentially wild African-American character emerged even in southern antebellum speculations on what emancipation would mean:

> According to [these theories], the Negro was by nature a savage brute. Under slavery, however, he was "domesticated" or, to a limited degree, "civilized." Hence docility was not so much his natural character as an artificial creation of slavery. As long as the control of the master was firm and assured, the slave would be happy, loyal, and affectionate; but remove or weaken the authority of the master, and he would revert to type as a blood-thirsty savage. (53–54)

Given this template, it is hardly surprising that in the white view, black people declined into their wild natures without a firm white hand on the reins, just like an untended field or an abandoned dog. George T. Winston, the President of North Carolina College of Agriculture and Mechanic Arts, summarized this supposed devolution in African-American identity from domesticated animal to beast in his 1901 address to the American Academy of Political and Social Science: "In slavery he was like an animal in harness; well trained, gentle and affectionate; in early freedom the harness was off, but still the habit of obedience and the force of affection endured and prevented a run-away. In Reconstruction came a consciousness of being unharnessed, unhitched, unbridled and unrestrained. The wildest excesses followed" (114).

These "wild excesses" reach their apotheosis in the obsessive and often psychopathically violent postbellum white paranoia over sexual contact between black men and white women. In this extraordinarily widespread fantasy, black men underwent a lycanthropic metamorphosis in the presence of white women, a change that entangled and intensified the broad range of racial, political, economic, cultural, and environmental pressures on postbellum white supremacy. And, once again, this violent delusion functioned symbolically by turning black men from docile antebellum animals into a generalized form of savage bestiality, yet another version of the floating black/animal "something" that both was human and wasn't. Take, for example, the violent de/evolution of the liminal animality of the African-American figure in Winston's description of these wildest excesses:

> But the social intercourse between the races in the South, which was so helpful to the blacks, has now practically ceased. The children of this generation no longer play and frolic together. White ladies no longer visit Negro cabins. The familiar salutation of "Uncle" or "Auntie" is no longer heard. The lady's maid sleeps no more by the bedside of her mistress. The Southern woman with her helpless little children in [the] solitary farm house no longer sleeps secure in the absence of her husband with doors unlocked but safely guarded by black men whose lives would be freely given in her defense. But now, when a knock is heard at the door, she shudders with nameless horror. The black brute is lurking in the dark, a monstrous beast, crazed with lust. His ferocity is almost demoniacal. A mad bull or a tiger could scarcely be more brutal. (108–9)

Winston (on many levels) doesn't quite know what/who he's talking about here; the passage is caught between the familiar nostalgia for the semi-human happy-darkies of the plantation pastoral, and the "nameless horror" of the floating identity of the bestial black man who threatens a spatial, sexual, and genetic invasion of the white/female. This "new" version of the What Is It? is described only in tangential and vague ways: he is a "black brute," a "monstrous beast," "almost demoniacal," a figure whose "lust crazed" brutality is in some uncertain comparative relation to the "mad bull or tiger." All "we" know for sure is that "he's" one more iteration of the human/animal hybrid that seemed to be the central way nineteenth-century whites, especially in the South, were able to think about black people; a creature who used to be a docile slave but had degenerated into a more primary savagery without white control, a savagery that fundamentally threatened the epistemological and genetic stability of white identity, that was bent on invading white territory, on corrupting white nature.[17]

This sharply bordered, but internally undefined, natural space of the Beast, in which white supremacy both imagined and contained blackness, simultaneously produced whiteness as an exteriority to that space. And accordingly, in the symbolic logic of the Beast, the Southern landscape that he stalked was once again reclaimed for whiteness. Under slavery (or its pastoral echo in Page and Harris), black people could signify the landscape because they, like it, were the possession of white people; when such domesticated figures spoke, it was only to express the love and gratitude of the whole Southern ecosystem to its white owners. But after the war, when white men found themselves in some limited competition with black men for ownership of that landscape, the pastoral equation of blackness and aspects of the agricultural landscape was refigured and concentrated in the ambiguous and endlessly threatening figure of the Beast. And the corollary of this unholy confluence of rape fantasy and racial/ environmental politics in the Beast-ing of black male identity was an ever more intense pastoralization of white women. The imago of a black man raping a white woman was naturalized as the image of a beast running rampant over the landscape—a naturalization that in turn echoed white anxieties over black farmers owning and working the Southern landscape for themselves and over black agricultural labor becoming mobile, empowered, refusing its "traditional" rootedness to a particular site.

The profoundly unhappy tangle of anti-black racism, violently insecure white male sexuality, and gendered and racialized pastoralism that we have seen develop throughout this study, here morphs yet again, into a form as ugly and dangerous as any that have come before. Take, for example, its narrative development—indeed, its *evolution*—in what is arguably the most infamous example of this new iteration of an old nexus, the rape/suicide/lynching at the center of Thomas Dixon's *The Clansman*.[18] First, his grotesque description of Gus, the future Black Beast Rapist:

> He had the short, heavy-set neck of the lower order of animals. His skin was coal black, his lips so thick they curled both ways up and down with crooked blood-marks across them. His nose was flat, and its enormous nostrils seemed in perpetual dilation. The sinister bead eyes, with brown splotches in their whites, were set wide apart and gleamed apelike under his scant brows. His enormous cheekbones and jaws seemed to protrude beyond the ears and almost hide them. (216)

This portrait is clearly meant to evoke and naturalize the same prejudices concretized in the ethnographic "science" of writers like Josiah Nott, the same sort of animalizing gaze that earlier transformed a black man into the Nondescript. Indeed, Gus functions almost as a checklist of the "scientific" signs of black animality—forehead, eyes, nose, nostrils, jaw, neck—a list down which the white reader moves, transforming—greenwashing—his or her preexisting prejudice into "objective" scientific truth, from irrational hatred and genuinely perverse sexual fantasy into the Natural Other.

Onto that perverse sexual fantasy:

> The door flew open with a crash, and four black brutes leaped into the room, Gus in the lead, with a revolver in his hand, his yellow teeth grinning through his thick lips.
>
> "Scream, now, an' I blow yer brains out," he growled.
>
> Blanched with horror, the mother sprang before Marion with a shivering cry:
>
> "What do you want?"
>
> "Not you," said Gus, closing the blinds and handing a rope to another brute. "Tie de ole one ter de bedpost."
>
> The mother screamed. A blow from a black fist in her mouth, and the rope was tied.
>
> With the strength of despair she tore at the cords, half rising to her feet, while with mortal anguish she gasped:
>
> "For God's sake, spare my baby! Do as you will with me, and kill me—do not touch her!"
>
> Again the huge fist swept her to the floor.
>
> Marion staggered against the wall, her face white, her delicate lips trembling with the chill of a fear colder than death.
>
> "We have no money—the deed has not been delivered," she pleaded, a sudden glimmer of hope flashing in her blue eyes.
>
> Gus stepped closer, with an ugly leer, his flat nose dilated, his sinister bead-eyes wide apart gleaming ape-like, as he laughed:
>
> "We ain't atter money!"
>
> The girl uttered a cry, long, tremulous, heart-rending, piteous.
>
> A single tiger-spring, and the black claws of the beast sank into the soft white throat and she was still. (303–4)

Dixon's overheated racial/sexual imagination here produces a violently pornographic scene calculated to arouse the passions of the reader, while wrapping that reaction in the plausible deniability of outrage and the eventual deaths by suicide and lynching of everyone involved. The real kink here is that this is not only six-way, mother/daughter, interracial rape with bondage, what Jacquelyn Dowd Hall in her book on lynching calls "folk pornography," but more fundamentally and simultaneously interspecial sex (150–51). Gus's overwhelming desire for white women (especially Marion, the fifteen-year-old daughter "ironically" only a few days from her début) makes him devolve suddenly from semi-human racist caricature into a generically animalized brute, from "ape-*like*" to "*the* beast" with his "tiger-spring" who sinks his "black claws" into the girl's "soft white neck." (And both women get even whiter under this assault—the mother is "blanched with horror," Marion staggers back, "her face white," her "blue eyes" "flashing.") Rape becomes literal predation; the sexual component of the scene is supplanted by the violence of the assault.[19]

Or so Dixon would like us to believe. But it is no accident that Dixon makes Gus's bestial devolution reach its nadir at the precise moment when his humanity, in an absolute genetic sense, is most evident. The "problem" of interracial sex was not, in fact, that it violated the natural order, but that it *didn't*, that it in fact demonstrated with all the explicit facticity of an infant that black and white were the same species. Since slavery had long declared that the "child follows the condition of the mother"—a belief that gave white men unfettered sexual access to black women in a way that subsumed their offspring and obliterated their paternal obligations under the very naturalized racial hierarchy that first facilitated the rape—sex between black men and white women threatened the foundation of the longstanding race/ nature system in a way that perhaps nothing else could.[20] White men could deny their children, white women could not, or at least not nearly as easily.[21] As a result, white women—specifically, white women's fertility—was the place where the centuries-old white ideology of black animality most conspicuously and materially collapsed. Accordingly, the Black Beast Rapist became an idée fixe in the postwar white imagination as well as the occasion, in lynching, for what was arguably the most psychopathic sadism and brutally violent suppression in the country's history.

The contradictory task for white supremacy was to evoke the question of such intimacy without asking it explicitly, and then to repress it without answering it. The product of such evocation and repression was, always, "righteous" violence. And so, when Marion and her mother wake up the next day, they immediately head off to kill themselves, pausing only to clean up the house and burn their clothes. As Marion says, "The thought of life is torture. Only those who hate me could wish that I live. The grave will be soft and cool, the light of day a burning shame" (306). For the women to live would be to pose the question white supremacy could not answer, to speak the "unspeakable outrage," to name Winston's "nameless horror." In killing themselves the women perform a sort of self-lynching that restores the natural racial hierarchy; just like Gus, they must die.[22] Dixon's description of their final moments both exemplifies the threat emancipated black people posed to white dominance of the pastoral landscape, and, in the women's sacrifice, the restoration of the women/landscape's racial purity:

> As they sat in brooding anguish, floating up from the river valley came the music of a banjo in a Negro cabin, mingled with vulgar shout and song and dance. A verse of the ribald senseless lay of the player echoed above the banjo's pert refrain:
>
> *"Chicken in de bread tray, pickin' up dough;*
> *Granny, will your dog bite? No, chile, no!"*
>
> . . . .
>
> A sparrow chirped in the tree above, a wren twittered in a bush, and down on the river's brink a mocking-bird softly waked his mate with a note of thrilling sweetness.
>
> "The morning is coming, dearest; we must go," said Marion. "This shame I can never forget, nor will the world forget. Death is the only way."
>
> They walked to the brink, and the mother's arms stole round the girl.
>
> "Oh, my baby, my beautiful darling, life of my life, heart of my heart, soul of my soul!"
>
> They stood for a moment, as if listening to the music of the falls, looking out over the valley faintly outlining itself in the dawn. The first far-away streaks of blue light on the mountain ranges, defining distance, slowly appeared. A fresh motionless day brooded over the world as the amorous stir of the spirit of morning rose from the moist earth of the fields below.
>
> A bright star still shone in the sky, and the face of the mother gazed on it intently. Did the Woman-spirit, the burning focus of the fiercest desire to live and will, catch in this supreme moment the star's Divine speech before which all human passions sink into silence? Perhaps, for she smiled. The daughter answered with a smile; and then, hand in hand, they stepped from the cliff into the mists and on through the opal gates of Death. (306–8)

Rather than representing the land, here blackness conflicts with it. Gus's bestial transformation has done its cultural and environmental work, separating blackness from the postbellum landscape while preserving the human/natural conflation at the heart of anti-black racism, and while leaving the field open for the two women to reclaim nature as a white signifier in a way that simultaneously naturalized gender hierarchy.[23] In sharp contrast to the white/natural bird songs that signify the women and their soon to be restored purity (the

"Sparrow chirp[s]" the "wren twitter[s]," and "a mocking-bird softly wake[s] his mate with a note of thrilling sweetness"), the sounds of a "Negro cabin" (the "pert refrain" of a banjo, a "vulgar shout and song and dance," a "ribald senseless lay," and a snatch of a minstrel song in which the chicken and dog seem to be coextensive with black domesticity) that float up from the river valley underscores the intrusive discordance of blackness into the women's white pastoral purity.

Marion is undoubtedly right that neither she nor the rest of the (white) world would ever forget the shame of sexual contact with a black man, and that her "death is the only way" for Dixon's patriarchal white supremacy to survive that contact intact. For what if Marion and her mother decided not to kill themselves, recognized that the "shame" was not theirs? What if they survived, like the countless thousands of black women who endured systematic racially focused rape, or like characters in black-authored texts such as Sappho Clark of Pauline Hopkins's *Contending Forces*?[24] What if *Marion* brought yet another "mulatto" child into the world? The absolute distinction between a corrupted and degraded black nature and a pure white one that was, as we have seen, a central metaphor for structuring white supremacy, would begin to give way.[25] Nature would no longer offer whiteness a refuge, like the nostalgic pastoral landscape of the Lost Cause, from a recognition of the constructedness of race and the saturation of the supposedly nonhuman environment by history, politics, and culture. The racially marked distinction between a pure and degraded nature upon which so much depended for so long would be undermined by and in Marion's living body. For Dixon, this is truly a fate worse than (their) death. So, instead, Marion and her mother join hands and step off into the soft sublime of some derivative Luminist landscape, with "the valley faintly outlining itself in the dawn," and the "first far-away streaks of blue light on the mountain ranges," and the pure and natural sexual fecundity of "the amorous stir of the spirit of morning [rising] from the moist earth of the fields below."[26] Their "corrupted" sexuality is downloaded into (forgive the pun), and purified by, the Southern pastoral landscape that in turn becomes the image and repository of a purified white female sexuality, the womb of whiteness. As a result, the vicious "defense" of white women by the white patriarchy acquires a fundamentally territorial—indeed natural—dimension that makes lynching and racial terrorism both an assertion of white supremacy generally, and of white male power over black men and white women in particular. In the place of asking the hard real questions about race, gender, sexuality, the control of agricultural capital, and so forth that Reconstruction brought so determinatively to the fore, Dixon invites his white readers to pull on their hoods, gaze at the beautiful landscape newly fertilized by the corpses of Marion and her mother, and just do what feels natural. Meanwhile, the women and the threat they represent fall permanently silent, disappearing into the supposedly unrepresentable transcendent purity of the natural scene, the "Divine speech before which all *human* passions sink into silence."

STRANGE FRUIT

Southern trees bear a strange fruit,
Blood on the leaves and blood at the root,
Black body swinging in the Southern breeze,
Strange fruit hanging from the poplar trees.

Pastoral scene of the gallant South,
The bulging eyes and the twisted mouth,
Scent of magnolia sweet and fresh,
And the sudden smell of burning flesh!

Here is a fruit for the crows to pluck,
For the rain to gather, for the wind to suck
For the sun to rot, for a tree to drop,
Here is a strange and bitter crop.
　　　　　　　　—Abel Metropol

This shift in the white characterization of black identity from antebellum docility to a postbellum savagery, supposedly catalyzed by emancipation and interracial desire, is itself transitional. The bio-epistemological instability of the What Is It?, dangerously heightened in the figure of the Black Beast Rapist, is grounded in the Beast's lynched body, in his conversion to the "strange fruit" of the pastoral landscape. In Winston and Dixon's exemplary works, this terminal black nonidentity follows naturally and immediately from the bestial conversion. Here's how Winston's earlier narrative ends:

The Southern woman with her helpless little children in [her] solitary farm house no longer sleeps secure in the absence of her husband with doors unlocked but safely guarded by black men whose lives would be freely given in her defense. But now, when a knock is heard at the door, she shudders with nameless horror. The black brute is lurking in the dark, a monstrous beast, crazed with lust. His ferocity is almost demoniacal. A mad bull or a tiger could scarcely be more brutal. A whole community is now frenzied with horror, with blind and furious rage for vengeance. A stake is driven; the wretched brute, covered with oil, bruised and gashed, beaten and hacked and maimed, amid the jeers and curses, the tears of anger and of joy, the prayers and the maledictions of thousands of civilized people, in the sight of school-houses, court-houses and churches is burned to death. (108–9)

The fatal telos of the black brute is the lynched, mutilated corpse of the "wretched brute," beaten, hacked, dismembered, and burnt alive. Similarly, the section of Dixon's novel that immediately follows the women's rape and suicide—"The Ku Klux Klan"—celebrates the establishment of systematic white racial terrorism that "naturally" evolves from Gus's crime, capture, and punishment. In the section's first chapter, entitled (of course) "The Hunt for the Animal," Gus is caught and put on "trial" by the Klansmen in their secret hideaway cave by the river, during which he is hypnotized and forced to reenact the crime:

Gus rose to his feet and started across the cave as if to spring on the shivering figure of the girl, the clansmen with muttered groans, sobs and curses falling back as he advanced. He still wore his full Captain's uniform, its heavy epaulets flashing their gold in the unearthly light, his beastly jaws half covering the gold braid on the collar. His thick lips were drawn upward in an ugly leer and his sinister bead-eyes gleamed like a gorilla's. A single fierce leap and the black claws clutched the air slowly as if sinking into the soft white throat. (323)

Before Gus can be executed, he must, once again, morph into his fully animal identity; the proof of his guilt and his animalization become the same thing. The centrality of this collapse is underscored in Dixon's bizarre repetition; and, indeed, before the hypnosis the dead mother's eyes are examined under a microscope where the image of Gus's "bestial figure," "huge black hand," and "massive jaws and lips" is burned (313–14). And Gus's miming *doesn't* reenact the rape at all, but, like the original description of the scene, substitutes for it his transformation into a predatory animal. At the very moment of sexual contact, when the supposedly absolute difference between the races is in fact most materially and brutally undone, that difference is most materially and brutally asserted in Gus's transformation. The transformation into the animal not only censors, but incorporates, subsumes, and signifies the sexual assault. I am, of course, not defending Gus's rape of the women, but rather arguing that the Klansmen are not punishing that crime as much as they are his bestial identity. Gus is lynched for being what he *is* as much as for what he has done. In this sense, the Klan's racial violence is, once again, always already a form of environmental violence: the Beast must be killed, black people must be tamed, the land must be physically and symbolically placed under the sign of an utterly submissive and feminized whiteness.

"Real" Lynching and "Real" Nature

Since Ida B. Wells's vitally important early studies—*Southern Horrors* in 1892, *A Red Record* in 1895, and *Mob Rule in New Orleans* in 1900—most scholars have agreed that, despite the endless and feverish claims of contemporary Southern whites, black men weren't lynched to "protect" white women from interracial sexual assault.[27] Indeed, as Leon Litwack notes, in only 19 percent of the roughly three thousand lynchings that occurred between 1889 and 1918 was the victim even *accused* of rape or attempted rape (24). This marked division between what whites said they were doing—punishing rape, protecting white women—and what they were in fact doing—wantonly killing black men for any and no "reason," is precisely the gap occupied by the Black Beast. Such statistics suggest that when Dixon transforms Gus's sexual violence into animal predation he is performing more than a simple censoring substitution, but manifesting how the Beast fused the rapist and blackness, making a natural hybrid Other outside the white/human moral universe that could be subjected to any form of violence. The Black Beast Rapist was a way of *not* answering the obvious question posed by Litwack's statistics— why did whites say lynching was punishment for rape when it wasn't?

The subsumption of rape, blackness, and lynching under the naturalized sign of the Beast, and the consequent, familiar association between racial and environmental violence that we see suffusing the imagination of Dixon and Winston, offers an important model for mapping the in-fact incomprehensible violence of the actual historical practice. The production of this trauma in lynching enacts with the most extreme intensity the reductive association of blackness and the speechless otherness of the natural world, the categorical silencing of African-American humanity, that as we have seen, has always been a fundamental part of the operation of white supremacy. The trajectory of the transformation of the articulate, emancipated (black) man into the raving Black Beast reaches its terminus in his lynched body, a gruesomely thoroughgoing and literal return of the human to meat and the land in its dismemberment, skinning, burning, and hanging from a tree.[28]

Anecdotal evidence underscores how lynching depended on a virulent updating of a much older association between black people and nature, the widespread white belief in what Litwack calls "the cheapness of black life in the south" in the late nineteenth and early twentieth centuries, the view among whites during this time of "black men and women as inherently and permanently inferior, as less than human, as little more than animals" (12). Litwack cites several examples of this view (though like other critics he never explicitly connects racial and environmental violence), from a former governor of Georgia, William J. Northen, who noted that in Georgia, he "was amazed to find scores and hundreds of [white] men who believed the Negro to be a brute, without responsibility to God, and his slaughter nothing more than the killing of a dog," to the proud assertion of a white Floridian that, "We Southern people don't care to equal ourselves with animals. The people of the South don't think any more of killing the black fellows than you would think of killing a flea . . . and if I was to live 1,000 years that would be my opinion and every other Southern man," to the recollection of two black Southerners, who asserted bitterly that "back in those days, to kill a Negro wasn't nothing. It was like killing a chicken or killing a snake. The whites would say, 'Niggers jest supposed to die, ain't no damn good anyway—so jes go on an' kill 'em," and "In those days it was 'Kill a mule, buy another. Kill a nigger, hire another.' They had to have a license to kill anything but a nigger. We was always in season" (12–13).

Undoubtedly white lynch mobs were motivated by a wide range of anxieties and fantasies, from a genuine if erroneous fear of black men raping white women, to repressed eroticism, fatuous genetic panic, economic dislocation, gender insecurity, and politically and socially opportunistic scapegoating. What aligns all these partial "explanations," though, is an agreement that the governing metaphor for black inferiority was the inferiority of the natural world, and that the natural relations of white and black mirrored the natural dominance of humans over animals and the environment. Under these assumptions, is it any wonder that the figure of the black male rapist was the central racial imago of white fear and hatred, an invasive species? Is it any wonder that this Black Rapist was always already a Beast? The fear of black male rape of white women was itself a metaphor for a more primary instability in the relations of black and white people and the natural world upon which so much had depended for so long, from slavery to agricultural production to racial hierarchy. Among other things certainly, lynching was a frenzied attempt to return the procreative black male body to an earlier status that slavery took for granted, indeed that slavery was built upon. This reimposition of slavery's governing metaphor took a gruesomely material form in the sadistic practices of the mob, as victims were hung from trees, burnt alive in what were commonly referred to as "nigger barbecues," castrated and forced to eat their genitals, their bodies flayed, transformed from human flesh into meat. The photographic postcards of lynching victims that circulated widely throughout the (white) nation, mostly showing the often mutilated victim hanging from a tree surrounded by approving whites, or the practice of collecting and publicly displaying the victim's charred fingers, toes, genitals, hair, and so forth, literally turned speaking subjects into natural objects.[29] The women's shoes made from the tanned skin of "Big Nose" George and proudly displayed in the lobby of Texas's Rawlings National Bank were not intended to signify George, for example, but the ontological status of blackness in general, a gruesome affirmative to the rhetorical question, "whether a man shall be treated as leather" that Emerson asked in criticizing Webster's vote for the Fugitive Slave Law. Lynching said "you are not human but nature, not text but context, not a speaking subject but the rawest of raw materials"; it provided an extreme and systematic example of the racist conflation of human and natural, the unbearable, unrepresentable material core of trauma that can't be laid to symbolic rest, that won't lay quiescent in memory's narrative, that always threatens to transform the natural world into a place of terror and degradation. Is it any wonder that "Strange Fruit" with its surreal, ghastly hybridization of the black body and the landscape has named lynching for more than fifty years?[30]

Obviously the contradiction between what whites claimed they were doing—defending white women against Winston's knock on the door or Dixon's Gus—and what they were in fact doing—regularly torturing black men to death in public, usually for reasons other than suspected sexual assault—invites investigation. The temptation for scholars is to provide an interpretative explanation for the practice, to reveal the "real" psychological, economic, or social motives for the racialized barbarity of these awful scenes, the actual motives masked by the rape claim.[31] Given the near-ubiquity of the practice by a very wide range of white participants, most of these explanations are likely to be "true" at least to some extent. Lynching undoubtedly did involve, for example, white economic anxiety over competition with and for black labor; did involve white sexual anxiety over and desire for the supposedly greater virility of black men; did afford a way for white women to solidify their political power; did allow white men to vent their frustration and anger at their impotence under unrestrained capitalism, and so forth.

But I want to resist that temptation to explanation, in part because such a wide array of talented critics have already taken up the question in a much more extensive and detailed way than I can here. In insisting on the multiple environmental resonances of the white obsession with the Black Beast Rapist, I do not intend to privilege my environmental reading of this terribly fraught and complex issue as providing some final hermeneutic diagnosis. I want, finally, to stress instead how lynching escapes full understanding. Indeed, lynching "represents" the absolute collapse of the possibility of understanding; its point is to produce such a collapse. Which is not simply to require our silence, but to insist on seeing critical, artistic, and other forms of representational discourse as necessarily fragmentary and marginal to the central trauma, and on not forgetting this intrinsic failure. Our attempts at explanation or representation are inherently inadequate to the speechlessness of the mutilated corpse, the total descent of the onlookers into the very sort of bestial frenzy of which they so frequently accused the victim. In short, lynching is virulently contagious trauma, an unassimilable event that escapes full symbolic encoding as part of the individual or collective social historical narrative, that won't turn fully from immediate agony into the language of grief and loss.

The material organization of the event itself represents this epistemological limit; once again we see traumatic experience organized spatially, closer to sculpture or topography than narrative. At the core of the lynching is the body of the victim itself, a locus of unbearable suffering burning at the center of the crowd or hanging above it. Literally unbearable; unlike slavery, the person who directly experiences the trauma of lynching does not survive, cannot remember it or anything. In this sense the trauma of lynching is always spectatorial and representational, always second order, always at least potentially trafficking in the sublime's voyeuristic relation to trauma. The victim serves as the event horizon of the possibility of human representation, that which can be seen but not survived, a list of tortures, suffering beyond survivability.[32] This is not to collapse lynching into its reception, but to note how that reception—all we have, but not all that was—rings an abyss, a real place we can only imagine. In this way the spatial structure of the lynching mirrors its epistemological structure.

That real place beyond final representation where, as DuBois says, "dark boy[s'] limbs [are] scattered to the winds by midnight marauders" (18), is the natural world. Lynching joins, finally and terribly, its victim to the extrahuman environment extending incomprehensibly beyond the last thought. The endless images of mutilated black bodies dangling from trees inevitably mark the woods for countless African Americans subsequently. To be alone in the forest, to feel identified with the landscape, to be vulnerable and intimate with the natural world is to risk, at least, triggering a traumatic return to such images. Toni Morrison captures this disjunction aptly—and testifies to its ongoing presence in African-American literary consciousness—at the opening of *Beloved*.[33] She narrates Sethe's conflicted recollection of the antebellum Southern landscape, a moment when the very enjoyment of natural beauty becomes a form of historical betrayal:

> [A]nd suddenly there was Sweet Home rolling, rolling, rolling out before her eyes, and although there was not a leaf on that farm that did not make her want to scream, it rolled itself out before her in shameless beauty. It never looked as terrible as it was and it made her wonder if hell was a pretty place too. Fire and brimstone all right, but hidden in lacy groves. Boys hanging from the most beautiful sycamores in the world. It shamed her—remembering the wonderful sighing trees rather than the boys. Try as she might to make it otherwise, the sycamores beat out the children every time and she could not forgive her memory for that. (7)[34]

A far cry from the "uncomplicated" union with the landscape that marks sublime experience, experience that, as a result, comes "naturally" to signify whiteness. It is these sublime experiences that I take up next.

7

WHITE FLIGHT

And then Tom he talked along, and talked along, and says, le's all three slide out of here, one of these nights, and get an outfit, and go for howling adventures amongst the Injuns, over in the Territory, for a couple of weeks or two; and I says all right, that suits me...But I reckon I got to light out for the Territory ahead of the rest, because Aunt Sally she's going to adopt me and sivilize me and I can't stand it. I been there before. (261–62)
—Mark Twain, *The Adventures of Huckleberry Finn*

Here in the famous conclusion to Twain's novel, the "Territory" of the American West performs what becomes its iconic role, offering a fantasy domain where "howling adventures amongst the Injuns" substitute for the constraints of female domesticity and "sivilization." The reader is invited to participate in Twain's seemingly gentle narrative irony, both appreciating Tom and Huck's boyish eagerness for Western adventure, while resting assured that any such adventures will take place within a larger context of narrative closure: Tom remains indefatigably privileged, Pap is dead, Huck is adopted and his fortune restored, Jim is free. In the place of the all-too-real cruelty, criminality, and racism of the Mississippi river towns Huck sees on his journey South with Jim, the Territory offers a mythic escape familiar to most Americans, a place Jane Tompkins memorably calls "West of Everything," where social entrenchment is magically lifted, and a fresh start is possible outside of the entrapments of history, politics, racism, economics, and the like.

Coming at the end of a novel so basically concerned with the impossibility of escaping such entrapments, however, where every move Huck and Jim make is bounded by a river flowing inexorably south away from freedom and ever-deeper into Slave Territory, such a promise of escape begs many of the same questions it purports to foreclose. The north/south geographic axis that provides the book's fundamental structure—and just as fundamentally, the structure of antebellum and postbellum America—skews west. The strictly limited zone of freedom offered by the Mississippi River, a natural space bordered by slavery and economic violence, is replaced by the lawless and vaguely defined western "Territory." The focus of racial conflict shifts abruptly from a white/black binary to a white/native one. And, more subtly but just as importantly, the narrative authority of these "adventures" shifts from Huck to Tom, and with that change, from realism to the derivative Romanticism that structures Tom's cruel creation of Jim's by-the-books "escape" in the novel's nauseating and parodic final episode.

As we have already seen in the discussion of transcendentalism and the slave narratives, this shift from a historicized and political settled nature to an extrahuman wilderness was part of a larger pattern in which whiteness recoiled from an engagement with various forms of naturalized black trauma. In leaving the book's major racial issues unresolved and instead gesturing toward a romanticized West supposedly external to such issues—an extrahistorical "howling" Western wilderness where boys could be boys—Twain offers a preview of one of the central ideological operations of white supremacy at the close of the nineteenth century and the start of the twentieth: a profound imaginative embrace of the Western Territory that functioned to repress the north/south divide that had so traumatically organized the country along a black/white color line for most of the century.

Without minimizing the terrible importance of the white/native struggle or the Mexican War in the construction of whiteness, the analysis that follows insists that slavery, the Civil War, Reconstruction, lynching, and the brutal establishment of Jim Crow provide another vitally important but hidden context for the white embrace of the West, a context whose importance is easily missed precisely because the purpose of that embrace was, in part, to obscure that context.[1] Out West, in the Territories, whiteness and the American geography could be about everything *but* that black/white binary, about the all-too-real genocide of the native population, about the Alamo, about the ecocide of the Western wilderness, about the establishment of a naturally dominant Anglo-Saxon aristocracy, but not about Huck and Jim on the river, or what happens to Jim afterward. As Fredrick Jackson Turner asserted in his famous 1893 address to the American Historical Association that first argued for the unique significance of the frontier: "the true point of view in the history of this nation is not the Atlantic coast, it is the Great West.... the slavery struggle...occupies its important place in American history because of its relation to westward expansion" and "when American history comes to be rightly viewed it will be seen that the slavery question is an incident" (3, 24). I do not want to repeat Turner's essentialist move here and argue for a different

"*true* point of view in the history of the nation." But Turner's assertion
that the real meaning of American history is the frontier rather than
slavery underscores how the entanglement between sublimity and
trauma that structured transcendentalism's response to "the slavery
question" persisted at the end of the century. I argued in the second
chapter that for transcendentalists like Emerson and Thoreau, "wildness" marked a psychic as well as geographic space far enough from
slavery to make the wild's promise of freedom seem fully sublime in its
intensity. Here, in a repetition of the pattern I have traced throughout
this study in which sublimity becomes a voyeurism or repression of
trauma, Turner's Great West signifies a point sufficiently distant from
the "incident" of slavery to render slavery's subsumption in a supposedly larger narrative of American self-definition part of what we might
call the national sublime, or the sublime of the nation. After all, anything big enough to subsume slavery, racial terrorism, and the Civil
War as an "incident" must be mighty big indeed. In fact, however, the
entanglement between slavery and the frontier provides the deep structure of Turner's inquiry: the choice for him is between whether (white)
America is defined by the trauma of slavery, or by the sublimity of the
Great West. Turner is arguing, in effect, that "we" should look at slavery from the perspective of the West—over the shoulder as it were—
and in doing so subsume it as a mere "incident" within a supposedly
larger national story of environmental conquest and triumph over the
native population. Given such a choice, the vogue for the West among
whites during this period is hardly surprising.[2]

But the ways white and black racial identities were constructed in
relation to natural experience did not, in fact, stop when white male
writers like John Muir began recording their intense identification with
the Western landscape. Rather, the West provided a place where whiteness could imagine its formation outside of the long terrible history of
the black/white racial binary that had been so central to the definition
of both whiteness and the American landscape back east.[3] This chapter
traces how what Toni Morrison calls an "abiding Africanist" context
persists in the Western sublime, how the history of black and white
racial struggle morphs into a newly—and allegedly—dehistoricized
form of whiteness that nevertheless retains the trace of that traumatic
history of slavery, war, and lynching.[4] It is the process of erasure that I
want to examine, the ways that nature was used to evoke and supplant
trauma, not simply to obscure or repress it. In insisting that the idea of
the West effaced the history of slavery, the Civil War, and postbellum
segregation, I want, ultimately, to offer one explanation for why African
Americans have found themselves "naturally" alienated from

contemporary wilderness-based mainstream environmentalism and ecocriticism, both of which have historical roots in the dehistoricized, and dehistoricizing, embrace of the sublime Western landscape that emerged at the end of the nineteenth century.[5]

As I noted in the introduction, recent ecocritical work (especially since William Cronon's important essay, "The Trouble with Wilderness") has started to point out how these sorts of sublime wilderness experiences have been largely limited to a group of privileged white men who found their own subjectivity writ large on the natural canvas.[6] Similarly, a number of recent critics have discussed how the Frontier, both as a site of wilderness experience and as an imaginary construct that presupposed a white perspective on the "savage," was central to the construction of what Theodore Roosevelt and others called the "Anglo Saxon" race, and Anglo-Saxon masculinity during this period.[7] Accordingly, I am less interested in how whiteness was *explicitly* claimed as a dominant racial identity by virtue of whatever bankrupt combination of social Darwinism, Lamarkian genetic theory, pseudo-history, and so forth a given elite white man was putting together to justify his privilege. Such explicit claims of white superiority have been appropriately marginalized for some time in contemporary America. Rather, I am interested in how whiteness took its current form, disappearing into the normative background while retaining its dominance, and while closing the door for "other" races to enact a similar disappearance. The white fantasy of the West, I will argue, marks a space in which African Americans are *conspicuously* absent, the creation of a natural space where the racial trauma that had organized the national geography for much of the nineteenth century could be left behind, and whiteness could vanish and become pervasive, become *natural* rather than historical.

The natural sublime was essential to this contradictory process. By aligning the subject with a transcendent natural landscape, one (supposedly) outside of history, that landscape and that sublime experience became, in turn, a sign of the subject's transcendent, extrahistorical identity. And by *not* paying attention to what sort of people, historically, were in a position to enjoy such experiences—by ignoring the long history of naturalized African-American trauma—sublime natural experience became a way of making whiteness invisible while retaining its social power. Bruno Latour comments on this process in his analysis of the formation of modern bourgeois identity:

> They [the Moderns] are going to be able to make Nature intervene at
> every point in the fabrication of their societies, while they go right on

attributing to Nature its radical transcendence; they are going to be able to become the only actors in their own political destiny, while they go right on making their society hold together by mobilizing Nature. On the one hand, the transcendence of Nature will not prevent its social immanence; on the other, the immanence of the social will not prevent the Leviathan from remaining transcendent. We must admit that this is a rather neat construction that makes it possible to do everything without being limited by anything. (32)

Latour's coupling of a "radically transcendent" (or, I would say, subtextual or extratextual) Nature, with a nature that functions ideologically to "mak[e] . . . society hold together," is precisely the operation that the sublime performs on the white subject, making the individual part of an enlightened community of nature lovers who just happen to be almost exclusively white.

In asserting this, I want to be very clear that I am not declaring nature-love itself to be intrinsically white, or accusing the natural sublime of being "really" a white supremacist plot. Rather, I am arguing that failing to recognize the historical racial context of natural experience leads almost inevitably to a naturalization of that context, and does so in a way that just as inevitably inserts an all-too-cultural element into that natural experience, one most white liberal environmentalists certainly would *not* embrace were they conscious of it. Forgetting about the racial and natural history this book has been tracing does not make that history go away, in other words—it just makes it disappear.

JOHN MUIR LEADS THE WAY: A
1,000 MILE WALK TO THE GULF

Save perhaps Thoreau, no figure in nineteenth-century American literature is more closely associated with the sublime embrace of the American landscape than John Muir, the founder of the Sierra Club, the first popular advocate for the nascent conservation movement, the person largely responsible for the formation of the national park system, the patron saint of American environmentalism whose vision of the ineluctable value of the wilderness and wilderness experience persists (rightly, in many ways) at the heart of the mainstream contemporary environmental movement. Muir taught an entire generation (of white people) to see the wilderness with awe and treat it with reverence, to understand the wild as a place of homecoming where individuals might renew themselves emotionally and spiritually. As he says at the opening of his book *Our National Parks*,

"Thousands of tired, nerve-shaken, over-civilised people are beginning to find out that going to the mountains is going home; that wilderness is a necessity; and that mountain parks and reservations are useful not only as fountains of timber and irrigating rivers, but as fountains of life" (*Eight Books*, 459). That those "overcivilised people" were (1) mostly, if not almost exclusively, white, and (2) were "going home" to a place most of them had never been, whose actual native inhabitants had been removed or killed, to (3) enjoy a wild experience that, despite its implicit universality—the wilderness is a "necessity," indeed a "fountain of life"—was in historical practice by no means universally available or universally appealing, should not make us simply dismiss Muir, his contribution, or the wilderness generally. But such a dismissal has hardly been the temptation for most subsequent critics of Muir; rather, the notion of the wild as a refuge from the ills of modernity, and the assumption that "thousands of tired, nerve-shaken, over-civilised people," stand for all humanity tends to pass without comment. Terry Gifford, for example, claims a panhistorical importance to this wilderness appeal in his Introduction to the recent single volume collection of Muir's eight "wilderness discovery books:" "John Muir's books will be reinterpreted by successive generations because they contain the possibility of accommodated man, at home in the universe, facing the difficult decisions, and knowing why," and goes on to assert that "part of the reason why is contained in Muir's opening words of *Our National Parks*, written over one hundred and ten years ago" (20). Muir's West is a universal home, a place where "difficult decisions" can be "faced," in part, I would argue, because one point of that home is to prevent some of the most difficult questions from ever arising.

Indeed, Muir's narrative of discovering the sublime West itself traces the process of forgetting the explicitly racialized geography of the east and south. While Muir is associated with the west—especially the Sierra Nevada and Yosemite Valley, the subject of his first and most popular published book, *My First Summer in the Sierras*—his career as a naturalist in fact began with a very long walk from north to south, followed by a boat ride west, a trip that provided the context for his later embrace of the West in ways that parallel Huck's axial shift at the end of Twain's novel. During the Civil War, Muir fled north to the Canadian wilderness in order to avoid being drafted into the Union Army. He returned at the war's end, and in 1867, just two years later, set out on a solo walk from Indiana to Florida, his first extended camping trip and the first time he recorded his natural experiences extensively in a journal, discovering the compositional process that led to his subsequent books (and to the posthumously published *1,000 Mile Walk to the Gulf*). This first long walk, in short, gave birth to Muir both as a naturalist and a writer.

From the very start of his career, Muir characterizes his journey in ways that assume an absolute separation between the natural world and the political and racial turmoil of the war and its immediate aftermath:

> I had long been looking from the wild woods and gardens of the Northern States to those of the warm South, and at last, *all drawbacks overcome*, I set forth (from Indianapolis) on the first day of September, 1867, joyful and free, on a thousand-mile walk to the Gulf of Mexico....
>
> My plan was simply to push on in a general southward direction by the wildest, leafiest, and least trodden way I could find, promising the greatest extent of virgin forest. Folding my map, I shouldered my little bag and plant press and strode away among the old Kentucky oaks, rejoicing in splendid visions of pines and palms and tropic flowers in glorious array, not, however, without a few cold shadows of loneliness, although the great oaks seemed to spread their arms in welcome. (119, my emphasis)

Nature is a third term here, an extrahistorical real to which Muir has special access. The trauma of the war, the horrors of slavery, the sharp division between north and south that constructed the geography of the place for its inhabitants, most especially the recently emancipated slaves, is here viewed from the outside, in every sense of the word.[8] The war becomes merely a vaguely referenced impediment to Muir's walk, a mere "drawback" that is "overcome," so that Muir can take to the road, "joyful and free." And Muir's description invites the reader to experience the landscape as he does, beckons us to see that racially and politically saturated landscape from the perspective of the "wildest, leafiest...least trodden...virgin forest," a place that, far from being traumatized, war-torn, riven by hatred, grief, and racism, instead "seems to spread [its] arms in welcome." Just two years earlier, to cover the territory Muir walked was conspicuously not a joyful or free experience; indeed the only people making such journeys were likely runaway slaves or members of the Union or Confederate armies, people for whom the great oaks signified the possibility of ambush, lynching, or a hiding place from patrols rather than the welcoming embrace of the extrahuman.

Muir's alignment with the natural world allows the (white, privileged) reader to adopt a viewpoint suddenly outside of the violent, racially saturated, intensely political, historical, even militarized, landscape instantiated by the suffering, enslavement, and death of so many for so long. While such a viewpoint is putatively available to any reader, it is hard to imagine such an extrahistorical escape readily available to someone who had experienced the traumatic history of the north/south and black/white division directly. An ex-slave, a veteran, a sharecropper might well appreciate the beauty of the trees, but, like Sethe, not be able to forget what happened in their shade. For them an earlier traumatic history would always be present along with that natural beauty. For Muir, someone who fled to Canada to avoid that traumatic history, the landscape appears restored to its natural, freely available, extra-political state. In this sense, to look at the territory from Muir's narrative perspective is to adopt the same sort of transparent vision that thrills Emerson some twenty-five years earlier as he walks the bare common, a perspective from which "to be master or servant" is a "trifle and disturbance," a mere "drawback."[9]

Muir sees both the trauma of the war and slavery, and the agonized recovery from that trauma, from that supposedly external and enfolding natural perspective. Indeed, as Muir writes several pages later, plant growth serves as an explanatory metaphor for how historical trauma can be counted on to just go away naturally:

> The traces of war are not only apparent on the broken fields, burnt fences, mills and woods ruthlessly slaughtered, but also on the countenances of the people. A few years after a forest has been burned another generation of bright and happy trees arises, in purest, freshest vigor; only the old trees, wholly or half dead, bear marks of the calamity. So with the people of this war-field. Happy, unscarred, and unclouded youth is growing up around the aged, half-consumed, and fallen parents, who bear in sad measure the in-effaceable marks of the farthest-reaching and most infernal of all civilized calamities. (144)

A clearer example of how Muir's natural gaze becomes—for the reader only—a way of not worrying about historical trauma is difficult to imagine. Here the trauma of the war will take care of itself, because "people" are like trees, and because the hard, persistent issues like racism and economic brutality, for example, are subsumed by Muir's governing natural metaphor. The unbearable alternative—the all too familiar viral transmission of parents' trauma to their children, the ways that historical violence resonates—is lost in the underbrush.

My point is not simply to wag my finger at Muir for his naïve or ahistorical botany. At some level—and it is an important level that I will return to at the end of the chapter—Muir is right that, as Thoreau said, "Nature has been party to no Missouri Compromise."[10] But access to that level is restricted in ways that neither the text nor the reader has to acknowledge in any conscious way; indeed, access is accomplished in the very act of forgetting the existence of those restrictions, in making the space at once universal, natural, outside of human history, while limiting that universal, natural, extrahistorical perspective to people of a very specific, nontraumatized, class, gender, and, most important, race. Certainly it is hard to imagine an African American, terrified of the widespread lynching at the time of the book's publication, seeing those Kentucky oaks spreading their arms in uncomplicated welcome, or enjoying the same sort of hospitality as Muir, seeking his bed as night fell at the door of various isolated farmhouses along his journey. Muir's narrative perspective unconsciously assumes that his delighted association with the natural world is itself "natural," escaping the human trauma signified by the north/south axis that organizes his walk. And that assumption thereby makes the inability to engage in that unselfconscious delighted association with nature an exception, a mark of damage, of unwelcome particularity, difference, otherness. Natural appreciation becomes a supposedly neutral test that determines a subject's character—the sort of neutral test that privileged whites just happen to pass in overwhelming numbers.

None of which is to say that Muir is unaware of the history of slavery, the Civil War, or that he does not see the presence of black people in the country through which he journeys. Throughout the account he reports again and again on conversations about the war with the (mostly white) people he meets, and on the ways the conflict has degraded the landscape and its inhabitants, and he is only too willing to portray black people in a variety of demeaning and stereotypical ways. But these conversations and descriptions, again, are narrated from the position of Muir as naturalist and amateur anthropologist; the human inhabitants and human history of the South become often amusing features superimposed over, or blended into, the real object of interest, the nonhuman landscape, particularly its flora.

While both white and black Southerners are viewed from the position of the extrahistorical naturalist, they are not, however, viewed in the same way. Whites are generally portrayed as homeowners who work the land by farming, prospecting, and the like, and are characterized (often humorously) in terms of the particularities of their conversation with Muir. While they do not usually share Muir's love of nature, they are, like Muir, *different* from it, like him capable of observing it, acting on it, and representing it—they are farmers, and prospectors, after all. By contrast, Muir often views African Americans as an extension of the natural world, following a similar sort of template that slavery adopted as its core mystification, and that subsequent authors of the Lost Cause would employ in narrators like Page's Sam and Harris's Uncle Remus.[11] Take, for example, Muir's description of his first encounter with African Americans, a woman and a boy who help him cross a river just a few paragraphs into the narrative:

> Emerging about noon from a grove of giant sunflowers, I found myself on the brink of a tumbling rocky stream (Rolling Fork). I did not expect to find bridges on my wild ways, and at once started to ford, when a negro woman on the opposite bank earnestly called on me to wait until she could tell the "men folks" to bring me a horse—that the river was too deep and rapid to wade and that I would "sartain be drowned" if I attempted to cross. I replied that my bag and plants would ballast me; that the water did not appear to be deep, and that if I were carried away, I was a good swimmer and would soon dry in the sunshine. But the cautious old soul replied that no one ever waded that river and set off for a horse, saying that it was no trouble at all.
>
> In a few minutes the ferry horse came gingerly down the bank through vines and weeds. His long stilt legs proved him a natural wader. He was white and the little sable negro boy that rode him looked like a bug on his back. After many a tottering halt the outward voyage was safely made, and I mounted behind little Nig. He was a queer specimen, puffy and jet as an India rubber doll and his hair was matted in sections like the wool of a merino sheep. The old horse, overladen with his black and white burden, rocked and stumbled on his stilt legs with fair promises of a fall. But all ducking signs failed and we arrived in safety among the weeds and vines of the rugged bank. A salt bath would have done us no harm. I could swim and little Afric looked as if he might float like a bladder. (120)

Muir's amused, detached description turns this child into a sort of subhuman natural curiosity. Rather than a young boy voluntarily helping Muir, the "little Afric" is a "bug," a "queer specimen," an "India rubber doll" with hair "like the wool of a merino sheep." And despite the earlier warning from the "negro woman" that Muir would "sartain be drowned" because "no one ever waded that river," Muir not only dismisses her knowledge of the local geography, but dismisses the very possibility of "little Afric" drowning: even if he could not swim, unlike any other human boy, this one looks like he would "float like a bladder." Nothing (or no one) to worry about here, no gratitude necessary, just some picturesque negro accents in the larger narrative of Muir's wilderness journey. Muir's racism comes in the way he looks, in how his language and his eye collapses dark-skinned humans into the natural landscape—the boy, reading this description, would be led to insist on his *difference* from that landscape, that he was *not* a bug, *not* a sheep, *not* made of rubber, fully capable of death by drowning and accordingly an appropriate subject of any adult's concern. But the boy, of course, has no voice here, and the reader, especially the white reader in 1900, is likely to follow Muir's lead, chuckling at the caricature of these just-emancipated slaves turned natural stereotypes, inoculated against the history of their suffering   indeed, against even the possibility of their drowning—and ready to continue enjoying the refined pleasures of Muir's ecstatic botany.

Muir's racist conflation of African Americans and the natural world reaches its nadir in Florida, a subtropical ecosystem he does not know well and where he does not feel at ease, a place he imagines is full of "robber negroes" enjoying what he thinks is "their" "natural" climate. In what is arguably the most racist moment in the narrative (and there are certainly competitors), Muir's vision collapses African-American subjectivity utterly into the wild landscape, a collapse that, in its totalizing association between blackness and the landscape itself threatens to destablize Muir's own project of making the natural world "home." As a result, Muir's description initially swerves wildly between degradation and sublimity:

> When within three or four miles of the town I noticed a light off in the pine woods. As I was very thirsty, I thought I would venture toward it with the hope of obtaining water. In creeping cautiously and noiselessly through the grass to discover whether or no it was a camp of robber negroes, I came suddenly in view of the best-lighted and most primitive of all the domestic establishments I have yet seen in town or grove. There was, first of all, a big glowing log fire, illuminating the overleaning bushes and trees, bringing out leaf and spray with more than noonday distinctness, and making still darker the surrounding wood. In the centre of this globe of light sat two negroes. I could see their ivory gleaming from the great lips, and their smooth cheeks flashing off light as if made of glass. Seen anywhere but in the South, the glossy pair would have been taken for twin devils, but here it was only a negro and his wife at their supper.
>
>   I ventured forward to the radiant presence of the black pair, and, after being stared at with that desperate fixedness which is said to subdue the lion, I was handed water in a gourd from somewhere out in the darkness. I was standing for a moment beside the big fire, looking at the unsurpassable simplicity of the establishment and asking questions about the road to Gainesville, when my attention was called to a black lump of something lying in the ashes of the fire. It seemed to be made

of rubber; but ere I had time for much speculation, the woman bent wooingly over the black object and said with motherly kindness, "Come, honey, eat yo' hominy." (150–51)

This passage is, in important ways, the inverse of the sublime experiences he enjoys in the West that we will turn to shortly, experiences that construct modern white subjectivity in and as a particular sort of vertically defined geography. Here, conversely, Muir journeys deep *into* the pine woods, into what Jon Smith calls an "engulfing" rather than transcendent landscape, and finds what I would argue is American ecocriticism's heart of darkness, a collapse of racial identity and the natural world against which Muir's (white) natural sublime will ultimately define itself.[12]

Muir's description of the scene is built around paradoxical binaries, a series of contradictions that underscore the impossible contradiction of the scene's underlying ideological function: to naturalize the construction of an essential black identity. For Muir, the Florida landscape produces blackness and blackness produces the landscape in a reflexive process. So the narrative is at once characterized by Muir's initial fear of "robber negroes," and by the hospitality, domesticity, and maternal tenderness he in fact beholds. The scene is both flooded with light—a fire that illuminates "more than the noonday sun"— and defined by the darkness of the surrounding landscape and its human figures—the clearing is at once the "best-lighted" and the "most primitive." The "two negroes" Muir initially sees at once epitomize a sort of diabolical or animalized blackness—they are "two devils," they have tusk-like "ivory," rather than teeth, "gleaming from [their] great lips"—and yet, at the same time, they are also described in angelic terms, as "a radiant pair" sitting "in the center of a globe of light," their "glossy" skin "flashing off light as if made of glass," giving off a look capable of subduing a lion. Both angel and devil, human and animal, these two figures quiver on the brink of sublimity, representing both a sort of powerfully surreal hybrid natural identity, and the all-too-familiar degradated ambiguity of the What Is It?.

Muir, in short, isn't quite sure what it is—for a while at least. The paradoxes he stacks up bespeak a deeper anxiety (indeed, I will ultimately argue, a formative one) over the relation between racial identity and natural experience. Simply put, he is caught between two contrary commitments: on the one hand, he clearly accepts uncritically the widespread racist assumption among whites that blacks are essentially closer to nature, less highly evolved, subhuman, animals, beasts, or in

Muir's words, "bugs," "rubber," "well-trained," "devils," and so forth. As we have seen, the brutal history of this conflation of African-American identity with the natural world was basic to the ideological operations of slavery and the white construction of black identity subsequently. On the other hand, however, Muir is just as (if not more, one hopes) deeply committed to his own identification with the natural, and to natural experience as "returning home" for "over-civilised" whites generally. The same basic structural experience—a potent merge between human and natural identity—once again produces racial identities at once intimately connected and utterly different, both a renewed form of white supremacy and its necessary black, subaltern inverse. A central function of passages like this is to perform the "ideological police action" I noted in the introduction, turning green into black and white, making absolute racial difference out of the same species, the same place.

Hence the "black lump of something lying in the ashes of the fire" that "seemed to be made of rubber" turns out to be a boy, a "black object" whose humanity is invisible to Muir until he is called forth from the earth by his mother before Muir's gaze:

> At the sound of "hominy" the rubber gave strong manifestations of vitality and proved to be a burly little negro boy, rising from the earth naked as to the earth he came. Had he emerged from the black muck of a marsh, we might easily have believed that the Lord had manufactured him like Adam direct from the earth.
>
> Surely, thought I, as I started for Gainesville, surely I am now coming to the tropics, where the inhabitants wear nothing but their own skins. This fashion is sufficiently simple—"no troublesome disguises," as Milton calls clothing—but it certainly is not quite in harmony with Nature. Birds make nests and nearly all beasts make some kind of bed for their young; but these negroes allow their younglings to lie nestless and naked in the dirt. (151)

Rather than recognizing his own culpable blindness to the boy's humanity in his inability to see him as different from the nonhuman natural background, Muir instead offers a racial origin story that reaffirms that very collapse of black identity into the landscape. After the black boy is called forth alchemically from the black earth before Muir's eyes in a direct transmutation of "rubber" and ashes into black flesh, Muir immediately reimagines the scene in universal terms as a kind of black creation myth: the Lord "manufactures...like Adam" the boy from "the black muck of a marsh." And in this fantasized second version, Muir tellingly shifts the assumed audience for the Lord's racial work from the first person singular to the first person (white) plural: "*we* might easily have believed" that this is where black people come from and that this what they are like.

But however demeaning this description is, the intimate bond between African Americans and landscape remains a possible source of dignity and empowerment, at least within Muir's broader ecocritical philosophy that sees the association of human and nature as immensely salutary. Just as we saw with the "black" narrators of Lost Cause fiction whose memories embodied Southern pastoral authenticity, Muir's collapse of blackness and land threatens, by the text's own logic, to destabilize the text's larger ideological project of providing whiteness a dehistoricized natural landscape to identify with after the trauma of the Civil War. And so Muir places blackness *below* the bestial; unlike "birds and nearly all beasts...these negroes allow their younglings to lie nestless and naked in the dirt." Suddenly black people are lower than the nonhuman natural, falling off the human/ animal continuum that had "justified" white supremacy for centuries, becoming degraded hybrid creatures like the domesticated sheep he decries throughout *My First Summer in the Sierras*.[13]

The resulting hierarchy—white/natural/black—provides, I would argue, one template for the long history of mainstream environmentalism ranking wilderness preservation above issues like lead paint, diesel particulates, industrial toxins, and the like, exposure to which is overwhelmingly correlated with both race and poverty. Surely this moment in Muir, the founder of the environmental movement, sheds light on James Cone's comment on the contemporary racial split in environmentalism that I quoted in the introduction: " 'Blacks don't care about the environment' is a typical comment by white ecologists. Racial and economic justice has been at best only a marginal concern in the mainstream environmental movement. 'White people care more about the endangered whale and the spotted owl than they do about the survival of young blacks in our nation's cities' is a well-founded belief in the African American community" (138). What Muir's passage demonstrates is a vital, and suppressed, part of the history of the division Cone describes so sharply. The misanthropy of mainstream environmentalism (not to mention adherents of so-called Deep Ecology) provides the rule—humans in general are an unnatural, parasitic, destructive species when they act out of harmony with nature—that then gets selectively applied along the all-too-familiar channels of race and class in a way that seems, to the white environmentalist, objective, extrahistorical, not racist.[14] The "people" whose environmental concern manifests as a love of wild nature and a sense of profound kinship with it are largely exempted from this parasitic designation. In contrast to these enlightened few are the parasitic swarms of "people," associated with subnatural urban and suburban environments who don't find an intimate association with nature elevating. An "accidental" racial segregation then shows up "naturally," a segregation that, I think, goes some way toward explaining the division in the contemporary environmental movement between "good" environmentalists and their invaluable wilderness, and the environmental concerns of urban poor people of color.[15] It's more than just an oversight, in other words, which does not mean it was conscious—far from it

None of this is to say, of course, that respect for and enjoyment of the natural world in all its beauty and otherness is not the birthright of every human no matter what race, or that environmentalism does not describe a profound collective and individual responsibility. But to make such natural experience the mark of exceptional, right-living human identity as environmentalism does, but not to pay very close and very explicit attention to the historical reasons why those experiences are hugely racially segregated, is to invite the sort of naturalized racist conclusions we see explicit in Muir's work.

ELEVATION: CALIFORNIA BY WAY OF CUBA AND NEW YORK

Muir's narrative doesn't stop where one might expect, at the southernmost point of his walk, but instead ultimately turns to the West, with its promise of freedom and a powerful individual (white) identity outside of the nation's traumatic racial history. But Muir's route to California is indirect in ways as unconsciously telling as the walk's deployment of nature as a term outside of the human racial history of the landscape. After walking to Cedar Keys on Florida's Gulf coast, he takes a boat to Cuba where he spends a month, hoping (in vain, as it turns out) to recover his strength sufficiently so he can continue his travels in South America. Cuba, the last slave society in the Western hemisphere, marks the southern extremity of Muir's north to south axial journey, a southern nadir like the one that turns Huck's imagination west.[16] And, like Huck, at this southern extremity Muir seems less cognizant of black humanity than ever. After several pages rhapsodizing about the Cuban fauna and the botanical garden in Havana, for example, Muir ends the chapter with a striking, and very rare, look at Afro-Cuban slave laborers:

> In Havana I saw the strongest and ugliest negroes that I have met in my whole walk. The stevedores of the Havana wharf are muscled in

true giant style, enabling them to tumble and toss ponderous casks and boxes of sugar weighing hundreds of pounds as if they were empty. I heard our own brawny sailors, after watching them at work a few minutes, express unbounded admiration of their strength, and wish that their hard outbulging muscles were for sale. The countenances of some of the negro orange-selling dames express a devout good-natured ugliness that I never could have conceived any arrangement of flesh and blood to be capable of. (169)

Once again, Muir is unable to see black people as human, or to celebrate them in terms remotely approaching his rapturous enthusiasm for any number of plants.[17] The slaves are entirely defined by their bodies, the "strongest and ugliest" he has ever seen, a sort of animalized and hyper-gendered physicality that gives the men the musculature of "giants" and, for Muir, the women an ugliness beyond what he previously conceived "any arrangement of flesh and blood to be capable of." Muir can't begin to see the political and social context in which these slave laborers are all-too-emplaced; that the men's muscles, for example, are formed by, and testify to, the hard labor Muir is witnessing, not by their negro giantism. And most tellingly, of course, Muir misses that these "hard outbulging muscles" *are* for sale. These are slaves, after all—but under Muir's naturalizing gaze the traumatic racial mess of their history is obscured and their suffering disappears as they blend into the exotic natural background. Muir journeys to one of the last slaveholding societies in the Western hemisphere just two years after the American Civil War—to an island that produced as much as a third of the world's sugar using slave labor, an island where between a third and a half of the population in the nineteenth century were enslaved—and then focuses his narrative almost exclusively on celebrating the island's natural beauty, inviting the (white) reader to a similar substitution of natural appreciation for political reality.

This substitution of uncreated nature for the bitterly constructed trauma of slavery and racism finds a much broader structural analogue in Muir's departure from Cuba. Muir's journey West—to his first sight of Yosemite and the landscape that he identified with so strongly and that so fundamentally shaped American environmentalism—begins in slavery. Muir sails from Cuba to New York, hiding below deck in order to avoid problems with customs officials:

Vessels leaving the harbor are stopped at the Morro Castle to have their clearance papers examined; in particular to see that no runaway slaves were being carried away. The officials came alongside our little ship, but did not come aboard. They were satisfied by a glance at the consul's clearance paper, and with the declaration of the captain, when asked whether he had any negroes, that he had "not a d____d one." "All right, then," shouted the officials, "farewell! A pleasant voyage to you!" As my name was not on the ship's papers, I stayed below, out of sight, until I felt the heaving of the waves and knew we were fairly out on the open sea. The Castle towers, the hills, the palms, and the wave-white strand, all faded in the distance, and our mimic sea-bird was at home in the open stormy gulf, curtsying to every wave and facing bravely to the wind. (170)

In a very real sense, then, Muir's journey replicates and inverts the structure of the slave narratives, in a way that might serve as a miniature of my argument in this chapter about how ahistorical natural appreciation came, for whites, to substitute for the brutal antebellum history and postbellum reality of racial trauma. Muir, the original white environmentalist writing his first book about his first extended wilderness experience, ends that narrative by taking the place of a fugitive slave, a white stowaway on a ship without "a d____d" "negro" onboard, fleeing slave territory for the definitional freedom awaiting him at the ultimate end of his journey in Yosemite and the West. All that the walk has taught the white reader about how natural identification might offer a place at once "outside" of race and entirely segregated here crystallizes; racial trauma isn't repressed here, quite, but utterly supplanted.

Muir's long walk from north to south, discovering "nature" along the way, and his retroping of the slave narratives in his escape from Cuba to New York, should historically contextualize the natural revelation that comes at the end of the narrative. This revelation, when Muir first sees the Sierra Nevada mountains, comes at the end of a long journey that is a fundamental part of its meaning. Too often, however, such moments of ecstatic appreciation of the natural landscape in Muir are read in dehistoricized isolation in a way that mirrors the very promise of ahistorical empowered subjectivity they offer Muir. (Indeed, there has been hardly any critical commentary on Muir's anti-black racism.)[18] Muir's natural sublime, his profound self-identification with the western mountain landscape in the Sierras, is not an escape from the "over-civilised" in general, or simply an individualized moment of rebirth in nature, but also a sublime escape from a very specific and profoundly traumatic history of slavery and racial guilt. And in a larger sense, then, the formative embrace of such sublime moments by mainstream environmentalism—Muir founded the Sierra Club, after all—explains, in part, the historical reasons behind both the overwhelming whiteness of the wilderness and the scarcity of African Americans in wilderness preservation movements.

When he finally arrives in the West in the final paragraphs of the *1,000 Mile Walk to the Gulf,* Muir claims a rebirth in an effusion that exemplifies the transformative power of Muir's natural sublime, one that should be read not only sui generis, but as the intimately connected inverse of Muir's vision of the African-American family by the campfire in Florida:[19]

> If you wish to see how much of light, life, and joy can be got into a January, go to this blessed Hollow. If you wish to see a plant-resurrection—myriads of bright flowers crowding from the ground, like souls to a judgment—go to Twenty Hills in February. If you are traveling for health, play truant to doctors and friends, fill your pocket with biscuits, and hide in the hills of the Hollow, lave in its waters, tan in its golds, bask in its flower-shine, and your baptisms will make you a new creature indeed. Or, choked in the sentiments of society, so tired of the world, here will your hard doubts disappear, your carnal incrustations melt off, and your soul breathe deep and free in God's shoreless atmosphere of beauty and love.
>
> Never shall I forget my baptism in this font. It happened in January, a resurrection day for many a plant and for me. I suddenly found myself on one of its hills; the Hollow overflowed with light, as a fountain, and only small, sunless nooks were kept for mosseries and ferneries. Hollow Creek spangled and mazed like a river. The ground steamed with fragrance. Light, of unspeakable richness was brooding the flowers. Truly, said I, is California the Golden State—in metallic gold, in sun gold, and in plant gold. The sunshine for a whole summer seemed condensed into the chambers of that one glowing day. Every trace of dimness had been washed from the sky; the mountains were dusted and wiped clean with clouds—Pacheco Peak and Mount Diablo, and the waved blue wall between, the grand Sierra stood along the plain, colored in four horizontal bands:—the lowest, rose purple; the next higher, dark purple; the next, blue; above all, the white rows of summits pointing to the heavens.
>
> It may be asked, What have mountains fifty or a hundred miles away to do with Twenty Hill Hollow? To lovers of the wild, these mountains are not a hundred miles away. Their spiritual power and the goodness of the sky make them near, as a circle of friends. They rise as a portion of the hilled walls of the Hollow. You cannot feel yourself out of doors; plain, sky, and mountains ray beauty which you feel. You bathe in these spirit-beams, turning round and round, as if warming at a camp-fire. Presently you lose consciousness of your own separate existence: you blend with the landscape, and become part and parcel of nature. (182–83)

These three paragraphs exemplify the hundreds of such sublime moments that punctuate, if not fundamentally structure, Muir's subsequent nature writing.[20] Here, as elsewhere, Muir testifies to an ecstatic experience in the wild religious in its intensity, a sublime experience in which the identities of self and nature become energetically interpenetrative, and which promises, in its resolution, to make that sublime landscape the symbol of a reconstituted and newly empowered subject.[21] In such experiences, the wealthy subject, his or her privilege naturalized in the notion of "traveling for health,"—is born again—"baptized"—in an extrahistorical, extrapolitical realm outside of "hard doubts," "carnal incrustations," the "choking sentiments of society," free from a world the subject is "so tired of." Uplifted, radically empowered, removed from history and time, transparent, Muir's personal transcendence is explicitly extended as an invitation to all others capable of passing the nature test, of losing themselves, history, and politics in this light-flood landscape.

That invitation, of course, implicitly and absolutely, is not intended for the African-American family in the Florida swamp, or other racially marked subjects for whom nature is all-too historical, for whom the merge with nature had long been synonymous with degradation, violence, and bondage. Certainly a revealing sort of inverted parallelism links this experience of the mountain sublime, and the earlier description of the African-American family and the tropical landscape they occupy.[22] Where the subject here loses his skin, his "carnal incrustation" in a flood of "spirit beams" emanating from this mystical "campfire," the black boy is utterly opaque by the light of his "campfire," defined by his "India rubber" carnal incrustation, his parents' black skin reflective rather than transparent. Where the unmarked white subject merges his preexisting civilized identity with the landscape, the boy *emerges* from the dirt and marsh to take his place in the hierarchy *beneath* the birds and beasts. Whiteness incorporates the transcendent power of mountains hundreds of miles away, makes them a "circle of friends;" the black family eats its hominy, labors in the swamp, signifies—for Muir and his readers, especially in 1867—part of the repressed "all" we get away from, when we get away from it all.

As we saw in Emerson's earlier ocular transformation, this experience of Romantic sublimity, of a powerful unmarked subjectivity "naturally" outside of history, culture, and race, serves as a idealized version of a certain normative—or "transparent"—form of white racial identity generally. This centrally important moment at once marks the sharpest difference between white and black, but does so without defining whiteness in an explicitly binary relation to blackness.

The mountains are where "people" find themselves, the swamp is where "negroes" come from.

Three things have changed since Emerson's moment, however. First, rather than being hyper-individuating, this transcendent experience is explicitly extended to, and formative of, a larger and racially normative white community. Muir's story is not his alone, but the start of a movement, a universal home. Second, this experience contrasts with a similarly normative vision of communal black genesis in nature, not from the earlier traumatic moment in Crèvecoeur that marked an individual white recoil from a similarly individualized black trauma. The "people" incapable of this moment of natural sublimity have already been marked in Muir's narrative. And third, rather than becoming, as Emerson says "part or parcel of *God*," in this experience of transcendence we become "part and parcel of *nature*," a substitution that, in the context of the larger passage's quasi-religious enthusiasm, divinizes the landscape and the subjects who merge with it. Such a move brings godhead much closer to home; rather than transcending the human in Emerson, Muir's transcendence is (all-too) human.

Put another way, this moment exemplifies not just *Muir's* sublime but the *white* sublime; it encapsulates the late nineteenth-century moment when whiteness moved from being a positive identity—an explicit claim of Anglo-Saxon superiority that sounds so safely benighted to our ears—to its much more insidious unmarked and ahistorical modern formulation. Muir's Sierras are a sublime place where whiteness can hide in plain sight, where the trauma of race is at once utterly effaced and an ambiguous and threatening other lurking just over the eastern horizon. By pretending to be a democratic home for all, a supposedly neutral test of spiritual advancement that produces a supposedly neutral—but in fact racially segregated—outcome the sublime wilderness functions both to mark and unmark race. The conclusion— that access to sublimity is racially marked and an experience that itself is a racial marking—is precisely what is avoided by the double gesture of the sublime, and precisely what I am insisting on here. While this moment in Muir, considered in isolation, is quite lovely and moving, we shouldn't *only* consider it in isolation; rather it is also the culmination of a narrative with a pronounced ideological agenda, the end of Muir's and the white reader's long walk away from the history of slavery and the Civil War that saturates the landscape of the East.

8

MIGRATIONS

And one morning while in the woods I stumbled suddenly upon the thing,
Stumbled upon it in a grassy clearing guarded by scaly oaks and elms.
And the sooty details of the s cene rose, thrusting themselves between
   the world and me...
              —Richard Wright, "Between the World and Me," 1935.

What's beauty anyway but ugliness if it hurts you?
              —Jean Toomer, *Cane*

While white America turned its gaze toward the sublime landscapes of the West dreaming of the sort of transparent extrahistorical freedom Muir "discovers" in the Sierras, in the late nineteenth century most African Americans remained where slavery and the failures of Reconstruction had left them: desperately poor and largely uneducated, intimately tied to the rural Southern landscape, and outnumbered by an increasingly violent white Southern population who controlled what few economic and natural resources were left. As we have seen throughout the previous chapters, that close tie to the landscape was a primary source of vulnerability and degradation, the conduit through which white supremacy had, from slavery onward, naturalized its brutally hierarchic relation to black people, justifying its exploitation and violence as a subset of a larger dominance of the nonhuman natural world.

It is in the context of that long history of naturalized trauma that this chapter examines several literary texts inspired by the Great Migration, a massive population shift starting around the First World War in which millions of African Americans relocated from the rural South to Northern cities.[1] Between 1910 and 1920, for example, the black population of New York City grew by 66 percent, by 148 percent in Chicago, 611 percent in Detroit, and by 500 percent in Philadelphia (Harrison 46). This widely studied movement produced an unprecedented flowering of urban black literature and art in Harlem, Chicago's

South Side, Washington D.C., and other urban areas above the
Mason-Dixon line in the early part of the twentieth century, a flowering that arguably changed black culture from one predominantly
rural-identified to one primarily urban-identified.[2] Reading this mass
movement through a green lens reveals two intersecting and profoundly conflicting environmental concerns that I will argue structure
several representative texts of the movement: (1) a reinvocation of the
anti-nature writing tendency of the slave narratives discussed in chapter three, in which detaching the author from a traumatic and degrading connection to nature was a formative trajectory of the
autobiographical project and (2) an often anguished longing for the
lost green world of the South and the deep connection to the land that
agrarian African-American culture fostered.

These two concerns are obviously in sharp conflict. On the one
hand African-American writers in the period confronted a longstanding white supremacist practice of conflating black people and
nature to the detriment of both, from the domesticated animality of
slavery, to the postbellum pastoralized idiocy of the Lost Cause narrators, the crudities of scientific racism, and the creation of the Black
Beast figure stalking the eroticized landscapes of the white supremacist imagination. And, as we have seen, lynching arguably served as
the telos of these white fantasies about black people's relation to
nature, at once the ultimate conflation of black body and landscape,
and the most horrific barrier possible to the sort of sublime escape
from history and politics that nature affords (white) people like John
Muir. On the other hand, this racist tradition did not eliminate the
experience of nature's beauty and solace, the profound connection
to the Southern landscape and the intimate knowledge of the natural world that comes from agrarian life. While celebrations of natural experience are almost wholly absent in the slave narratives and
other antebellum African-American literature, a careful embrace of
the beauty of the rural Southern landscape emerges in the literature
of the Harlem Renaissance as Northern black writers looked back
from a relatively safe distance. This newfound appreciation of nature
was not, however, the uncomplicated ecstasy we saw in Muir, nor
the uncritical sentimentality of Lost Cause pastoralism; the connection with the land recorded in the Harlem Renaissance remained
dangerous and painful, making nature a locus of vulnerability as
well as comfort and homecoming, simultaneously an intensely political and historicized site of suffering and oppression, and the sign of
the possibility of difference, of a world outside of such unhappy
human constructions.

The interweaving of natural beauty and trauma in African-American texts from this period is clearly conversant with, and critical of, both the sublime and the pastoral modes, intervening on the naturalizing processes of racial identity formation that have been the central subject of this book. For a northern African-American writer to look south at a rapidly disappearing rural culture that was also a possible point of cultural origin, a site of authenticity and tradition marked by beauty as well as terrible violence and degradation, was to participate, at some level, in the sort of mix of temporal and spatial dislocation, desire, and loss fundamental to the structure of both sublimity and nostalgia. As I have argued in the introduction and elsewhere, a critical difference between sublimity and trauma lies in the position of the subject in relation to an inexpressible Other that threatens annihilation. In trauma the subject is subsumed and the Other's inexpressibility subsequently supplants the subject's self-expression; in sublimity the subject is positioned "further out," and the rupture in signification becomes the sign of a reconstituted and newly empowered individual or collective/racial identity. In this sense, for an African American in Harlem to write at a distance about the horror and beauty of black life in the rural South was to occupy a sublime position long reserved for whites. Similarly, if the sort of pastoral nostalgia we see in Lost Cause writers like Bagby, Page, and Harris makes the temporally displaced antebellum Southern landscape and the "black" narrators who give it voice the mark of (supposedly) authentic origin, then the moments embracing the vanishing pastoral life we see in texts by Hurston, Toomer, and others, for example, are, arguably, attempts to intercede on a longstanding white supremacist project of naturalizing and mythologizing Southern history and race relations. To read such moments in this larger political context avoids seeing them as simply participating in the tradition of pastoralizing rural poverty and suffering; for an African-American writer to lay claim to a pastoral landscape or sublime experience was, especially at this time, almost always an intensely political act, if not, indeed, an ideological intervention, even when those politics are not explicit in the text.

While black writers in this period were deeply engaged with sublimity and the pastoral, they were, in other words, doing something substantially more complex than putting a black face on a white tradition. While moments of genuine natural appreciation emerge for the first time in African-American texts from this period, they certainly do not describe an embrace of natural experience in anything like the ways white people valorized sublime or pastoral experience. Indeed, the trajectory of black nature writing in the Harlem Renaissance moves, on the whole, toward the same sort of "de-naturing" of black identity that we saw in the slave narratives. The process is more painful, however, in part because the loss of nature is, newly, seen as a genuine loss. However appealing natural beauty and a connection to the land might be, to affiliate with nature remains threatening; the rural landscape is best viewed from the safe position of the urban artist, looking south with a sense of nostalgia that does not quite wish for a return. In an echo of the early nineteenth-century embrace of the wilderness by Eastern whites, it is only when the natural landscape is lost that it can be safely mourned. This fact, however, should not be taken to mean that the appreciation of the natural world in these texts is artificial, but that it is always historical, always contextualized by the longstanding and pervasive danger of that association. What emerges is a new sort of nature writing that is committed both to an explicit recognition of a terribly unhappy racial history grounded in natural experience and to an explicit recognition of the secondary trauma that primary history entails, if not necessitates: the additional loss of a deeply felt and in many ways salutary relation to nature.

In the remainder of this chapter, I take up texts from three African-American authors that illustrate this reimagining of the pastoral mode: two versions of a short story by Angelina Weld Grimké about an infamous 1918 lynching incident, the "Kabnis" section of Jean Toomer's *Cane*, and three episodes in Zora Neale Hurston's *Their Eyes Were Watching God*.

Losing the Forest for the Trees: Angelina Weld Grimké's Natural History

In 1919 and 1920 Angelina Weld Grimké wrote two little-known short stories, "Blackness" and "Goldie," based on the horrific 1918 lynching of pregnant Mary Turner (and ten other African Americans) in Valdosta Georgia, in which her still-living unborn child was cut from her body and stomped to death.[3] This particularly gruesome event, with its destruction of a mother and the wanton slaughter of a categorically innocent life, had provoked widespread outrage in Northern newspapers and black journals after Walter White's vivid description in the NAACP's 1919 *30 Years of Lynching*.[4] Indeed, this murder arguably became a sort of paradigmatic lynching in African-American writing at this time, the subject of two of Grimké's stories and several of her poems, a source of panic for Kabnis in the last part of Toomer's *Cane*, and an event that, according to Barbara Foley, *The Crisis* (a leading

African-American journal of the time) "continually reverted to…as an archetypical instance of Southern barbarism" (187).

Given the spectacularly shocking quality of the event's violence, Grimké's characterization of the event is somewhat surprising. Both versions mediate the event, focusing on the lynched woman's brother (named "Victor Forrest" in "Goldie," but left unnamed in "Blackness") and his journey south from his urban home in the north to find out why his sister has disappeared. The drama in both stories is not the lynching itself, but the how the discovery of the sister's lynched body affects the dead woman's Northern brother. This effect is characterized almost exclusively in terms of his growing alienation from the natural world, particularly a horrified relation to trees.

At the beginning of "Blackness," for example, the unnamed brother offers a prequel of the later effects of his traumatic discovery in terms of both a bond with the Southern landscape, and a horrified recoil from it. The brother relates to Reed (his interlocutor and the story's narrator) the nauseating details of his trip south in the overcrowded and filthy "pig-pen" Jim Crow car—which produces a degradation that precisely recalls slavery's pastoral reduction of the subject to the status of domesticated animal—and then declares there is nevertheless "a beauty still left in the South—that even the polluting touch of the white man can never spoil" (232). But that appreciation for the beauty of the Southern landscape moves immediately into a traumatic qualification of that natural embrace, a trauma that quickly spreads to Reed:

> "Beauty! In the South?"
> "Yes, Reed, beauty in The South."
> "It must be nature, then, you're meaning."
> "I am. They may never spoil, try as they may, the beauty of the days and of the nights, those of the dawns, and those of the dusks. Each has a loveliness, all its own, you know here, so much more genial are they, so much more exquisite, so much softer. Nor can they spoil the beauty of the bird songs, nor of the flower-blooms, nor the beauty of the wave-like, wave flung changing green on green of the little [hi]lls and of the mountains; nor can they spoil the beauty, either, of their peace to tired eyes made weary with long waiting."
> "Why," I exclaimed softly though, "you are a poet."…"[b]ut you are not forgetting?"
> "Forgetting[?]"
> "Yes, one more at least of the beautiful things there."
> "What?"
> "Why, the trees?"

> I was certain, at that, I heard him draw in his breath sharply and suddenly.
>   I strained my eyes. I could not see that he moved.
> "You do not think them beautiful?" I persisted.
> "Once," he said finally.
> "But not, now?"
> "No." And I know from the tone, I was to ask no more. Later I was to
>   understand; and since that night no tree has been or ever will be quite
>   the same to me again. (232–33)

The brother's memory in the compositional present of how the lynching transformed his view of trees reflects a painful loss of the natural world finally shared by both men, and arguably the black reader as well. Three vitally important historical points of the African-American relation to the natural world are quickly traced here: (1) the ongoing and degrading link between the pastoral and slavery (2) a deep appreciation of nature's beauty outside the "polluting touch of the white man," and (3) a traumatic intervention where racial history violently reenters that appreciation, where the memory of the sister's lynching makes nature not only a source of solace but the trigger for a "shuddering" recollection of unbearable suffering.

In this sequence, the natural gets violently rehistoricized, the pristine landscape suffers a sudden, shocking racial "pollution" as the extrahuman is wrenched into signifying the possibility of white supremacist violence. Rather than the awareness of nature leading to sublimity, moments of sublimity themselves collapse into trauma.[5] As a result, when the brother describes to Reed his long walk from the train station to his sister's house the night before he discovers their bodies, the mere unvoiced suspicion of what might be awaiting him makes the initial invocation of the sublime unsustainable:

> "Reed," he said, "it was one of those beautiful nights about which I
> have told you. There was no wind, no moon, no clouds. The skies were
> crowded with stars large white ones and little white ones. It was such a
> relief to be at last alone amid all this goodness of quiet and beauty and
> cleanness that I refused to think at all for a while just to absorb it, drink
> it all in, as it were, if you understand.... Presently I began to wonder,
> as I walked along, my eyes on the stars, whether perhaps someone in
> one of those white worlds another just as I might not be walking along
> under other stars because to him out of the silence a will had called.
> Who knows? And suddenly the whole thing, the voice, the woman, I,
> myself, what I was to find, what I might need to do seemed utterly
> unimportant, insignificant and God very far off and unreal.... The
> only sounds I heard were little leaf ones, the noise made by a cracking
> twig or of a dry leaf rustling under some stealthy, tiny woodland foot.

On either side of me tall black trees, nothing more, line on line, row on row, deep on deep. Trees, Reed."

He paused and I shuddered involuntarily and quite unaccountably.

"And, then, little by little, all the thoughts and fears I had been refusing steadily to entertain came back, not singly but together." He paused. "I need not, I think tell you what they were." (239)

The brother almost immediately moves from a quintessentially sublime suspension of individual experience and collective political realities under the gorgeous night sky, a beauty that leads him to "refuse to think at all for a while," that gives him a profound sense of his "utter unimportant[ce]" and "insignifican[ce]," to an equally overwhelming return of "all the thoughts and fears I have" coming back "not singularly but together." It is the sight of the trees on the edge of the road that serve as the trigger for the collapse of the sublime into the traumatic, as they shift from being part of the extrahuman to signifying the totality of his all-too-human worries, worries entirely embedded in a racial history so well known he does not have to name them to Reed or the reader. In the context of this story and this history, we all know what is coming, what the trees mean.[6]

This pattern of traumatic violence erupting in moments of natural appreciation provides the essential tension in the subsequent descriptions of how the brother comes to discover the bodies, forming a template for natural experience that gets applied repeatedly, a repetition that itself underscores the essentially traumatic structure of this template. The description of the discovery is drawn out over several pages as the narrator oscillates between moments of intense natural appreciation interrupted by what he calls "the duet": three creaking noises in succession, one higher pitched, one lower, and then both sounding together. After every interruption he takes another step closer to discovering the source of the noises—the lynching ropes rubbing a tree limb as the bodies sway in the breeze. This almost ritualistic call and response sequence continues for several pages in Grimké's text, as continuing moments of the brother's appreciation of nature repeatedly produce the same trauma-filled reply, leading him inexorably closer to the unbearable sight deep in the woods. Here is the climactic moment:

"Reed, I wish I could tell you of the breath taking, poignant beauty and wistfulness of it all, the pale twilight everywhere, the freshness, the softness of the greens—the deep blue and purple shadows, the frailest gossamers of mist softly iridescent. The wonder of the bird songs here there and everywhere with every bird well hidden, well

I can't, I sat there drawing it in. And then the breeze blew…'Creak! Creak! Creak!' Only a short distance farther, I knew, and I had it to do. I moved the branches aside, they resisted, but I went on…

'Creak! Creak! Creak!' And I knew that between me and *it* whatever it was, was only now this thin screen of delicate and beautiful and green leaves. I put up my hands to them and the I noticed an inch worm making his awkward, energetic and seemingly important journey along the leaves and the twigs. I watched him a long time, and just beyond were the creaking and the stillness.

I closed my eyes and pulled the branches aside.

'Creak! Creak! Creak!'

Nothing between, now, but my closed eyelids.

I stepped forward; I opened my eyes—and I saw."

His deep and shuddering breathing was the only sound to be heard for some time. At last that quieted down.

"It was—those two?" I asked, and my voice was strange in my ears.

"Yes. Each with a rope around the neck—strung up—onto the same limb—that made the creaking—. Their faces swollen, distorted, unrecognizable—awful!—and naked—both of them."

He paused, drew in another shuddering breath. I leaned forward. It was he striking one knee with a clenched fist. For the first time his words came brokenly in little gasps.

"Her beautiful golden body—swaying there—ripped open—"

I cried out at this but he did not pause.

"Ripped open—I say—and under her poor little swaying golden feet—her child—unborn—beautiful—tiny hands and feet perfect— one little hand reached up—as though—appealing—the little head— blotted out—crushed—its little brains"—

"Stop!" I cried out. "Oh Stop!" (241–44)

In this terrible sequence the beauty of the forest is indelibly marked by the violence of lynching, making nature signify not an escape from human history but possibility of the most brutal immersion in it. Bird songs are supplanted by the creak of the rope, green leaves only temporarily shield the narrator's eyes from the terrible truth, natural appreciation is rendered here as ultimately only a distraction from the discovery of the "swollen, distorted, unrecognizable, awful" heart of the forest.

Grimké clearly intends this traumatic revelation to resonate far beyond its effect on the anonymous brother. The horror of the scene, and its all-too-real historical reference, is shared by both Reed and the audience, almost inevitably diminishing the possibility of a contemporary black reader enjoying a Muir-like unselfconscious peace if he subsequently found himself walking alone in the Georgia woods. And such a diminishment might itself be complex in the same ways that Grimké's story records: neither simply a fearful recoil nor, certainly, a straightforward embrace of a beautiful landscape but a complex, contradictory, and painful vacillation between appreciation and anxiety that finally fuses natural beauty and trauma into a profoundly unnatural hybrid. The result of such an experience would, nevertheless, likely be an avoidance of the woods subsequently, as the experience of vacillation turned natural beauty definitively from the promise of solace to the threat of terror.

Grimké's second version of the story which records how the alienation of the brother and Reed in "Blackness" is neither specific to them nor to the site of the hanging, but ultimately inherent in the generic natural setting itself. While in "Blackness," the brother's walk from the train station to the cabin at night demonstrates the difficulty of sustaining a sublime appreciation for the woods in the face of the possibility of racial terror, in "Goldie" the same moment of interaction with nature takes a more definitively gothic turn from the start. Rather than a specific set of unspoken worries about the fate of his sister, triggered by the trees on each side of the road, the brother in "Goldie"—tellingly now named "Victor Forrest," and now the subject of Grimké's third-person narration—immediately finds the entire forest surreally terrifying:

> Singular fancies may come to one, at such times: and, as he plodded forward, one came, quite unceremoniously, quite unsolicited, to him and fastened its tentacles upon him. Perhaps it was born of the darkness and the utter windlessness with the resulting great stillness; perhaps—but who knows from what fancies spring? At any rate, it seemed to him, the woods, on either side of him, were really not woods at all but an ocean that had flowed down in a great rolling black wave of flood to the very lips of the road itself and paused there as though suddenly arrested and held poised in some strange and sinister spell. Of course, all of this came, he told himself over and over, from having such a cursed imagination; but whether he would or not, the fancy persisted and the growing feeling with it, that he, Victor Forrest, went in actual danger, for at any second the spell might snap and with that snapping, this boundless, deep upon deep of horrible, waiting sea, would move, rush, hurl itself, heavily and swiftly together from the two sides, thus engulfing, grinding, crushing, blotting out all in its path, not excluding what he now knew to be that most insignificant of insignificant pigmies, Victor Forrest. (282–83)

Here the instability of the natural reference in an explicitly racialized context is dramatically underscored: rather than being a source of extrahistorical Truth, the forest is imaginatively transformed into an apocalyptically destructive "great rolling black wave of flood," one only held back by a curiously described magic spell. And here we see another terrifying moment in which a sublime landscape threatens to become traumatic, to collapse the observational distance necessary for sublimity and to plunge the black observer into a traumatic union with that landscape, "engulfing, grinding, crushing, blotting out all in its path." Here, too, the threat has "spread;" in "Blackness" it was initially located in the sister's body, markedly separated from the brother by the "thin screen of delicate and beautiful and green leaves" that stand between him and the scene of lynching. In "Goldie" trauma has become inherent in the forest itself, threatening the brother in *advance* of the discovery of the brutal murder. Forrest never gets to view this forest from a position of "relative safety;" there is no pastoral moment at all in the story, only a sort of suspended violence temporarily held back by a "strange and sinister" spell. This strange and sinister spell that keeps the furiously destructive "black wave" temporarily at bay is, symbolically, white power:

> But there were bright spots, here and there in the going—he found himself calling them white islands of safety. These occurred where the woods receded at some little distance from the road.
> "It's as though," he thought aloud, "they drew back here in order to get a good deep breath before plunging forward again. Well, all I hope is, the spell holds O.K. beyond."
> He always paused, a moment or so, on one of these islands to drive out expulsively the dank, black oppressiveness of the air he had been breathing and to fill his lungs anew with God's night air, that, here, at least, was sweet and untroubled. Here, too, his eyes were free again and he could see the dimmed white blur of road for a space each way; and, above, the stars, millions upon millions of them, each one hardly brilliant, stabbing its way whitely through the black heavens. And if the island were large enough there was a glimpse, scarcely more, of a very pallid, slightly crumpled moon sliding furtively down the west.— Yes, sharply black and sharply white, that was it, but mostly it was black. (283)

The spell produces "white islands of safety," like the stars "stab- bing...whitely through the black heavens," where Forrest can at least *feel* safe from the threatening black forest/wave. Grimké's portrayal of a "sharply black and sharply white" nature, where the forest is associated with racist fury and black suffering, and is contrasted with a explicitly white sense of security in its midst, underscores how deeply natural experience and racial experience construct each other. Forrest's feeling of safety on those "white islands" is a quintessentially white experience of nature, a temporary space where he can "drive out expulsively" the "black oppressiveness...he had been breathing," a natural space where he can imagine himself safe/white.

But Forrest's feeling of safety is both misplaced and short-lived. He is black, and, at least in these stories, Grimké is certainly no Romantic naturalist. While the brother in "Blackness" escapes execution for killing his sister's murderer, "Goldie" ends with a report of Victor's own lynching, "d[ying]," as the other two had died, upon another tree" (305). And in a paragraph coda to the completed narrative, Grimké invests Victor's subjective fear with an even more surreal third-person omniscient vision, one in which the forest loses its extra-human natural reference altogether and becomes a sort of repository of traumatic racial history:

> There is a country road upon either side of which grow trees even to its very edges. Each tree has been chosen and transplanted here for a reason and the reason is that at some time each has borne upon its boughs a creaking victim. Hundreds of these trees, there are, thousands of them. They form a forest—"Creaking Forest" it is called. And over this road many pass, very, very many. And they go jauntily, joyously here—even at night. They do not go as Victor Forrest went,—they do not sense the things that Victor Forrest sensed. If their souls were not deaf, there would be many things for them to hear in "Creaking Forest." At night the trees become an ocean dark and sinister, for it was made up of all the evil in all the hearts of all the mobs that have done to death their creaking victims. It is an ocean arrested at the very edges of the road by a strange spell. But this spell may snap at any second and with that snapping this sea of evil will move, rush, hurl itself heavily and swiftly together from the two sides of the road, engulfing, grinding, crushing, blotting out all in its way. (305–6)

While this forest appears natural to the "very very many" who pass "jauntily" and "joyously" through it, like Muir on his long walk, it is, of course, anything but the sort of morally uncomplicated transparent natural signifier that people like Muir experience. To pass blithely is to have a "soul" both "deaf" to black suffering and "deaf" to white crime, to imagine that nature is not always already historical; it is to have what is arguably a typical white experience of the landscape. Indeed Grimké's vision eliminates the extrahuman reference of nature entirely: by day, every tree in this forest is in fact a carefully transplanted gallows, a materialization of the history of

American lynching, while at night this gruesome monument itself dematerializes into a collation of the evil in the hearts of every lynch mob.[7] The Creaking Forest is a sort of totalization of the naturalized racial trauma this book has been tracing, an ocean of unbearable suffering and limitless brutality that threatens to become mobile. The transparency essential to the metaphors of natural sublimity deployed by white writers from Emerson to Muir, turns decidedly opaque as Grimké imagines nature as a sort of weaponized trauma, suddenly turning on its white makers, engulfing the "position of relative safety" essential to the experience of the white natural sublime. Nature becomes at once the sign of unbearable black suffering and psychopathic white supremacist rage—by day a landscape of gallows, by night, a compendium of all the terrifying emotions of the lynch mob—an awful hybrid that reflects the contradictory (un)natural trauma events like the Turner lynching produced. This is antinature writing with a (literal) vengeance, not only the complete collapse of sublimity into trauma, but a fantasy of turning the long history of naturalized racial degradation and victimization into an apocalyptic assault on the equally long and deeply imbricated history of naturalized white supremacy. Lynching functions in these stories as a toxin, an absolute physical and psychic contamination of the natural well-spring of white self-definition. In the transition from "Blackness" to "Goldie" we see how fragile even the cautious and limited embrace of nature that first emerges in the Harlem Renaissance was.

CANE: DISLOCATION

Grimké's stories underscore, in the most dramatic possible fashion, how traumatic racial violence still irreducibly marked African-American natural experience in the late nineteenth and early twentieth centuries. A hidden danger of a surreal metaphor like the Creaking Forest, however, that straightforwardly (if powerfully) replaces nature with lynching is the ease with which it leads to the inverse of Muir's mistake, making nature simply historical instead of really transcendent. Nature is always both textual and extratextual, and the impossibility of doing full justice to that contradictory duality in our representations does not mean such a duality is not in fact always present. Grimké gestures toward this duality in her insistence on the brother's initial pleasure in nature in "Blackness," but certainly both stories' narratives of discovery, and the larger way "Goldie" rewrites

"Blackness" in a thoroughly traumatic mode, make lynching the Truth of the forest. And in turn, to make the trajectory from "Blackness" to "Goldie" the Truth of the African-American experience of nature in this period would be to adopt a straightforward, if powerful, narrative of rejection while ignoring a much more fraught, contradictory, and painful process of separation and continued alliance. Such a move is particularly tempting to a contemporary critical perspective uninformed by ecocriticism, one that dismisses the value of nature and natural experience and thereby misses the agony of the African-American migration away from a landscape both beloved and terror-filled. If nature simply signifies traumatic history, it is easy enough to celebrate a departure from it to the very real cultural richness and freedom of the city, and to see evocations of a rural African-American pastoral experience as little more than nostalgia, or a green romanticism about suffering.

Such a temptation haunts critics of Jean Toomer's *Cane*, one of the best-known and most studied works of the Harlem Renaissance. Toomer's invocations of the Southern rural landscape certainly threaten to pastoralize Southern black poverty and labor; what Foley calls a "lush lyricism...achieved only through a fetishization of labor processes" (183).[8] Springing from three months he spent living in rural Georgia, teaching school and temporarily escaping from the exhausting duty of providing care for his chronically ill grandparents in Washington, D.C., Toomer writes *Cane* from the perspective of a romantically invested outsider, an urban Northerner looking toward a rural African-American origin at once real, mythological, and dying. Heavily invested in a landscape and a rural lifestyle that he was, nevertheless, profoundly separate from, Toomer was often ready to mourn with a faintly patronizing nostalgia the passing of an agrarian way of life that millions were desperate to leave.[9]

At the same time, however, Toomer's simultaneous engagement with, and separation from, the Southern pastoral landscape uniquely positioned him to see what was being lost in that passing. Indeed, given the traumatic threat of violence and degradation that a connection with the landscape had long posed to African Americans, such a contradictory stance may have been essential to such a recognition. An urban author who did not have Toomer's deep feeling for the landscape might find it understandably easy simply to repudiate a connection with nature that had long been a source of degradation. Likewise, a rural African American of the time was likely already planning an escape north to a better job and greater freedom, a difficult task that would not have been made any easier by an intensely focused appreciation for what he or she lost in doing so. Toomer critically articulates the unstable space between an urban repudiation of the natural and a traumatic immersion in it, a zone of transition between north and south that holds both agony and appreciation in a painful and temporary suspension.[10]

The structure of *Cane* itself reflects this suspension. Toomer divided the work into three sections: the first focuses on sketches of the rural South, often written from the perspective of a Northern observer, that shift abruptly between a lyric pastoral and terrible violence; the second section is set in the urban North, incorporating sudden imaginative transport to a Southern pastoral landscape; the final section, "Kabnis," is Toomer's autobiographical narrative of an aspiring and emotionally unstable African-American writer from Washington D.C., teaching school in rural Georgia and searching for artistic inspiration and "authentic" cultural experience. Every location in *Cane* is predicated on the loss of another location, carries with it the danger, trauma, and compromise necessary for survival. Location is dislocation in *Cane*; African-American culture is, in the book, always strung out between North and South, between urban and rural life, between a safer life in the city purchased at the loss of centuries of African-American rural culture and a profound connection to the land, and an immersion in a black Southern pastoral that continually threatened degradation and white supremacist violence. The inevitability of loss implied by such an impossible choice—an inevitability that depends both on an embrace of the natural and a recognition of the terrible danger in such an embrace—is central to both Toomer's aesthetic project, and the Harlem Renaissance generally.

We can see this painful oscillation in stark clarity in the final section, "Kabnis," Toomer's fictionalized account of the rural Southern experiences that led him to write *Cane*.[11] The section opens with Kabnis killing a chicken that has found its way into his cabin, an all-too-literal and, to him, insulting intrusion of the pastoral. He then stumbles outside to an immensely difficult appreciation of the Georgia countryside at night:

> Kabnis: "Hell of a fine quarters, I've got. Five years ago; look at me now. Earth's child. The earth my mother. God is profligate red-nosed man about town. Bastardy; me. A bastard son has got a right to curse his maker. God…"
> Kabnis is about to shake his fists heavenward. He looks up, and the night's beauty strikes him dumb. He falls to his knees. Sharp stones

cut him through his thin pajamas. The shock sends a shiver over him. Tears mist his eyes. He writhes.

"God Almighty, dear God, dear Jesus, do not torture me with beauty. Take it away. Give me to an ugly world. Ha, ugly. Stinking like unwashed niggers. Dear Jesus, do not chain me to myself and set these hills and valleys, heaving with folk-songs, so close to me that I cannot reach them. There is a radiant beauty in the night that touches and...tortures me. Ugh. Hell. Get up you damn fool. Look around. Whats beautiful there? Hog pens and chicken yards. Dirty red mud. Stinking outhouse. Whats beauty anyway but ugliness if it hurts you? God, he doesn't exist, but nevertheless, He is ugly. Hence, what comes from Him is ugly. Lynchers and business men, and that cockroach Hanby, especially." (85)

Kabnis's description of himself as the bastard product of a union between "the earth [his] mother" and a profligate hard drinking white ("red-nosed") God-about-town, both engages with and eschews the template for sublime white natural experience. To be born from the union of mother Earth and God, to be presented with a night so "radiantly beautiful" it strikes one dumb and brings one writhing and crying to one's knees, would almost inevitably be a climactically wonderful and self-defining experience in a white-centered text, especially a text written in this period. While Kabnis's appreciation of the natural beauty of the scene *is* sublime in its intensity, that appreciation is also—and ultimately—"torture" rather than ecstasy, a temptation to forget about the poverty, violence, and degradation in the "ugly" landscape of "hog pens and chicken yards...dirty red mud...[and] stinking outhouse[s]" to which Kabnis brutally calls his and our attention. The answer to his anguished question, "Whats beauty anyway but ugliness if it hurts you?" is, of course, "N/nature," a locus of sustained contradiction, a word referring to a "radiant beauty" he "cannot reach," and an all-too-historical locus of traumatic racial history.

Kabnis' temporary ecstasy is itself dangerous; however terrible it is to lose an appreciation of nature's beauty (or, in fact, to have it taken), such a loss is not as threatening as forgetting what has been done in its name. And so, again, natural beauty comes to trigger the trauma of lynching rather than sublimity by the end of the scene:

Kabnis has stiffened.... He totters as a man would who for the first time uses artificial limbs. As a completely artificial man would.... His gaze drifts down into the vale, across the swamp, up over the solid dusk bank of pines, and rests, bewildered-like, on the court-house tower. It

is a dull silver in the moonlight. White child that sleeps upon the top of
pines. Kabnis' mind clears. He sees himself yanked beneath that tower.
He sees white minds, with indolent assumption, juggle justice and a
nigger…Somewhere, far off in the straight line of his sight, is Augusta.
Christ, how cut off from everything he is. And hours, hours north, why
not say a lifetime north? Washington sleeps. Its still, peaceful streets,
how desirable they are. Its people whom he always halfway despised.
New York? Impossible. It was a fiction. He had dreamed it. An impotent nostalgia grips him. It becomes intolerable. He forces himself to
narrow to a cabin silhouetted on a knoll about a mile away. Peace.
Negroes within it are content. They farm. They sing. They love. They
sleep. Kabnis wonders if perhaps they can feel him. If perhaps he gives
them bad dreams. Things are so immediate in Georgia. (85–86)

Instead of either a sublime merge with nature, or a degrading and
violent one, Kabnis *separates* from nature—indeed, becomes "a
completely artificial man"—and, in his imagination, flees north to a
sort of lost urban pastoral in the "still, peaceful streets" of Washington
and the "impotent nostalgic fiction" of New York. This longing for
the urban North is itself the inverse of his recoil from nature, both in
the earlier passage and in the profound alienation from rural African-
American culture he feels at the end of this one. New York is an
"impossible dream" for Kabnis, while he himself is the source of bad
dreams for the pastoral culture around him. Completely artificial, cut
off from both city and country, Kabnis is only *tormented* by the
"promise of a soil-soaked beauty" around him, as Lewis, another
Northern character, says later in the book (98). Unable to transform
"these hills and valleys, heaving with folk songs, so close to [him]
that [he] cannot reach them" into art, Kabnis is, in Lewis's words,
"uprooted, thinning out. Suspended a few feet above the soil whose
touch would resurrect him" (98).

   While Kabnis's experiences reflect Toomer's, Toomer went on to
write one of the influential works of the Harlem Renaissance; *Cane*
ends with Kabnis in a sort of incoherent despair, lying in a dirt floor
basement after a drunken night, railing impotently against the legacy of slavery by heaping insults on an aged black man. Kabnis's
suspension "a few feet above the soil" describes a distance at once
too far and too close; he can neither embrace the rural without risk-
ing degradation, nor can he separate from it, at least not without
losing the immense cultural and aesthetic possibilities it possesses.
Toomer's suspension above the natural world of the South is
different, at once much more distant and, as a paradoxical result,
much closer. In the process of writing about living in the rural

South—not in living there—he produced a work with a structure that itself reflected the sort of separation necessary for its creation: an absolute, even elegiac, authorial distance from the land and rural black life that could, at least temporarily, hold Grimké's engulfing trauma at bay with something other than a "white spell." The dangerous and fragile beauty Toomer revealed in that distance and embrace produced *Cane,* and, with it, an even more acute sense of just how much was lost in the necessary disassociation between African Americans and the natural world.

ZORA NEALE HURSTON'S
PARTIAL SOLUTION

Kabnis's agony and frustration at the loss of an articulable bond with nature is a loss central to African-American natural experience in general, a loss on which Toomer builds *Cane. Cane* represents only a temporary and unsustainable moment, however, when "distance and embrace" could be balanced before the sort of collapse we see in the final scenes of Kabnis. When nature comes to function as a trigger for historical trauma, for something unnatural, constructed, and all-too-human, the temptation is inevitably to disassociate from nature altogether, thereby avoiding both the anguish the primary historical trauma nature triggers, and the secondary pain of losing the beauty and solace of the natural world in that triggering. That these two losses are irreconcilably contradictory—one precipitates escape from a nature-based horror; the other grieves at the natural loss inherent in that escape—makes the pain of the experience all the more persistent. Sethe's tortured memories of "boys hanging from most beautiful Sycamores in the world," a "shameless beauty" that "make[s] her want to scream," that I noted at the end of chapter six underscores how this doubled trauma remains agonizing even in contemporary African-American novels like *Beloved.*

Their Eyes Were Watching God, Zora Neale Hurston's 1937 novel set in an all-black community in rural Florida, asks perhaps a harder, and certainly more dangerous question: what sort of African-American art might spring from an alliance with the Southern landscape? Is there an alternative to Kabnis's misery and terror, or an outside to the raft of demeaning black rural stereotypes, from slavery to Uncle Remus to the Black Beast? Certainly some of her critics have not thought so, or at least not thought that she found such an alternative. Hurston's seeming embrace of Southern rural black folk culture in part led contemporaries like Richard Wright to dismiss her prose as "facile sensuality.... that

[only] manages to catch the psychological movements of the Negro folk-mind in their pure simplicity," a "sensory sweep" that "carries no theme, no message, no thought," and has been sharply questioned by present-day critics like Hazel Carby, who views Hurston's engagement with nature as largely childhood nostalgia and an invitation to racial and gender essentialism.[12] Celebrations of Hurston's novel are far more common, though; at least since its rediscovery in the 1970s, the work has drawn widespread critical praise for its portrayal of a strong female character coming to voice and claiming her independence and sexuality.[13] Debates have raged subsequently about the extent to which Janie's triumph might serve as a model for less advantaged black women and how much that triumph naturalizes class and sexual preference, and about Hurston's contradictory stance as an anthropologist taking notes on her own community.

As important as this critical dialogue has been, however, another vital reading emerges by viewing the novel in the context of the historical intersection of race and nature. While it is certainly the case that the novel's natural setting functions symbolically—the pear tree orgasm is a metaphor for Janie's emergent sexuality, the mule stands for the position of black women, the rabid dog that bites Tea Cake serves as a metaphor for his violence and Janie's own repressed rage, the hurricane is anything and everything, except for a hurricane, and so forth— Hurston's pervasive engagement with nature in the novel should also be considered on its own terms, as an important intervention on the long, largely unhappy, historical intersections between nature and race. Hurston's rural Southern upbringing gave her a profound appreciation for the natural world and the black folk culture that lived close to it. At the same time, the extensive anthropological training she received at Columbia University under Frank Boas produced a sort of safe observational distance from an association with the landscape, the contradictory mix of alliance and leave-taking that we have seen at the heart of other Harlem Renaissance nature writing and as a fundamental structure of natural sublime experience generally.[14]

It is no accident, then, that Hurston frames Janie's autobiography with two moments in which the border between her subjectivity and the natural world is in the sort of dynamic flux characteristic of sublimity and trauma: first, her ecstasy under the pear tree that marks the beginning of her quest for erotic and emotional freedom and her first subjection to the trauma of domesticated animalization that afflicts Nanny; and second, the tremendous hurricane at the end of the novel that destroys the black pastoral community at Lake Okeechobee and results in Tea Cake's deadly case of rabies. Both incidents represent moments when the naturalization of race is most traumatically evident *and* when such racial definitions are radically unsettled; experiences, as Sharon Davie says "which one cannot pin down, fix, with rational thought, that which one can name only to unname, or to name again, or to fail at naming, or to succeed through admitting failure" (447). Put another way, such moments reveal both the radical promise of the natural sublime and the terrible danger of it falling into trauma, a duality at the center of this book's inquiry, and one that structures Hurston's work in ways critics have yet to explore fully. Viewed through this lens, Hurston's engagement with nature is not simply a retreat from critical politics into a sham folk authenticity, but the staging of a high-stakes confrontation between an extrahuman natural Other and the most historically degrading naturalized stereotypes of African Americans. Such a confrontation, like nature generally, at once evokes the origin of some of the ugliest racial politics, and the possibility of an Outside to those politics. This is the sort of intersection—and the sort of author—to which eco-criticism must start paying attention if it genuinely wants to make the love of nature an integral part of a broader radical critique. The road to that Outside goes through the Creaking Forest; Hurston knows this, and *Their Eyes Were Watching God* illustrates just how danger-ous, and potentially redeeming, a walk on that road can be.

The pear tree scene that marks the turn in the novel from Janie's introductory framing conversation with Pheoby to the narrative's third-person omniscient voice conjoins an ecstatic moment of union with nature that puts John Muir to shame, and, immediately follow-ing, the incarnation of Nanny's long traumatized discourse conflat-ing mules and black women in Janie's forced marriage to Logan Killicks. First, consider the ecstatic moment Janie says her "conscious life" "commenced":

> It was a spring afternoon in West Florida. Janie had spent most of the day under a blossoming pear tree in the back-yard.... It had called her to come and gaze on a mystery. From barren brown stems to glistening leaf-buds; from the leaf-buds to snowy virginity of bloom. It stirred her tremendously. How? Why? It was like a flute song forgotten in another existence and remembered again. What? How? Why? The singing she heard that had nothing to do with her ears. The rose of the world was breathing out smell. It followed her through all her waking moments and caressed her in her sleep. It connected itself with other vaguely felt matters that had struck her outside observation and buried themselves in her flesh. Now they emerged and quested about her consciousness.

> She was stretched on her back beneath the pear tree soaking in the alto chant of the visiting bees, the gold of the sun and the panting breath of the breeze when the inaudible voice of it all came to her. She saw a dust-bearing bee sink into the sanctum of a bloom; the thousand sister-calyxes arch to meet the love embrace and the ecstatic shiver of the tree from root to tiniest branch creaming in every blossom and frothing with delight. So this was a marriage! She had been summoned to behold a revelation. Then Janie felt a pain remorseless sweet that left her limp and languid.
>
> After a while she got up from where she was and went over the little garden field entire. She was seeking confirmation of the voice and vision, and everywhere she found and acknowledged answers. A personal answer for all other creations except herself. She felt an answer seeking her, but where? When? How?... Oh to be a pear tree—*any* tree in bloom! With kissing bees singing of the beginning of the world! She was sixteen. She had glossy leaves and bursting buds and she wanted to struggle with life but it seemed to elude her. Where were the singing bees for her? Nothing on the place nor in her grand-ma's house answered her. She searched as much of the world as she could.... [l]ooking, waiting, breathing short with impatience. Waiting for the world to be made. (10–11)

Something significant is lost if we read this scene as simply encoding Janie's sexual awakening, preparing the way for her first kiss with Johnny Taylor. Rather than the landscape only reflecting Janie, in this passage she also comes to reflect it; this is erotic nature writing as much as (or more than) it is naturalized eroticism. Janie's sexuality is part of the spring landscape: it emerges from her intimate observation of budding and pollination, a natural process external to her, but one with which she aligns her own "vaguely felt matters...buried...in her flesh." Her orgasm in the second paragraph is an aftershock of the union of bee and tree, a moment of alliance rather than simply projection.[15] The "revelation" that "she had been summoned to behold," is not only her own desire writ large; indeed, her frustration in the final paragraph stems from an intensely felt separation between the sexual fecundity of the natural world and her own objectless desire, a frustration springing from a longing to participate in the larger natural "marriage" she sees all around her, to "be a pear tree—*any* tree in bloom," to receive "a personal answer" like "all other creations."

But of course she cannot be a pear tree, and the landscape will not answer, but remains always just outside of the text, "a mystery," "a flute song forgotten in another existence and remembered again," "sing-ing...that had nothing to do with her ears," the "inaudible voice of it all."[16] Janie's frustration is built into the natural sublime, an intensely meaningful moment of simultaneous connection and alienation, where expression fails in the very gesture that makes it imperative.[17] That such a frustration is aligned with and readily resolved by a transformation into the libidinal—in this case in the form of Johnny Taylor—does not mean it was simply that from the start, that all the blossoms and uncertainty are just so much decoration around the facticity of teenage lust, as Nanny so reductively and destructively understands the scene. What is lost in such an assertion is not only the beauty and energy of the natural scene that Janie perceives so passionately, but the representational lacuna inherent in natural sublime experience, a sudden, eruptive, failure of language in which everything is temporarily called into radical question. That such eruptions resolve in ways that often produce essentialized knowledge does not mean that such conclusions are inherent in the eruptive moment itself.

At the same time, it is revealing to see which ideological first responders rush in to make sense of such gaps in representation. Nanny's response to Janie's sublimity imposes a familiar historical template, one that renders instability between an African-American subject and the natural world dangerous and degrading. Nanny (who is tellingly described as "look[ing] like the standing roots of some old tree that had been torn away by storm" [13]), replaces Janie's sublime marriage of bee and blossom with the naturalized trauma at the heart of her slave experience: "[D]e white man throw down the de load and tell de nigger man tuh pick it up. He pick it up because he have to, but he don't tote it. He hand it to his womenfolks. De nigger woman is de mule uh de world so fur as Ah can see" (14). Here gendered oppression and slavery's agricultural metaphors for subjectivity supplant Janie's romantic vision. When Nanny tells Janie her life history subsequently, a similar conceit conflating African-American subjectivity with a domestic animal is repeatedly invoked: "You know, honey, us colored folks is branches without roots and that makes things come round in queer ways.... Ah was born back due in slavery so it wasn't for me to fulfill my dreams of whut a woman oughta be and to do. Dat's one of de hold-backs of slavery.... Ah didn't want to be used for a work-ox and a brood-sow and Ah didn't want mah daughter used dat way neither" (16).

For Nanny, Janie's moment of eroticized natural sublimity is reducible to her burgeoning sexual desire, a desire that in turn inevitably threatens to degrade her to the status of a mule. In a well-meaning but terribly misguided universalizing of her own traumatic history, Nanny subsequently forces Janie to marry Logan Killicks, a union that ironically threatens to produce in Janie the very animal status

Nanny fears. Killicks, a farmer Janie insults as having "toe-nails [that] look lak mule foots" (24), tries to force Janie to tote her own cooking wood and to haul manure, and puts her to work plowing behind a new mule "all gentled up so even uh woman kin handle 'im" (27). The figure of the human/mule hybrid haunts the next several chapters, embodying the naturalized trauma of slavery in a way that Hurston clearly means her novel to address. When her second husband, Joe Starks, buys and "frees" Matt Bonner's abused, fiercely stubborn, perpetually starving mule (the subject of endless amusing stories on the front porch of the store), Janie's gratitude is poignant in its excess, an excess that reveals her too-deeply felt connection to the animal:

> Jody, dat waz uh mighty fine thing fuh you tuh do. 'Tain't everybody would have thought of it, 'cause it ain't no everyday thought. Freein' dat mule makes uh mighty big man outa you. Something like George Washington and Lincoln. Abraham Lincoln, he had de whole United States tuh rule so he freed de Negroes. You got uh town so you freed uh mule. You have tuh have power tuh free things and dat makes you lak a king uh something. (58)

This moment of identification with the mule is also the first moment when Janie comes to voice, the first moment she speaks at length in the store; a member of the crowd immediately comments "Yo' wife is uh born orator, Starks. Us never knowed dat befo'. She put jus' de right words tuh our thoughts" (58). The "free-mule," as it is called subsequently, represents, then, both the terrible legacy of slavery's natural commodification and the end of Janie's association with speechless and degraded animality. Hence the surreal moment at the end of the chapter, when the mule's death and funeral is presided over by talking buzzards, an anthropomorphized natural farewell to a ter-rible history—what Kathleen Davies calls "a stunning recuperation of the 'inaudible voice,' giving Nature the last laugh" (152)—and hence Joe's decline and death soon afterward. In the first half of the novel, then, Janie's pear tree sublimity falls into the trauma of slavery's essential conceit, a traumatic repetition of a much older and wide-spread pattern in the relation of African Americans to the natural world. Hurston consciously evokes this traumatic natural pattern, and with the death of the mule and Joe Starks, she at least partially exorcises it, making room for Janie's embrace, in every sense, of the pastoral in the figure of Tea Cake.

In both the introduction and conclusion of the novel Hurston offers a portrait of an untraumatized relation between African-American subjects and the natural environment, a Garden she in turn uses to stage the primary traumatic experiences that historically emerged from that relation. Janie's involvement with Tea Cake in the latter part of the novel, and her life on the muck as part of an almost idyllic African-American agrarian community, trades the individual ecstasy of the pear tree for an extended portrait of an initially unalienated African-American pastoral. This pastoral in turn provides a stage for confronting the terrible postbellum development of slavery's animalizing conceit, the white supremacist transformation of the domesticated pastoral animal/slave into the "savage" and violently hypersexual Black Beast discussed at greater length in chapter six.

At first, Janie's life on the muck is idyllic. The land itself is preternaturally fertile:

> To Janie's strange eyes, everything in the Everglades was big and new. Big Lake Okechobee, big beans, big cane, big weeds, big everything. Weeds that did well to grow waist high up the state were eight and often ten feet tall down there. Ground so rich that everything went wild. Volunteer cane just taking the place. Dirt roads so rich and black that a half a mile of it would have fertilized a Kansas wheat field. Wild cane on either side of the road hiding the rest of the world. People wild too. (129)

The same fecundity of the land that makes crops grow to two and three times their normal height produces a similar fecundity in the folk culture and economy that is linked to it. As Tea Cake promises Janie, "Folks don't do nothin' down dere but make money and fun and foolishness" (128), a claim Hurston confirms in her third-person romantic encomium to muck culture: "Blues made and used right on the spot. Dancing, fighting, singing, crying, laughing, winning and losing love every hour. Work all day for money, fight all night for love. The rich black earth clinging to bodies and biting the skin like ants" (131). Transnational culture flowers, the music is terrific, life is passionate, money comes (relatively) easy, Janie's voice is celebrated, she has great sex; folk life on the muck is Arcadian. Janie even becomes an accomplished hunter, indeed a sort of black female update on Natty Bumpo: "She got to the place she could shoot a hawk out of a pine tree and not tear him up. Shoot his head off. She got to be a better shot than Tea Cake. They'd go out any late afternoon and come back loaded down with game" (131).

In a different novel—a more conventional white one—the tremendous hurricane that blows in and disrupts the pastoral community would perform the iconic function of the natural sublime, providing the sort of climactic experience that would conclusively demonstrate Tea Cake and Janie's love and fortitude. If Hurston had done this, it would be (even) more appropriate to criticize her for an uncritical and essentializing reification of black rural culture as the privileged mark of racial authenticity. In such a conventional novel, Tea Cake and Janie would have survived the hurricane through a combination of luck, bravery, and skill, and returned, sadder, wiser, and married, to rebuild their pastoral community on the muck with the other intrepid survivors. But this is not what happens, of course, in part because Hurston is so keenly aware of the troubled history of African Americans and the natural world.[18]

The proper response to Hurston's storm in fact is practical and humble—flight—rather than a stereotypically white and masculine bravado. Instead of toughing it out, Hurston makes it very clear that Tea Cake should follow the example of the Native Americans and the Bahamains and run away. He fails to do this, however, precisely because he has internalized the very white supremacist attitudes that are themselves aligned with the will to environmental dominance:

> "De Indians gahn east, man, It's dangerous."
>
> "Dey don't always know. Indians don't know much uh nothin', tuh tell de truth. Else dey'd own dis country still. De white folks ain't gone nowhere. Dey oughta know if it's dangerous. You better stay heah, man. Big jumpin' dance tuhnight right heah, when it fair off." (156)

Tea Cake's foolishness here is not just his own, but a blind obedience to a similar conflation of racial and environmental dominance on the part of early European settlers discussed in the second chapter. As Curren comments, "In touch with nature and aware of its awesome power for both creation and destruction, the tribal lore of the Indians and Bahamians is actually more rational than white, Western thought, since the latter is lettered with illogical racial prejudices and a magical belief that money and technology can conquer natural forces" (19).

Tea Cake's argument—that white might makes whites right about the weather, or the "Indians" would still own America—is no less dangerous for being ludicrous. Indeed, his confidence that white knowledge of, and dominance over, nature is so complete it leads to a curiously anticlimactic passivity in the face of the storm. Tea Cake, Janie, and a friend named "Motor Boat"— the name surely a sublime-deflating pun on Hurston's part—play dice in their cabin until the storm picks up and the waters rise, whereupon they do nothing but helplessly stare at the cabin door, hoping it is God's will (their eyes are watching Him) that they survive:

> [T]he monster began to roll in his bed. Began to roll and complain like a peevish world on a grumble. The folks in the quarters and the people in the big houses further around the shore heard the big lake and wondered. The people felt uncomfortable but safe because there was the seawalls to chain the senseless monster in his bed. The folks let the people do the thinking. If the castles thought themselves secure, the cabins needn't worry. Their decision was already made as always. Chink up your cracks, shiver in your wet beds and wait on the mercy of the Lord. The bossman might have the thing stopped before morning anyway....
>
> A big burst of thunder and lightning that trampled over the roof of the house. So Tea Cake and Motor stopped playing. Motor looked up in his angel-looking way and said, "Big Massa draw him chair upstairs."
>
> "Ah'm glad y'all stop dat crap-shootin' even if it wasn't for money," Janie said. "Ole Massa is doin' *His* work now. Us oughta keep quiet."
>
> They huddled closer and stared at the door. They just didn't use another part of their bodies, and they didn't look at anything but the door. The time was past for asking the white folks what to look for through that door. Six eyes were questioning *God*.
>
> Through the screaming wind they heard things crashing and things hurtling and dashing with unbelievable velocity. A baby rabbit, terror ridden, squirmed through a hole in the floor and squatted off there in the shadows against the wall, seeming to know that nobody wanted its flesh at such a time. And the lake got madder and madder with only its dikes between them and him. (158–59)

No action-packed rescue, no contending with wind and wave, just three people and one baby rabbit in a cabin, looking fearfully at a door, wondering what God has in store for them. Hurston here substitutes a curiously passive portrayal of her characters—in love, in a hurricane, at the end of the novel, after all—for the more typical heroic model, a curious and deliberate refusal to engage the sublime template. Importantly, this passivity is directly connected to the same internalized white supremacy that led Tea Cake to his foolish decision to ignore the warnings of the Native Americans and Bahamians and ride out the storm.[19] The "folks" falsely believe the natural sublime is under white control—the "castles" are safe so the cabins must be, the "bossman might have the thing stopped before morning,"—and that accordingly their only role in the face of natural force is resignation: "the folks let the people do the thinking.... Their decision was already made as always. Chink up your cracks, shiver in your wet beds and wait on the mercy of the Lord." Fate itself becomes coextensive with a white nature/God, an "Ole Massa" upstairs, before whom "folks" "oughta keep quiet." Hurston's sublime nature, and the possibility of heroic struggle with it, is subsumed by the historical conflation of natural mastery and white supremacy.

When Janie, Tea Cake, and Motor Boat are forced to flee the cabin by the rising waters, Hurston continues to pique and deflate her reader's expectations for character-defining, novel-ending heroics. Her description of the storm itself certainly presents the natural sublime adversary in anthropomorphized fury: "The monstropolous beast had left his bed. The two hundred miles an hour wind had loosed his chains. He seized hold of his dikes and ran forward until he met the quarters; uprooted them like grass and rushed on after his supposed-to-be conquerors, rolling the dikes, rolling the houses, rolling the people in the houses along with other timbers. The sea was walking the earth with a heavy heel" (161–62). Despite the possibility for dramatic confrontation, Hurston continues to eschew a climactic battle. After taking shelter in another house on higher ground, Tea Cake again makes a bad decision, this time to leave Motor Boat behind (!) and swim for it. (And as it turns out, Motor Boat sleeps safely through the rest of the storm, in the top floor bedroom of the floating house). Swimming through the flood waters and assisting Janie utterly exhausts Tea Cake. As a result, at the start of the novel's final scene of man-against-nature sublime confrontation, Tea Cake is asleep on the ground and Janie is sheltering him from the storm, first with a piece of roof. Hurston once again deflates the reader's expectations; instead of stereotypical male heroism in the face of natural disaster, Hurston gives us a realistic and tender scene: an exhausted man asleep on the ground who doesn't possess an infallible knowledge of the natural world, and a woman who is not simply helpless, but who also does not quite know what she is doing in the storm.

Hurston's repeated juxtaposition of an anthropomorphized sublime storm—the monstropolous beast—and realistic characters who don't engage in the (white) narratives of combat and self-definition such a storm invites, reaches its disastrous climax when Janie is blown into the water. In the course of rescuing her from a rabid dog who is riding atop the cow she is using as a life preserver, Hurston forces Tea Cake into the narrative of combat and self-definition with nature that so often characterizes the sublime:

> Janie achieved the tail of the cow and lifted her head up along the cow's rump, as far as she could above water... The dog stood up and

growled like a lion, stiff-standing hackles, stiff muscles, teeth uncovered as he lashed up his fury for the charge. Tea Cake split the water like an otter, opening his knife as he dived. The dog raced down the backbone of the cow to the attack, and Janie screamed and slipped far back on the tail of the cow, just out of reach of the dog's angry jaws. He wanted to plunge in after her but dreaded the water, somehow. Tea Cake rose out of the water at the cow's rump and seized the dog by the neck. But he was a powerful dog and Tea Cake was over-tired. So he didn't kill the dog with one stroke as he had intended. But the dog couldn't free himself either. They fought and somehow he managed to bite Tea Cake high up on his cheek-bone once. Then Tea Cake finished him and sent him to the bottom to stay there. The cow relieved of a great weight was landing on the fill with Janie before Tea Cake stroked in and crawled weakly upon the fill again.

    Janie began to fuss around his face where the dog had bitten him but he said it didn't amount to anything.... He flopped to the edge of the fill as if the storm wasn't going on at all. "Lemme rest awhile, then us got tuh make it on intuh town somehow." (166)

The final moment of conflict involving Janie, Tea Cake, a cow, and a rabid dog replays the collapse of sublimity into trauma we have seen played out relentlessly in representations of African-American relations to the natural world. Without taking away from the courage and prowess Tea Cake displays here, it hardly represents a moment of unambiguous triumph. Indeed, there is a sort of surreal and undignified quality to the initial scene: Janie's head is pressed against the "rump" of a frantically swimming cow who is, in turn, being ridden by a huge dog. Tea Cake struggles with the dog atop the cow, finally killing it and rescuing Janie—at the cost of being bitten by a visibly symptomatic rabid dog—and then after immediately and mistakenly discounting the bite's danger, lies back down on the ground in the middle of a hurricane, "as if the storm wasn't going on at all." This is heroism, but one rendered all-too-realistic, hardly the moment when some masculine self leaves behind the dross of civilization to be reforged in the smithy of the natural sublime. Indeed, the bleak irony of how this scene falls short of the expectations created by sublime confrontations with nature is palpable in Tea Cake's subsequent conversation with Janie:

    "You was trice noble tuh save me from dat dawg. Tea Cake, Ah don't speck you seen his eyes lak Ah did. He didn't aim tuh jus' bite me, Tea Cake. He aimed tuh kill me stone dead. Ah'm never tuh furgit dem eyes. He wuzn't nothin' all over but pure hate. Wonder where he come from?"

"Yeah, Ah did see 'im too. It wuz frightenin'. Ah didn't mean tuh take his hate neither. He had tuh die uh me one. Mah switch blade said it wuz him."

"Po' me, he'd tore me tuh pieces, if it wuzn't fuh you, honey."

"You don't have tuh say, if it wazn't fuh me, baby, cause Ah'm *heah*, and then Ah want yuh to know it's uh man heah." (167)

There will not be "uh man heah" for long, however, as the dog's bite infects Tea Cake with rabies. But the dog's still undiagnosed disease here manifests in perhaps a truer form than when explained and contained as a labeled pathogen. What is terrible about rabies, of course, is not simply its universal fatality in its later stages of development, but its very particular effect on its sufferers: human and animal alike are transformed into unreasoning, savage, and uncontrollably violent beasts whose only urge is to attack and infect others. Rabies is a multiply invested representation, not just the incarnation of the sublime natural other that Tea Cake proves his manhood by defeating, but symbol of something utterly terrible— "nothin' all over but pure hate,"—a power "frightenin' " even to the generally imperturbable Tea Cake. Viewed in the context of the longstanding traumatic association between African Americans and the natural world, a context Hurston's whole novel has asked us to consider, the dog's bite infects Tea Cake not only with rabies, but, I want to argue, with the terrible white supremacist history that transformed black men into the Black Beast discussed at length in chapter six.[20]

By the end of the novel, Tea Cake becomes, in fact, that bestial figure, an alchemical transformation catalyzed by an eruptive moment of contact with the natural other.[21] The hero becomes an animal and the natural sublime falls once again, terribly and intimately, from a moment of individual self-definition into a larger traumatic history:

> " 'Bout the only think you can do, Janie, is to put him in the County Hospital where they can tie him down and look after him."
>
> "But he don't like no hospital at all. He'd think Ah wuz tired uh doin' fuh 'im, when God knows Ah ain't. Ah can't stand de idea us tyin' Tea Cake lak he wuz ah mad dawg."
>
> "It almost amounts to dat, Janie. He's got almost no chance to pull through and he's liable to bite somebody else, specially you, and then you'll be in the same fix he's in. It's mighty bad." (177)

The doctor's warning to Janie confirms how the disease has itself changed Tea Cake into what "almost amounts" to a "mad dawg" who needs to be tied up. This stress on how the beast's identity is irrevocably supplanting Tea Cake's own comes repeatedly in the novel's close:

> Tea Cake was lying with his eyes closed and Janie hoped he was asleep. He wasn't. A great fear had took hold of him. What was this thing that set his brains afire and grabbed at his throat with iron fingers? Where did it come from and why did it hang around him? (178)

> Janie fooled around outside awhile to try and think it wasn't so. If she didn't see the sickness in his face she could imagine it wasn't really happening. Well, she thought, that big old dawg with the hatred in his eyes had killed her after all. She wished she had slipped off that cowtail and drowned then and there and been done. (178)

> Tea Cake had two bad attacks that night. Janie saw a changing look come in his face. Tea Cake was gone. Something else was looking out of his face. (181)

> He gave her a look full of blank ferocity and gurgled in this throat. She saw him sitting up in bed and moving about so that he could watch her every move. And she was beginning to feel fear of this strange thing in Tea Cake's body. (182)

Hurston takes pains to distinguish the mad from the "real" Tea Cake. There are two identities here; one the loving, flawed, brave individual the novel has developed for a hundred some pages; the other a reductive categorical stereotype that reduced all black men to savage animals. That grotesque reduction—"pure hate"—rewrites Tea Cake in its image, engrafts itself onto, or into, Tea Cake's body, forcing him to signify doubly. Hurston clearly demonstrates the interlinkage between sublimity and trauma here; rather than the sublime's subsumption of the natural other as a sign of the empowered individual, we get trauma's collapse of the subject into that natural other, a return of the horrific postbellum identification of blackness and the bestial that fueled lynch mobs for decades.

Reading the novel in this historical context makes its ending much less conclusively triumphant than it might be otherwise. Janie's shooting of Tea Cake manifests the intractability of the traumatic history triggered by moments of intimate contact with the natural world, from the pear tree's ecstasy paired with the legacy of slavery's animalized degradation, to the sublime's fall into the postbellum history of the bestialization of blackness and the rise of lynching. There is nothing else for her to do to end the cycle but shoot Tea Cake, to end trauma's transmission by killing another innocent victim of it. As she says in her own defense in court:

> She tried to make them see how terrible it was that things were fixed so that Tea Cake couldn't come back to himself until he had got rid of that mad dog that was in him and he couldn't get rid of the dog and live. He had to die to get rid of the dog. But she hadn't wanted to kill him. A man is up against a hard game when he must die to beat it. (187)

While Janie is exonerated by the white jury, and eventually by her own people as well, the historical trauma Hurston evokes is hardly containable by a single "not guilty" verdict. Despite the temptation to read the end of the novel as celebrating Janie's hard-fought freedom and independence, such readings overlook the fact that Tea Cake bites Janie before he dies:[22]

> The pistol and the rifle rang out almost together. The pistol just enough after the rifle to seem its echo. Tea Cake crumpled as his bullet buried itself in the joist over Janie's head. Janie saw the look on his face and leaped forward as he crashed forward in her arms. She was trying to cover him as he closed his teeth in the flesh of her forearm. They came down heavily like that. Janie struggled to a sitting position and pried the dead Tea Cake's teeth from her arm. (184)

As Robert Haas points out, according to the medical science of the day, Tea Cake's bite put Janie at significant risk for rabies, an infection that often would not manifest itself for weeks, months, or years, an incubation period that could extend well after the novel's end. (And this is confirmed by the doctor's own warning to Janie earlier in the book: "he's liable to bite somebody else, specially you, and then you'll be in the same fix he's in.") Hurston means to leave open the very real possibility that despite the important measure of independence and self-possession that Janie achieves at the end of the novel, she will herself go mad and die, that her voice and independence will be swept away and that she will herself incarnate the seemingly endless violence and animalized trauma that indelibly marks the history of African-American natural experience. That such an ending would feel horrible, forced, unnatural, brutal—as pointless and familiar as Tea Cake's—might well be Hurston's point. Certainly it is a fine argument for moving to the city.

Coda: Prospects for an
Antiracist Ecological Sublime

To call attention to the specific historical ways that sublime experience functioned in the formation of race is not the same as declaring such a reading exhaustive. It would be more than merely reductive to dismiss the natural sublime or wilderness experience as simply a white cover-up. To swing from an uncritical white masculinist Romanticism, to a reflexive sort of demystification of the sublime that insists on a total retextualization of nature helps neither racial politics nor the planet. Nor does it begin to do justice to the fundamentally contradictory sorts of experiences and possibilities named by the sublime. Within ecocriticism, such a binary oscillation between true belief and demystification replicates the sort of theoretical tail-chasing we see in the seemingly endless debates over whether nature is really a transcendent Real or just another ideological construction, and what the right ratio between construction and transcendence is, and how to tell the difference, and so forth.

As I have argued throughout this book, the word "nature" always has at least two simultaneous referents: a sub-textual material Other at once indescribable, real, and constitutive of human identity in the most physically fundamental way, and a massive ideological/linguistic fantasy about that sub-textual real. The natural sublime might be defined as a transition between the two referents, as the subject moves from a radically destabilizing sense of a world utterly external to human language—an experience that, at least potentially, relativizes both subject and culture—to the inverse of that radical destabilization in which subject and culture are reconstituted as transcendent, a process itself then hidden under the veil of the natural. The thrill of the sublime is, at least in part, the transition from a radical destabilization of human textuality to a radical naturalization of it, all while providing a natural(ized) origin for the in-fact newly instantiated subject. The attempt to deploy the destabilizing experience of an extratextual world in the service of an environmental politics is, almost inevitably, to couple the two senses of "nature" in ways that risk rendering one's individual experience and politics transcendent. And however tempting such a coupling is, most especially after a breathtaking hike in the Sierras, it is intellectually confused, an illegitimate conclusion, a power-grab. Nature and nature are not the same thing, despite the pleasures of speaking ex cathedra, the joy of "finding" oneself a universal subject. To represent the extratextual is always already the act of crossing between the two referents of nature.

This fact does not necessitate an abandonment of the natural sublime, however, though it does call on subsequent descriptions to be explicitly self-conscious about the limits of representation, and explicitly aware of how enmeshed those experiences and those representations are in the observing subject's context of historical, political, and racial privilege. Otherwise, like Muir in *A 1,000 Mile Walk to the Gulf*, we think we've left "it" all behind, when, in fact, we've hidden "it" in plain sight, indeed, made "it" a transcendent principle of self and land. Certainly privileged white people should be aware of the historical role the experience of the natural sublime has played in naturalizing white privilege. And certainly white ecocriticism needs to continue to move toward a more deeply historicized understanding of how natural experience has not only been defined by, but has itself defined, whiteness. Without such a consciousness, whiteness will just keep finding and reifying its invisible and pervasive power on the mountaintop, will keep missing the inevitable moment when Nature becomes nature, when Nature becomes whiteness.

At the same time, the slowly increasing diversity of the environmental movement, the work of writers like Toni Morrison and critics like Robert Bullard and James Cone, the recovery of Black frontier experience by Michael Johnson and others, and even the recent shift in African American settlement patterns from north to south, indicates that the long history of naturalized trauma may not be as virulent as it was. Historically and culturally, we may have arrived at a point of relative safety, a moment where the experience of the natural sublime might be successfully deployed against the very racial trauma it triggers. The eruptive experience of uncertainty and connection at the heart of the natural sublime, the genuine contact with something outside of history and human textuality, a natural Other of which we are all irrevocably a part, certainly opens up the possibility of reimagining history, race, embodiment, and everything else, if only for a moment. Despite the inevitable fall into textuality, the sublime still names a moment of contact with the radically extratextual Nature, still points to a something—an everything, indeed—outside our text. The brief but total suspension of human context that intense natural experience can provide should be immensely useful to any effort to think outside the terrible history that forms us, that we so often helplessly repeat. Indeed, if such moments of emptiness, possibility, and connection are not a vital part of our politics, then we really have given up.

NOTES

1 INTRODUCTION: THE SUBLIME AND THE TRAUMATIC

1. For more on the history of this foundational event for the environmental justice movement, see Pulido's invaluable analysis and Cole, as well as Hofrichter (especially Faber and Bullard), Shrader-Frechette, and Rhodes.

2. Leo Marx hinted at this division twenty years ago in his contribution to Bercovitch and Jehlen's important collection *Ideology and Classic American Literature*. Marx's essay ends by noting how the political possibilities of a natural allegiance are curtailed by the racial and class limitations of the nature's appeal: "To provide the basis for an effective ideology, in other words, adherents of pastoralism would have to form alliances with the hitherto disadvantaged carriers of emergent values—those for whom 'the recovery of the natural' as yet has, in itself, little or no appeal" (66).

3. See, for example, Cronon's *Uncommon Ground* (especially Cronon, "Trouble"), Ross, Bennett's *Nature of Cities*, Armbruster, Buell's *Endangered World*, and Mazel for recent critiques of wilderness-focused ecocriticism. Guha offers an explicitly "third world critique."

4. Moore, et al. first directed me to this quote (42). See Stuart Hall for the original citation.

5. Qtd. in Solnit, 220. Moore, et al. initially brought Solnit's book and this quotation to my attention; see, fn 63 to p. 55. Note that in fact Muir knew well the history of the spot, providing a portrait of the surrender quite sympathetic to Tenaya and the Miwoks in his *My First Summer in the Sierras*. See especially 115. What is striking is how easily the historical knowledge Muir has seems to give way to a fantasy about Yosemite being unmediated, unpopulated, Natural, ahistorical, his place. It is almost uncanny how it does, in fact, seem to Muir like no one has ever been there, how hard that belief in an untouched nature presses even in the face of his historical knowledge of an all-too-human history of slaughter and dispossession.

6. The literature on the history of native genocide(s) is far too extensive to note exhaustively here and is, regardless, outside the scope of this book. See, though, Adamson and Dreese for recent work on ecocriticism and Native American literature and culture. Ecofeminism also is too rich and diverse a critical movement to document completely; however, Gaard's collections, Murphy, Devine, Diamond, Mies, Norwood, Plant (especially

King), Plumwood, Shiva, and both Haraway books (but especially, for me, *Simians, Cyborgs, and Women*), are certainly all important contributions. Kolodny's works on the pastoral gendering of the American landscape, and on women and the frontier deservedly remain influential.

7. For the whiteness of the wilderness, see especially Cronon's "Trouble," DeLuca, Braun, Evelyn White's account, and the Reed and Evans articles in Adamson. Again, the risk of focusing on whiteness is that it can exclude other ways the wilderness is reserved for particular groups—not just for white people in general, but whites who are also rich and male in particular. But the correlation of those additional components does not mean, necessarily, that whiteness does not play its own role. I have not been able to find hard demographic data on wilderness usage broken down by gender, class, and race. Anecdotal evidence certainly suggests the predominance of white people—male and female, well and poorly equipped—on the hiking trail and at the campground, however, and the relative scarcity of black people. This study suggests some of the historical reasons behind that pattern, in addition to inequalities in wealth and leisure time, or gendered difference.

8. Several recent collections of ecocritical work have articles engaging African-American perspectives (though almost exclusively focused on twentieth-century and contemporary writers). See Mayer's collection, especially Christine Gerhardt and Barbara Cook's essays on the slave narrative. Ingram's recent collection, especially Martin's essay, is also important for my purposes. In Armbruster, see Bennett on the slave "anti-pastoral," Dodd's essay on Michael S. Harper, and Wallace and Armbruster on *Beloved*. White's engaging personal account is in Jordan and Hepworth. See also hooks and Alice Walker in Barnhill, Cone, and the Moore collection, especially the Introduction, and the essays by Gilroy, Braun, and Di Chiro. Gerhardt's "Greening" provides a useful summary, and connects ecocriticism, race, and postcolonial theory in ways that should initiate an important discussion. Hicks's essay calls for "an ecocriticism of color" and offers a valuable ecocritical reading of duBois, Richard Wright, and Booker T. Washington. Wendel Berry's *The Hidden Wound*, written in 1970 when he was thirty-four, represents an early, earnest, flawed, and sincere attempt to address both his racially divided childhood and to speculate on the larger ecological consequences of that division. See Debian for a critique. Adamson, Stein, and Evans's *Environmental Justice Reader*, is perhaps the best place to start an inquiry into environmental justice ecocriticism.

Myers's *Converging Stories* focuses more directly on the history of the relation between racism and natural experience in America. He argues that what he calls "ecocentricity"—a view that sees the human as profoundly interconnected to and responsible for the nonhuman natural—is "the basis for both ecological sustainability and social justice" (10). Conversely, Myers argues that to view humans as separate from and dominant over nature is part of the same view that constructs whiteness as separate from and dominant over people of color: "Euroamerican racism and alienation from nature derive from the same source and result in the joint and interlocking domination of people of color and the natural world" (15).

While I admire much of Myers's work, my approach is in many ways the inverse of his, differing in at least two specific and substantive ways. First, my analysis views moments of merge with the natural world and a strong identification of subject and landscape as also deeply implicated in racist hegemony, from the relatively strong environmental commitments of the Nazis, to the ways whiteness became normative and white supremacy was naturalized in the texts I discuss in this book. Ecocentricity is, in my view, no proof against racism; indeed versions of it seem to me fundamental to the creation of whiteness as an unmarked, normative, "natural" supremacy. Second, I see the separation between the human and natural as in fact more marked in African-American culture than in Euroamerican, a legacy of the terrible practices of slavery, lynching, scientific racism, and of the hard-won triumphs of the Great Migration and the founding of vibrant urban African-American communities in New York, Chicago, and elsewhere. I think Myers largely overlooks this separation in his analysis. When he argues, for example, that "the separation of the Euroamerican self from people of color and the rest of the natural world is an ecologically untenable position," (13) he misses, I think, how in making "people of color" part of the "rest of the natural world," from which whites are alienated, he invokes a conflation that has historically been much more fraught than his general call for human/natural unity would acknowledge.

9. Note, for example, that what is arguably the foundational collection for ecocriticism, Glotfelty and Fromm's *Ecocriticism Reader*, contains no essays that engage with African-American experience or cultural production. Elizabeth Dodd has recently noted "the absence of black writers from existing ecocritical discussion," and goes on to speculate about the possible reasons for this "absence":

    I suspect that African American writers may not have embraced nature writing (creative writing in the autobiographical naturalist tradition) since what Robinson Jeffers called Inhumanism (the literary attempt to deflect attention away from human beings, or what Glen A. Love calls eco-consciousness) might not be appealing for writers who already feel politically, economically, and socially marginalized. Further, academic inquiry, including the work of ecocritics, already expects black literature to focus on the social realm; literary studies categorizes black literature as offering an interest in environmental similar to the interest in socioeconomic environment that characterized naturalist novels at the close of the nineteenth century. (177)

10. In this sense my project is part of the larger project Paul Gilroy calls for in his recent essay "After the Great White Error...the Great Black Mirage": "we will need to reconstruct the history of 'race' in modernity, offering multiple genealogies of racial discourse that can explain how the brutal, dualistic opposition between black and white became

entrenched and has retained its grip on a world in which racial and ethnic identities have been anything but stable or fixed" (73).

11. For more on such taxonomies, see especially Wheeler, Gossett, and Fredrickson.

12. As Hazel Carby notes, "racism, in its appeal to the natural order of things, appears as a transhistorical, essentialist category, and critiques of racism can imitate this appearance" (*Reconstructing Womanhood*, 18–19).

13. Gilroy subjects the uncritical acceptance of racial categories of subjectivity to a withering critique in a recent essay, decrying,

> ...how people become intimidated by and resigned to the mystifications of raciality and its narcissism of minor differences; how they try to make the refusal to see beyond reified racial categories into a measure of their political virtue; and how, while usually according racial difference a routine and empty measure of recognition as a social and historical construction, they are only too happy to lose the capacity to imagine its unmaking, its deconstruction, its transcendence, or even the possibility of its eventual descent into irrelevance. These problems have been compounded by a voguish reluctance to trespass on the imagined communities of oppressed groups who may have seized the discursive categories through which their subordination has been transacted or imposed and then lodged them in the centers of their "wounded" solidarity and the carnival of identities that it supports. This compensatory commitment to unanimity cannot succeed for long. (86)

Of course, neither Gilroy's statement here, or mine in the text to which this footnote refers, should be taken as declaring that race doesn't function in materially important ways or that "giving it up" is something easily done.

14. The Hill quotation is referenced in the original passage from Ware and Back. It is originally from Hill's similarly intelligent and witty introduction to his edited collection in which he notes "Whiteness becomes something we both claim (single out for critique) and avoid (in claiming whiteness for critique, what else can we be, if we happen to be identifiably white?)" (3). Hill's most recent book, *After Whiteness*, asks how this central issue in recent scholarship on whiteness—"the troubling sense that the critical study of whiteness was destined to come up against the limits of modern epistemology"—might serve to "advance the agenda of a post-white analytic...to assess how we presume to know and value a thing by the fact of its not being there" (9).

15. I want to acknowledge here how intellectually indebted this project is to Morrison's *Playing in the Dark*. Her reading of how "white" literature engages with and denies what she calls an "Africanist presence," catalyzed my thinking about how natural sublimity has functioned historically as in part a conspicuous suppression of a racial context.

16. As Montag writes about this process in his essay on whiteness and the Enlightenment, "the human norm, of course, is always glimpsed only

negatively: it is what allows us to see the deficient and abnormal without itself being seen," an invisibility he connects to whiteness's negative identity, asserting that whiteness "may be nothing more than the principle in relation to which all (other) races, nations, and peoples are classified and hierarchized" and that "[w]hiteness is itself the human universal that no (other) race realizes" (291–92). This assertion of whiteness's emptiness is hardly original to either Montag or to me; indeed, versions of it are almost a commonplace in the critical literature on the subject. My contribution here is only to point out how easily "whiteness studies" can lose sight of this fundamental emptiness, "unmasking" whiteness as "another" racial identity like "blackness."

17. Though note how often those features are defined in terms of absence—white men can't jump, can't dance, have bad style, small penises, and so forth. And the places where white power is grounded—corporate America and national politics to take two obvious examples—take pains *not* to name themselves explicitly as "white culture."

18. In Stokes's engaging work, heterosexuality provides that "other abstraction," what he calls his "primary angle of vision on whiteness" (13). My angle here is ecocritical; there is, of course, room for both, and many more. In general, viewing whiteness through the lens of a particular form of cultural and/or individual practice, rather than trying to theorize about it more generally, has produced, to me, the most interesting work on the subject. Hence, for example, the influence of Lott's terrific book on blackface minstrelsy and working-class culture and Gubar's important recent study of contemporary cultural performances in the blackface tradition, or Hale's invaluable study of the specific cultural and physical practices that produced whiteness and segregation in the decades after the war.

19. Scholarship on whiteness has exploded in the last decade or so (though it is arguably now imploding). A full bibliographic note on the subject would run many pages, and is, regardless, outside the specific focus of this study. Hill's collection is certainly a good place to start an inquiry into the major debates in the field, and serves as an intelligent and thorough introduction to some of its major theorists. Hill's latest book offers a densely argued and always intelligent discussion of the topic; see especially 173–84. Stokes's Epilogue (178–92) provides a very useful and clear summary of the major currents in whiteness studies and an insightful analysis of the intellectual difficulties that it faces. Ware and Back's coauthored book offers a thoughtful introduction to some of the contemporary tensions in whiteness studies as well. George Yancy's two collections were also influential in my thinking about the subject; I take up Yancy's work directly later in the book. See also Dyer for fascinating examination of white imagery and Taylor for a breathtaking and often brilliant study of whiteness from cave paintings to Eminem (though largely focused on the period from Columbus's voyages to the beginning of the eighteenth century).

Roediger's work has been enormously influential, since his important *Wages of Whiteness* was published fifteen years ago that took up the issue of working-class white identity. Like Roediger's work, Saxton's book focuses on class and whiteness in an early American context, though he is more interested in how whiteness was tied up with the creation of national citizenship. For a critique of Roediger's labor history, see Wiegman's "Whiteness Studies." For an analysis of contemporary labor issues and the construction of whiteness, see Lipsitz; his work is particularly valuable for refusing the black/white binary by engaging with the racial experience of Asians and Latino/as in the course of his analysis.

The so-called New Abolitionist movement attempts to shift whiteness studies from theorizing to practical antiracist action, calling on whites to refuse the privileges white identification affords. Ignatiev's journal *Race Traitor* is at the center of this movement, whose appealing motto is "Treason to Whiteness is Loyalty to Humanity." The movement is rightly admired, and rightly criticized, I think for a certain naïve utopianism, though given my explicit sense that there isn't a morally pure position for whites to speak about whiteness, or not to speak about it, I'm perhaps less troubled by that utopianism than others have been. Ignatiev's book on how the Irish achieved white "status" is invaluable both for its insights on the specific topic of Irish American history, and for its analysis of how whiteness has been created historically in America.

20. Ecocriticism's commitment to a nonhuman natural world that both exists incomprehensibly outside of human representation and of which we are, nevertheless and irrevocably, a part, provides an important check on the reflexive critical dismissal of such assertions as "essentialist." Only the naïve believe in the possibility of an entirely unmediated or Absolute experience of nature, and only the most anthropocentric theoretical idealists would deny nature's independent existence altogether. Nevertheless a debate between how much to stress nature's nonhuman facticity and how much to stress its human construction has sprung up, mirroring a similar debate in feminism, studies of race, gender, and sexuality, and other criticism interested in identity, as Mazel, among others, notes.

Mazel adopts a thoroughgoing poststructuralist approach to nature throughout his book; see especially xi–xxv and 59–92 for a stimulating attempt to bring Judith Butler's theories of embodiment and performitivity to bear on the construction of nature. In addition to Mazel, other important constructivist approaches include Cronon, and the more recent Branch, Tallmadge, and Herzogenrath collections. A more essentialist emphasis can be found in the Soulé collection, which offers a variety of often quite nuanced defenses of nature as including an extratextual and ahuman element. The deep ecology movement (see especially Devall) also often rejects poststructualist approaches as anthropocentric. Leopold's classic argument in "The Land Ethic" (201–26) and Nash's history also argue for treating nature as having intrinsic and extra-human value.

Regardless of which emphasis I have assigned them, most of these accounts blend a sense of nature as text with a sense of it being also an independent existent with claims and rights of its own. I believe it is both things, of course; an argument for one or the other side, or for a particularly fixed ratio between them seems unfruitful to me. See Levin for an important statement on the need for such a combination. Along these lines I also particularly admire the Gaard ecofeminism collection, Buell (especially his call for "aesthetics of duel accountability" discussed from 83–114 in *Environmental Imagination*) and both Evernden books.

21. Recent essays by Hitt and Cronon provide important exceptions.
22. See Robbins for sweatshops, Klein for cigarettes.
23. Studies specifically focused on the American sublime include Wilson's book and Arensberg's collection (in which Pease's essay is particularly valuable).
24. Lyotard's "unpresentable" (a concept found throughout *The Inhuman* and *Lessons on the Analytic of the Sublime*, and elsewhere in Lyotard's work) or Žižek's "insupportable, real, impossible kernel" from which ideology (as the "social reality") (45) protects us might serve as examples.
25. While Kant resolves the sublime eruption decidedly in favor of the noumenal, as Armstrong notes, "the unpresentable is not quite the same opportunity for celebration it has become among postmodern critics" (225). Kant's noumenal sublime is not ultimately an embrace of the Uncertain, but a mark, at whatever distance, of the Divine.
26. The work speculates more widely on the capacity of a range of cultural and racial groups to experience the sublime as well, though the "Negroes of Africa" are clearly ranked at the bottom, just below the "savages of America." This passage is taken from an excerpt in Eze, from Goldthwaite's translation.
27. Doyle is also acute on the relation between these two accounts of sublimity in Kant, seeing them as part of a larger process of turning sublimity from a potentially subversive and democratic impulse into an explicitly racialized nationalism. Judy's analysis of Kant's racism is densely argued and very worthwhile; see especially 108–47.
28. This gesture by which whiteness is created in relation to the natural sublime at the same time that blackness is "naturally" excluded arguably persists in modern form. As Braun suggests in his intriguing writing on contemporary adventure recreation and extreme sports, the absence of the figure of the "'nonwhite' adventurer" is "not only, or even primarily, and economic or sociological matter but an ideological matter: within the discursive terrain of 'adventure' in the United States today, the figure of the black or Latina adventurer *has no proper place*" (178).
29. LaCapra (199) introduced me to this concept in Freud.
30. Barbara Freeman, conversely, assimilates trauma, specifically African-American trauma, to the discourse of the sublime in the final chapter of her book, arguing that "Africanism" (in the sense Toni Morrison uses the term in *Playing in the Dark*, as a "dark abiding presence" that constitutes the (white) American canon) functions in a way that "mirrors...the Kantian sublime: to contain the fear of boundlessness

and primal terror; to give the unnameable a name and thereby defend against it; to aggrandize (or create) identity, but only at the expense of a scapegoated other; and to keep the fear of unrepresentability at bay" (108). Even when noting possible differences between sublimity and trauma, Freeman subsumes trauma under sublimity, noting that "as in Lyotard's famous remarks about the sublime, trauma also attests to the fact that something unpresentable exists," (125) and that "trauma raises in history the same issues that the sublime raises in aesthetics— the experience of an event whose magnitude exceeds representation" (136). Freeman's eliding of the two does not make her by any means an insensitive reader of *Beloved*, but at least for my project, the distinction between the two forms is sharper. For more on Freeman's understanding of the unpresentable as central to Lyotard's sublime, see 181.

31. Both Burke and Kant incorporate aspects of this requirement in their definition of the sublime. For example, Burke writes "When danger or pain press too nearly they are incapable of giving any delight, and are simply terrible; but at certain distances, and with certain modifications, they may be, and they are delightful, as we every day experience," (40), and Kant, in the *Critique of Judgment* insists that "the sight of" sublime nature "is the more attractive, the more fearful it is, provided only that we are in security" (100).

32. For an engagingly written analysis of Romanticism's relation to the natural world that is more concerned to establish affinities between the movement and ecocriticism, see especially Bate's study of Wordsworth.

33. As Doyle asserts sharply, "the Romantic sublime is importantly constituted ... by its function to transform a revolutionary racial discourse into a hegemonic one" (26).

34. See especially her chapter "Us is Human Flesh," 117–49 that draws on early twentieth-century WPA interviews with ex-slaves to address this issue at length.

35. In focusing on the *entanglement* of these discourses, I hope to avoid what Anne Cheng rightly warns is the danger of using trauma to discuss race: "trauma, so often associated with discussions of racial denigration, in focusing on a structure of crisis on the part of the victim, misses the violators' own dynamic process at stake in such denigration" (12). Cheng instead builds her very worthwhile analysis around "melancholia" and its internalization of grief and loss, that "expresses itself in both violent and muted ways, producing confirmation as well as crisis, knowledge as well as aporia" (12).

2 The Colonial Pastoral, Abolition, and the Transcendentalist Sublime

1. As Branch notes, "we ... need to study earlier American conceptions of nature in order to better understand how certain misguided and

destructive ideas gained prominence in our culture; environmental degradation during the past half century has often been the consequence of
earlier American environmental attitudes such as fear of wilderness; narrow adherence to theological imperatives of predestination and conversion; ignorance of functional interrelationships in ecological systems; and
the sanctioned exploitation of women, indentured servants, Native
Americans, and African Americans" ("Before," 93). In the context of this
recognition, he then offers an ecocritical reading of two very early writers,
William Wood and Cotton Mather.

2. Wilton and Barringer note how many elements of the painting make the
Biblical landscape signify the American: "with a few tropical additions,
[the Garden] resembles the Catskill or Adirondack landscape" and "the
natural bridge and the deep waterfall, as well as the lofty mountains, had
been identified as key elements of American scenery" (93).

I had the good fortune to spend a day at Wilton and Barringer's "American
Sublime" exhibition at the Philadelphia Academy of Fine Art, a remarkable
collection that was important to the initial formation of this project. The
exhibition volume, which includes plates of most of the works and important
introductory essays by both scholars, is invaluable for anyone interested in
the American sublime. See also Bryan Wolf for an earlier, and still very
worthwhile, analysis of the sublime tradition in American painting.

3. For white settlers this was true; for the Native population, of course, the
American wilderness was neither American nor a wilderness, but a familiar place, their home. As Nash notes in his introduction:

We should pause to recognize that at the time of European
colonization, there were already hunting and gathering people in
the New World who did not recognize the wilderness/civilization
distinction. Indeed, the "wilderness" may, in retrospect, be the
wrong word to characterize North America at the time of European
contact. But the colonists *did* use it, and they carried the full set of
pastoral prejudices. Living on the edge of what they took to be a vast
wilderness, they re-experienced the insecurities of the first farmers
and town builders. There was, initially, too much wilderness for
appreciation. Understandably, the wild people of the New World
seemed "savages," and their wild habitat a moral and physical wasteland fit only for conquest and transformation in the name of progress, civilization, and Christianity.

Evidence that civilization created wilderness is found in the attitudes of the so-called Indians that the European settlers found in
the New World. It made no sense for them to distinguish wilderness
from civilization or to fear and hate what they did not control in
nature. Chief Standing Bear of the Ogalala Sioux explained that by
tradition his people "did not think of the great open plains, the
beautiful rolling hills and the winding streams with their tangled
growth as 'wild.' Only to the white man was nature a 'wilderness'
and...the land 'infested' with 'wild animals' and 'savage people.'"

The "wild West and the frontier" were products of the pioneer mind; so was the idea of wilderness. (xiii)

While Nash's "pause" and his "understanding" are, I think, a bit too quick, and he fails to explain fully why the Indians' familiarity with the wilderness didn't also lead to them fearing and hating it, his general point is important and insightful.

4. Qtd. in Nash, 23.

5. There have been a number of important studies of the role of pastoral ideology in the formation of early American culture and environment; indeed, the accomplishment of this body of scholarship is so impressive it has occasionally overshadowed other important ways of understanding the American natural landscape such as the wilderness or the sublime. Two works have proven particularly influential, Leo Marx's *The Machine in the Garden*, which traces the ongoing collision between the pastoral dream and industrialization in America, and Annette Kolodny's landmark study, *The Lay of the Land*, which analyzes the ways the pastoral impulse gendered the land as either an all-providing Mother or a sexually available Virgin, marking (male) environmental practice as either infantile regression or erotic aggression. I am grateful for their work, and it is not my intention here to replicate it. My purposes are more general and more explicitly ecocritical than either of theirs—less literary than Marx's, and less engaged by gender psychology than Kolodny's. I am largely concerned with how the pastoral ideal the colonists held so dear collided with a wild that *wasn't* pastoral, that was, indeed, a largely intact ecosystem, one that certainly bore far fewer marks of human intervention than what these early settlers soon created.

6. Timothy Sweet offers an important counterweight to this argument in his book, tracing some of the salutary ecological effects of what he calls the "georgic"—a pastoral landscape that integrates human labor. His introduction offers an especially worthwhile summary of recent ecocriticism of the pastoral mode (1–28). Sarver's book is also worthwhile in this regard. See Stoll for a convincing argument about the importance of soil conservation practices to nineteenth-century American history, an issue that especially shaped southern slave and sharecropping agriculture.

7. For more on these early views, see Fredrickson, especially 71–97, and Gossett, especially 3–54. Wheeler's book, while focusing on eighteenth-century British culture, is a fascinating introduction to ideas that had great currency in America as well. She traces, among other things, how skin color emerged during this period as the uniquely privileged mark of race. On climate see especially 2–48. Racist views about the effects of climate persisted, of course, after their early popularity had passed; Huntington's massive *Climate and Civilization* (first published in 1915, revised in 1924) might serve as a generic example.

8. Note too that this notion of a tamed landscape as a sign of racial identity, "civilization," and the concomitant right of possession, was later used to justify slavery and "prove" the inferiority of black Africans, who supposedly had failed to develop their continent's "natural resources."

9. As many critics have noted, male gender anxiety was, of course, also often central to this process. See, for example, Dollow.

10. For a thoroughgoing study of how profoundly the construction of whiteness and territorial expansion were linked, see Horsman.

11. For more on race relations during this period, see (in addition to Saxton), Glasrud's collection and Sweet's *Bodies Politic*. Kazanjian's book provides a theoretically dense and rewarding study of the formation of citizenship in early America. See also Babb's chapter, 46–88.

12. As Crèvecoeur describes the process:

> He who would wish to see America in its proper light, and have a true idea of its feeble beginnings and barbarous rudiments, must visit our extended line of frontiers where the last settlers dwell, and where he may see the first labors of settlement, the mode of clearing the earth, in all their different appearances; where men are wholly left dependent on their native tempers and on the spur of uncertain industry, which often fails when not sanctified by the efficacy of a few moral rules.... They are a kind of forlorn hope, preceding by ten or twelve years the most respectable army of veterans which come after them. In that space, prosperity will polish some, vice and the law will drive off the rest, who uniting again with others like themselves will recede still farther; making room for more industrious people, who will finish their improvements, convert the loghouse into a convenient habitation, and rejoicing that the first heavy labors are finished, will change in a few years that hitherto barbarous country into a fine fertile, well-regulated district. Such is our progress, such is the march of the Europeans toward the interior parts of this continent. (46–47)

13. As Moore, Pandian, and Kosek write, "Inherently duplicitous, the term 'landscape' refers both to th[e] visual perspective and to the geographical territories that are seized by it. Landscapes articulate both culture and nature, seer and scene. But equally at stake in landscape are the embodied practices that transform the objects of a proprietary gaze. A multiplicity of situated practices—of cultivators and pastoralists, slaves and colonists, labor migrants and adventure travelers—shapes both terrain and identity" (11).

14. Pease, conversely, distinguishes Emerson's sublime in this passage from Kant's version of the mode, as well as from the romantic/egotistical sublime and from what he sees as a semiotic core to Weiskel's interpretation:

> Unlike the Kantian negative sublime defined as Nature's excess of signification simultaneously breaking down the capacity of the understanding and awakening reason as the only agent of comprehension, and unlike the romantic or egotistical sublime arising out of an excess of self, the Emersonian sublime does not elevate either nature of the self to the status of the sublime. Nor, as was the case with the semiotic sublime, does it intensify the

sensed arbitrariness in the relationship between self and world. In qualifying the four assertions preceding it, the statement, "the currents of the Universal Being circulate through me," intensifies the sense of transition, the give and take between Nature and the self. In moving from the "transparent eyeball" (more akin to an ear in its power to covert objects into currents of universal Being) to the "me" that forces pass through, the individual crossing the bare common has become less a person than a site of passage, a personification of the confluences between self and nature.

From another perspective, it might be said that in "the transparent eyeball" sequence, the speaker unintentionally fulfills the wish imbedded in the question from the introductory paragraph to "Nature," "Why cannot we also enjoy an original relation with Nature?" But this unintentional fulfillment leads to quite an unusual state of affairs. The "transparent eyeball" converts the self who would enjoy Nature and the Nature to be enjoyed into the give and take released by the original question. With neither self nor Nature around to enjoy it, we can only say that the speaker answers the question by himself becoming the original relation between self and nature. (43–44)

I would qualify Pease's statement in a few ways. First, and least important, while I think the differences he points to between Emerson and Kant/Wordsworth/Weiskel are accurate, here I see Weiskel as offering a formal, as well as semiotic, description of the sublime. Second, while I agree that transition ("a site of passage") is the focus of the sublime rather than Emerson's ego or a specific natural object, I read that transition as motivated by a desire to repress two interlocked, extant and well-established material relations with nature: slavery, and the accompanying transition from whiteness identifying with the pastoral to its identification with the wild.

15. See Branch, "Indexing" for a summary of these different views.
16. While to my eye the humor here is accidental, Buell finds a "deliberately comic bubbliness" in the passage (*Emerson*, 94).
17. Sadly, it often functions as "an elaborate social subterfuge," that makes "both whites and nonwhites" see themselves and their world as "naturally given, unchangeable ways of being." Terribly sadly for those who, like me, love and defend it. Again, my statements here shouldn't be taken as dispositive, though I think the fact that whiteness and wilderness experience have historically functioned in these way is undeniable. That they have also functioned in other ways and that the extrahuman natural is not simply a white plot is as central a commitment as any I have; my ultimate interest here is not to establish a racial essence for nature but to disestablish one.
18. While Thoreau's commitments to abolition were more clear-cut than Emerson's, both certainly despised slavery and explicitly and publicly aligned themselves with the abolitionist cause.

19. Melville, a much more suspicious observer of the sublime, makes explicit how the politics of race can produce this natural transformation in his 1860 poem "Misgivings":

When ocean-clouds over inland hills
Sweep storming in late autumn brown,
And horror the sodden valley fills,
And the spire falls crashing in the town,
I muse upon my country's ills—
The tempest bursting from the waste of Time
On the world's fairest hope linked with man's foulest crime.
Nature's dark side is heeded now—
(Ah! optimist-cheer disheartened flown)—
A child may read the moody brow
Of yon black mountain lone.
With shouts the torrents down the gorges go,
And storms are formed behind the storm we feel:
The hemlock shakes in the rafter, the oak in the driving keel. (34)

In this brink-of-the-Civil-War poem, Melville explicitly conjoins America's promise ("the world's fairest hope") with slavery ("man's foulest crime"), and as a result, nature turns from "fair" to its "dark side," to "late autumn brown" and the "moody brow" of the "black mountain lone." The horror of slavery and the coming violence of the war are imaged as a series of terrible storms overwhelming the land and sea, rewriting nature's signification totally, from "inland hill" to "sodden valley," from mountain to gorge. And there is no shelter from this storm, no natural or extranatural place of retreat. Even the utterly domesticated nature signified by the "hemlock" rafter and "oak" keel are shaking.

20. The distance between Emerson and the practice of slavery was also typical of what Buell calls "the tendency in the early nineteenth century for white New England to disassociate itself from its own African American presence" (*Emerson* 247). See *Emerson*, 241–87, for Buell's typically thorough and subtle discussion of the ambiguities in Emerson's commitment to the Abolitionist cause, and his views on racial essence and the possibilities of equality.

3   "BEHOLD A MAN TRANSFORMED INTO A BRUTE": SLAVERY AND ANTEBELLUM NATURE

1. I discuss the terrorism and trauma of lynching in chapter six.
2. Johnson, *Soul by Soul*, 26.
3. As Johnson notes,

The seasonality of the slave trade was tied to the cycles of the larger agricultural economy. In the upper South, exportation had to wait until after harvest, because hands were needed in the summer and fall to tend the crops; in the lower South, buying was delayed until after harvest because that was when buyers had money available to pay for slaves. The rhythm of the trade marks its centrality to the economy of slavery; the historic role of the slave trade in binding the diverging fortunes of the upper and lower South into mutual interest was yearly recapitulated in the season cycle of interregional trade. (*Soul by Soul*, 49)

4. See especially Johnson, *Soul by Soul*, 4.

5. Or, as Baker asserts in "Figurations," Douglass's conversion from slave to free is principally an economic transaction: "Having gained, contractually, the right to hire his own time and to keep a portion of his wages, Douglass eventually converts property, through property, into humanity" (167).

6. Saidiya Hartman's analysis inverts, or compliments, mine, focusing on how "benevolent correctives and declarations of slave humanity *intensified* the brutal exercise of power upon the captive body rather than ameliorating the chattel condition" (5, my emphasis).

7. In Toni Morrison's *Beloved*, for example, Schoolteacher's pseudo-scientific categorization of Sethe's "animal characteristics" and her literal milking by his sons pains her more than the whippings she endures. And when Paul D really wants to hurt her later in the book he lashes out with the admonishment—"You got two feet, Sethe, not four," an insult that puts a wilderness between the lovers: "and right then a forest sprang up between them; trackless and quiet" (165).

8. My emphasis. Note though that the arrows, square brackets, and other forms of enlivening punctuation are found in Walker's text.

9. Especially in this latter process, the slave narratives enact what Eng and Kazanjian call "the politics of mourning," a "creative process mediating a hopeful or hopeless relationship between loss and history" (2).

10. In this I both anticipate my final chapter, "Migrations," and agree with Hazel Carby in her criticism of what she feels is an overemphasis on the rural "folk" origins of African-American literature:

A mythology of the rural South conflates the nineteenth and twentieth centuries and two very distinct modes of production, slavery and sharecropping, into one mythical rural folk existence. Of course, the ideological function of a tradition is to create unity out of disunity and to resolve the social contradiction, or differences, between texts. Consequently, not only are the specificities of a slave existence as opposed to a sharecropping existence negated, but the urban imagination and urban histories are also repressed. Our twentieth-century vernacular (the blues, if you like) is reinterpreted as emerging from a shared rural heritage, not as the product of social displacement and migration to the city. The fact that imaginative recreations of the "folk" including the ex-slave, are themselves produced and distributed primarily within the urban environment and for urban consumption is not critically examined. ("Ideologies of Black Folk," 127)

In this sense, I read the text of slave narrative as itself a sort of migration, as enacting figuratively (and not only on the level of plot) the departure and disconnection of the author from the southern landscape. This process does not involve a "return to roots," or "finding oneself," but the creation of identity in a deliberate uprooting, or derooting.

11. As Judy notes about Douglass's literacy, "The myth that Douglass in fact violates... is the underlying assumption that where there is illiteracy there is no evidence of thought, which was one of the authoritative arguments for justifying the enslavement of Africans, an argument which runs something like: they had no literacy, therefore could not be shown to have thought, which is an essential peculiar condition of humans, so they cannot be shown to be fully human" (104).

12. For more on Bibb's nature imagery from an environmentally concerned perspective, see Gerhardt's insightful "Border Ecology."

13. Though Spillers connects this perpetual difficulty in representing slavery not to the difficulty of representing natural experience, but to how widely the experience of slavery varied from person to person, place to place, and time to time.

14. A notable exception to this is Bennett's important article that views Douglass's narrative as an "anti-pastoral" and is explicitly willing to recognize how his work provides an important critique of American nature writing (198).

15. This moment when the remembered traumatic past threatens to overwhelm the compositional present is one of only two such episodes in the 1845 *Narrative*. The other is, tellingly, also a moment when natural experience is linked to a failure of representation in a way Douglass finds definitional of the trauma of slavery. Douglass describes listening to the slaves singing in the woods as they went on errands for their master:

> I did not, when a slave, understand the deep meaning of those rude and apparently incoherent songs. I was myself within the circle; so that I neither saw nor heard as those without might see and hear. They told a tale of woe which was then altogether beyond my feeble comprehension; they were tones loud, long, and deep; they breathed the prayer and complaint of souls boiling over with the bitterest anguish. Every tone was a testimony against slavery, and a prayer to God for deliverance from chains. The hearing of those wild notes always depressed my spirit, and filled me with ineffable sadness. I have frequently found myself in tears while hearing them. *The mere recurrence to those songs, even now, afflicts me; and while I am writing these lines, an expression of feeling has already found its way down my cheek.* To those songs I trace my first glimmering conception of the dehumanizing character of slavery. I can never get rid of that conception. Those songs still follow me, to deepen my hatred of slavery, and quicken my sympathies for my brethren in bonds. If any one wishes to be impressed with the soul-killing effects of slavery, let him go to Colonel Lloyd's plantation, and, on allowance-day, place himself in the deep pine woods, and

there let him, in silence, analyze the sounds that shall pass through the chambers of his soul,—and if he is not thus impressed, it will only be because "there is no flesh in his obdurate heart" (24, my emphasis).

And yet, both these moments of textual breakdown are, to me at least, also some of the most powerful in the *Narrative*, examples of what Eng and Kazanjian call the "counterintuitive" idea of "imput[ing] to loss a creative instead of a negative quality" (2).

16. For Althusser, writing in his classic essay "Ideology and Ideological State Apparatuses," interpellation is the primary way ideology transforms individuals into literal subjects; indeed, "the existence of ideology and the hailing or interpellation of subjects are one and the same thing" (175). In his view, an individual's response to the call of an authority "recruits" him or her, transforming that person into a subject, because "he has recognized that the hail was 'really' addressed to him, and that 'it was *really him* who was hailed' (and not someone else)" (174).

17. That relatively "innocent" childhood starting point is itself, of course, often built on an earlier trauma suffered by the mother when her child was taken from her. Douglass points out how it was "common custom" to separate mothers from their children before the child's first birthday, leaving the mother distraught and the child parentless. Spillers notes how "the enslaved must not be permitted to perceive that he or she has any human rights that matter. Certainly if kinship were possible, the property relations would be undermined, since the offspring would then 'belong' to a mother and a father" ("Mama's Baby," 75).

18. I read Douglass's narrative as generic here, in the sense that he is invoking and troping on a transracial myth of development from a "natural" or pastorally associated boyhood innocence. Other writers—Booker T. Washington in *Up from Slavery*, for example—seem more explicitly aware of their condition from the start. Washington's childhood home, for example, is not a "snug cottage" but a drafty cabin with a wood floor. For more on this distinction between Washington and Douglass, see Andrews.

19. As Sundquist declares, "The whip permeates and defines slaveholding paternalism, breaking across the white-black boundary to contaminate and enslave all" (110).

20. Prince's narrative was, like many of the slave narratives, including Northup's, dictated to a white auditor and subsequently edited. It is impossible to know with any great certainty how much an editor shaped the language of a given narrative, though Prince's work, especially in passages like this, retains the cadence of oral delivery, at least to my ear. Her editor and publisher, Thomas Pringle, certainly claims to have had very little influence on the work:

> The narrative was taken down from Mary's own lips by a lady who happened to be at the time residing in my family as a visitor. It was written out fully, with all the narrator's repetitions and prolixities, and afterwards pruned into its present shape; retaining, as far as

was practicable, Mary's exact expressions and peculiar phraseology. No fact of importance has been omitted, and not a single circumstance or sentiment has been added. It is essentially her own, without any material alteration farther than was requisite to exclude redundancies and gross grammatical errors, so as to render it clearly intelligible. (*Six Women's Slave Narratives*, iii)

In Prince's case, I am willing to trust her, Pringle, and my own ear enough to do some limited close work with the text, though not to the same extent that I do with texts like Douglass's, Bibb's, or Jacobs's whose authorship is not in question. In the case of Northup's narrative, I often detect the heavier editorial hand of David Wilson, Northup's amanuensis. Take the following passage, for example:

Imagination cannot picture the dreariness of the scene. The swamp was resonant with the quacking of innumerable ducks! Since the foundation of the earth, in all probability, a human footstep had never before so far penetrated the recesses of the swamp. It was not silent now—silent to a degree that rendered it oppressive,—as it was when the sun was shining in the heavens. My midnight intrusion had awakened the feathered tribes, which seemed to throng the morass in hundreds of thousands, and their garrulous throats poured forth such multitudinous sounds—there was such a fluttering of wings—such sullen plunges in the water all around me—that I was affrighted and appalled. All the fowls of the air, and all the creeping things of the earth appeared to have assembled together in that particular place for the purpose of filling it with clamor and confusion. Not by human dwellings—not in crowded cities alone, are the sights and sounds of life. The wildest places of the earth are full of them. Even in the heart of that dismal swamp, God had provided a refuge and a dwelling place for millions of living things. (300)

James Olney asserts directly that "the style of the narrative...is demonstrably not Northup's own" and comments wryly on one sentence in the passage above ("My midnight intrusion ...") that "when we get such a sentence we may think it pretty fine writing and awfully literary, but the fine writer is clearly David Wilson rather than Solomon Northup" (162). Certainly it would seem that anyone who in fact spoke in the inflated manner of the passage would be unlikely to need an amanuensis.

Even if Northup wrote the passage himself, the question of its "authenticity" remains a vexed, if not impossible one, since the very notion of an authentically "black" text inevitably raises the specter of racial essentialism. In addition, the fact that the narratives were largely intended to move white audiences to the abolitionist cause raises the question of authenticity regardless of the color of the hand holding the pen. I'm inclined, as a result, largely to abandon questions of authenticity as unanswerable and inherently problematic. Rather, I take a more low-flying approach, looking for moments in the narratives in which the writing seems constructed out of the confrontation with nature and trauma in a given scene, rather than, as in the case of the Northup quotation above, out of a preexisting style. Since I certainly don't want to abandon the narratives as a vital source of information about African-American experiences of nature in the antebellum South, I make my judgments on how closely to read a given passage based on the editorial history of the text and my own ear—an unsatisfactory combination, but perhaps the best one can do under the circumstances.

21. For an argument that sees slavery as the reduction to monetary value, see, for example, Boesenberg's essay. She argues that,

> …quite literally, freedom and personhood depended on money in a slaveholding economy. The profit motive, which had occasioned the slaves' transatlantic passages in the first place, was inscribed in the social structures of the 'peculiar institution' with startling consistency. Treated as chattel and assigned a cash equivalent, the slaves were depersonalized further by the degree of abstraction inherent in monetary language, which screens contextual relations and reduces vastly different activities, objects, and relations to a common denominator. (117)

For me, that common denominator is the natural world.

22. The market's transformation of slave into money not only depended on an association between the slave and the natural world, it paralleled a similar transformation from nature to money in the process of turning "natural resources" into agricultural and other natural commodities that were sold in the marketplace for cash.

23. Note again, too, how this is itself built on Prince's mother's own trauma, her forced participation in the first "choosing" of Prince at the auction.

24. And this reduction to meat in slavery recalls a similar reduction the suspended slave in the passage from Crèvecoeur suffers, and returns again in a passage from Douglass that closes the chapter. The whole question of how animal rights activism and vegetarianism engages racial and gender oppression is a fascinating one, but outside of my immediate focus here. Interested readers might start by looking at Adams's *The Sexual Politics of Meat,* and Cary Wolfe's recent *Animal Rites: American Culture, the Discourse of Species, and Posthumanist Theory.*

25. For an insightful analysis of the sexual violence and commodification in the auction of slave women, see Saidiya Hartman, especially 37–42.

26. Of course male slaves were, undoubtedly, also subject to sexual abuse by white men and women alike, and black women by white women as well. Accounts of the auctioning of male bodies are often, to my eye, particularly suffused with repressed eroticism. Whitman, for example, arguably "outs" the auction in Section Seven of "I Sing the Body Electric," as I discuss in my essay "Whitman and Race ('he's queer, he's unclear, get used to it')" (307–12). This sexual subtext is not made explicit in the slave narratives, however, and it seems to me unlikely that sexual contact between black men and whites, or black and white women was nearly as common as between black women and white men—hence this section's focus.

27. Though, as Spillers points out in "Changing the Letter," the "peculiar institution" also fundamentally undid the distinction between inner and outer spaces, between domestic and field: "The horror of slavery was its absolute domesticity that configured the 'peculiar institution' into the architectonics of the southern household. So complete was its articulation with the domestic economy that from one angle it loses visibility and becomes... 'natural' to the dynamics of culture ..." (28).

28. See Johnson, *Soul by Soul*, 113.

29. In noting this contradiction, I am certainly not claiming that the power differential between master and slave was not itself part of the erotic charge for the master, that the master was not a rapist or a sadist, or that he somehow "really" desired an equal partner. Rather, the contradiction itself was eroticized. The sharper this contradiction—the more violent and total the domination, the more "pure" the beauty—the more powerful the sado-sexual charge the distinction carried.

30. This continuum might be represented by two iconic figures of enslaved female sexuality: On one side put Hiram Power's 1847 statue The Greek Slave, an alabaster nude of a conventionally comely white Christian woman supposedly about to be sold in a Turkish auction. This statue served both as a rallying symbol for the Abolitionist movement and an opportunity for titillation—it was the most viewed work of sculpture in nineteenth-century America, and provoked enormous controversy, largely because the woman was simultaneously white, nude, and a slave. Her vulnerability provides an invitation to a sort of sadistic voyeurism while providing the plausible deniability of moralizing pity. On the other side, put a "real" figure, Sara Baartmanm, the so-called The Hottentot Venus, an African woman who was displayed in Europe in 1810, whose supposedly oversized genitals and buttocks both made her an object of intense sexual fascination/repulsion and an example of African animality. Taken together these figures limn the impossible range of the sexual fantasy slave women were forced to embody by white men.

31. Boesenberg's analysis of how the explicit commodification of black women as their sexuality could threaten white women is worth noting in this context. She writes,

> The image of the prostitute, the woman whose profession makes *explicit* the cash nexus structuring male-female relations, thus becomes for the respectable woman, the fiend against whom her own position must be secured and defended. If white Southern women's ostensible purity also masked anxieties about their own economic independence, one might argue that the female slave, whose body was *already* sold, represented a similar "problem" for the wives of slaveholders. (121)

32. Elizabeth Fox-Genovese's study of black and white women in the antebellum period provides an insightful and very readable account of this often intimate and always exploitive relation. See especially 372–96 for an examination of Jacobs' narrative. Bernhard's collection offers a series of essays that together insist on the interconnections between the

identities of differently raced and classed southern women. In this sense, Rable's exclusive focus on white women limits his otherwise useful work. For her part, Clifton sees the quest to understand the antebellum plantation as fundamentally involving cross-gender and cross-racial inquiry, and offers a wealth of images from the period in addition to her straightforward historical narrative. For a reader fresh to the topic, Clinton's book would be a good place to begin his or her inquiry.

33. Hazel Carby insists on the interwoven construction of black and white female sexuality:

> In order to perceive the cultural effectivity of ideologies of black female sexuality, it is necessary to consider the determining force of ideologies of white female sexuality: stereotypes only appear to exist in isolation while actually depending on a nexus of figurations which can be explained only in relation to each other. Therefore, I will discuss and analyze ideologies of white Southern womanhood, as far as they influence or shape ideologies of black womanhood, and will argue that two very different but interdependent codes of sexuality operated in the antebellum South, producing opposing definitions of motherhood and womanhood for white and black women which coalesce in the figures of the slave and the mistress. (20)

As should be clear from the following references, Carby's analysis of this issue in *Reconstructing Womanhood* has instructed my own thinking about this passage in Jacobs.

34. As Carby puts it, the slave woman's "reproductive destiny was bound to capital accumulation; black women gave birth to property and, directly, to capital itself in the form of slaves, and all slaves inherited their status from their mothers" (*Reconstructing Womanhood*, 24–25).

35. Again, Carby's work in *Reconstructing Womanhood* is relevant here, especially 20–39 for an acute analysis of how power, race, and sexuality played out in the relation between slave mistress and female slave. On the scapegoating of black women for their own rape by white men, Carby writes:

> The effect of black female sexuality on the white male was represented in an entirely different form from that of the figurative power of white female sexuality. Confronted by the black woman, the white man behaved in a manner that was considered to be entirely untempered by any virtuous qualities; the white male, in fact, was represented as being merely prey to the rampant sexuality of his female slaves. A basic assumption of the principles underlying the cult of true womanhood was the necessity for the white female to "civilize" the baser instincts of man. But in the face of what was constructed as the overt sexuality of the black female, excluded as she was from the parameters of virtuous possibilities, these baser male instincts were entirely uncontrolled. Thus, the white slave master was not regarded as being responsible for his actions toward his black female slaves. On the contrary, it was the female slave who was held

responsible for being a potential, and direct, threat to the conjugal sanctity of the white mistress. (*Reconstructing Womanhood*, 27) While there was undoubtedly more variation to white female response than Carby acknowledges here—Mrs. Flint, like many white southern women, is furious at her husband's sexual interest in Jacobs—Carby's larger point about "blaming the victim" is well taken.

36. Valerie Smith suggests how the generic plot of the slave narrative was better suited to traditional male experiences, especially (though she does not remark on it particularly) traditional male *natural* experience.

    As the writer of a slave narrative, Jacobs's freedom to reconstruct her life was limited by a genre that suppressed subjective experience in favor of abolitionist polemics. But if slave narrators in general were restricted by the antislavery agenda, Jacobs was doubly bound by the form in which she wrote, for it contained a plot more compatible with received notions of masculinity than with those of womanhood. Like the archetypical hero of the bildungsroman or the adventure tale, the representative hero of the slave narrative moves from the idyllic life of childhood ignorance in the country into a metaphoric wilderness, in this case the recognition of his status as a slave. His struggle for survival requires him to overcome numerous obstacles, but through his own talents (and some Providential assistance), he finds the Promised Land of a responsible social position, a job, and a wife. The slave narrative extols the hero's stalwart individuality. And the narratives of male slaves often link the escape to freedom to the act of physically subduing the master. (216)

37. As Valerie Smith puts it: "Given the constraints that framed her ordinary life, even the act of choosing her own mode of confinement constituted an exercise of will, an indirect assault against her master's domination" (212–13).

38. See Barbara Cook's fascinating essay that, among other topics, examines Jacobs's loophole as a forerunner of the environmental justice movement's intervention on mainstream environmentalism.

39. As Kawash notes, "the space of the garret is invisible, unserveilled, unregulated. It is a space excluded by the space of slavery; and this very exclusion marks the limits of slavery's totalizing premise of opposition between person and property" (76). Kawash's reading of Jacob's loophole significantly influenced my own.

40. Which is not to say, of course, that being confronted with a pack of hungry wolves doesn't appropriately produce enormous stress—but stress that, "normally," would lead Bibb to focus on those wolves exclusively, and not on his memories of slavery.

41. See both Dixon's book and his essay in the Davis and Gates collection for a very different view of how slaves related to the natural world. Some, but perhaps not all, of my differences with Dixon may be explained by the sort of "nature" each of us is referencing; his "nature" is, I think, more symbolic and less material than mine. But a concept as ambiguous

as "nature" of course leaves ample room for both of our positions to coexist.

42. As Elizabeth Dodd writes in discussing landscape in African-American literature, "actions become embodied in the landscape, surviving their actors and remaining in their original location" (181).

43. See Osofsky 14–15 and 17 for more on these local escapes.

44. Indeed, as Bennett notes, "the only consistent *pastoral* vision in early African-American culture is of the Promised Land waiting beyond this mortal coil" (199).

4   Trauma, Postbellum Nostalgia, and the Lost Pastoral

1. At least a boy without Douglass's combination of genius, iron will, and extraordinarily good luck.

2. And this association was, of course, itself a subset of a larger crisis for white supremacy that Emancipation catalyzed: the supposedly essential freedom of whiteness had long been defined relationally, as the inverse of slavery's abjection. As Saidiya Hartman asks, "If slave status was the primary determinant of racial identity in the antebellum period, with 'free' being equivalent to 'white' and slave status defining blackness, how does the production and valuation of race change in the context of freedom and equality?" (118)

3. Bay suggests that whites' commitment to this form of ecologically destructive commodity agriculture was not necessarily shared by African-American farmers after the war: "Both Southern planters and Northern businessmen wanted to see the South return to producing cotton for export, and both feared that free black laborers would favor the cultivation of staples for their own subsistence over the cultivation of cotton" (146).

4. On this issue, see Leys.

5. As Yellin writes: "*Swallow Barn* is generally characterized as the book which first embodied the pattern of the plantation novel" (10). Yellin's chapter (49–62) on Kennedy provides a worthwhile introduction to the racism of both the novel and its author.

6. See Tara McPherson's recent work for an engaging and insightful analysis of contemporary Southern nostalgia.

7. Page's comments and the quotation can be found in his "Social Life in Old Virginia," 147–48. The original is in Bagby, 3–4.

8. As Moore's "Introduction" notes, "notions of nature often function by effacing the very traces of their fabrication through human labor," and "[t]his naturalization of identities and differences is one of the most powerful means by which race works" (9).

9. Not only is whiteness naturalized here, but gender as well, to some extent; this is a horse*man*. And, as Jane Censer notes in her study of the construction of postbellum white southern womanhood, white women often had a much more ambiguous relation to the rural setting than

white men did: "While twentieth-century popular fiction tends to dwell on the affection of aristocrats for their ancestral acres, the attitudes of nineteenth-century privileged women toward plantations were far more ambivalent" (138).

10. See Ritterhouse for an analysis of "the process of constructing social memory" in the Lost Cause, outside of the specific context of trauma that I bring to bear here.

11. In calling this fantasized past a "seamless narrative," I do not mean "narrative" to suggest historical or temporal development. As Romine insists, rightly: "the antebellum literary mind devoted its principal energy toward preserving a pastoral vision of chattel slavery that resisted insertion in a historical sequence or plot. More specifically, the plantation itself did not translate effortlessly into narrative; the literary plantation was in every way a less stable institution than its rhetorical counterpart" (66–67).

12. As Clinton notes, "white voices enter the text only to frame the 'verbatim' black chronicles, published wholly in dialect. As linguists have reminded us, this 'black English' is really white racist rendering of African-American language. 'Wuz' for 'was' and 'dere' for 'there' were not the spellings used by blacks; rather, the way in which whites consistently misspelled black speech conveyed a sense of racial superiority. Whites' perfect grammar and spelling are the bookends that enclose these 'black voices' and are meant to provide stark contrast" (202).

13. Censer lays the blame for the initial construction of this devoted retainer figure at Page's feet: "[P]rivileged women did not lead the way in inventing these devoted slaves of the past. It was Thomas Nelson Page, rather than his female counterparts, who limned the description of the old servant who was so devoted to his master that he too reminisced about the good old days and the grandeur of the planter family" (75). Though certainly, as Censer notes, white women soon adopted Page's vision, particularly in the figure of the Mammy.

14. Indeed, as Clyde N. Wilson's "Introduction" to the 1991 edition of *In Ole Virginia* demonstrates, the sort of history Page represents retains contemporary currency. Wilson, a historian at the University of South Carolina and a member of the right-wing southern heritage group The League of the South, offers an essay to me remarkable for its seemingly uncritical embrace of Page's worldview.

15. As Romine notes, such a reliance rendered unstable the whole postbellum white supremacist project of (re)building a supposedly lost organic community:

> To establish itself as an organic order—that is, a natural rather than a constructed or instrumental one—the community and its representatives must therefore establish two things, the natural basis of division and the collective basis of unity. Division, then, is defined from the top down, while unity is asserted from the

bottom up. Because deprivileged groups are required to participate consensually in the social order, they acquire a certain power to disrupt community, which can never overtly announce itself as a form of coercion. (7)

16. As Hagood notes: "He [Page] designates African Americans as the representatives of the Southern periphery and not only empowers Southern whites but also transfers the rich capabilities of empowerment inherent in the peripheral position to former slaves. Presenting African Americans as legitimate regionalized figures raises their status to a level of visibility and control of the narrative that imbues them with a narrative strategy as potentially subversive and powerful as that of aristocratic white Southerners themselves" (427).

17. In saying this, I don't mean to suggest, of course, that some absolute racial authenticity is possible, either in or out of the text. But that said, there is a real, if blurry, difference between authors like Pages whose portrayal of black people makes them little more than symbols of his own self-serving racist fantasies, and authors who are genuinely interested in representing the lived experience of black people. Giving up on an absolute notion of authenticity doesn't have to mean giving up on a relative one.

18. For more on the degradation of southern land under slave agriculture, see Steinberg and Genovese.

19. As Romine comments about the relation between the slave and the plantation (as Page imagines it): "the plantation absorbs the abstract slave with his instinctive will to power and transforms him into a concrete bulwark of conservatism and positive commitment to the status quo" (88).

20. Sundquist, for example, notes how "Harris was the first to pay careful tribute to the great complexity of inherited African American folklore," though "came perilously close to perpetuating the sentiment that blacks were indeed closer to the animal kingdom" (341). I differ here largely in my emphasis: first, rather than "coming perilously close," it seems to me Harris in fact builds his stories on a black/animal conflation at the core of slavery. Second, I see that conflation as essentially connected to a larger white supremacist eco-racial project of rehabilitating the structures of antebellum racism after the war. That said, my focus is also much narrower; Sundquist's analysis of Harris, like the rest of his book, is not readily reducible to summary, a tribute to its remarkable breadth and subtlety. See also Rittenhouse for a more sympathetic and perhaps less dismissive discussion of Harris's racial views. Mixon provides a well-known defense of Harris on this issue. For a comprehensive introduction to Harris criticism, see Bickley and Keenan. Bickley's collection of essays is also useful.

21. "Patter-rollers" are patrols, the groups of (generally) poor whites who looked for and challenged black people who were off the plantation without white supervision.

5 TRAUMA AND METAMORPHOSIS IN CHARLES CHESNUTT'S CONJURE TALES

1. On this topic see also Fabre's collection. In the introduction by O'Meally and Fabre, they note:

    The legacy of slavery and the serried workings of racism and prejudice have meant that even the most optimistic black Americans are, as the expression goes, "born knowing" that there is a wide gulf between America's promises and practices. For blacks this tragic consciousness has spelled a cautious and critical attitude toward unfolding experience—a stance toward history that is braced by the awareness that the past, as Faulkner put it, has never really *passed*. (3)

2. See Martin for a comparative study of Page and Chesnutt's engagement with the "plantation myth."

3. Of course, such historical trauma and other forms of violently produced alienation can give dispossessed and traumatized groups greater insight into the historical context of their moments, can denaturalize "contemporary" cultural practices, and can be a vital source of the avant-garde, but that is different from the issue of periodization.

4. As Paul Gilroy notes, the trauma of slavery echoes through African-American art: "though they were unspeakable, these terrors were not inexpressible, and...residual traces of their necessarily painful expression still contribute to historical memories inscribed and incorporated into the volatile core of Afro-Atlantic cultural creation" (*Black Atlantic*, 73). As noted, Eyerman's important work on how the trauma of slavery propagates through postbellum African-American culture informs my own reading in this chapter and throughout the latter half of the book. See also Erikson's essay on community trauma in Caruth.

5. Sundquist's deservedly influential long chapter, "Charles Chesnutt's Cakewalk," in *To Wake the Nations* (271–453) understands Chesnutt's work as part of the larger hybridization of African and European influences that constructed African-American culture. See especially 323–406 for a discussion specifically focused on *The Conjure Woman*. McWilliams argues in part that the fluidity of conjuration and the proliferation of narrative frames that Chesnutt employs works against the essentialist understanding of identity upon which racism depends. See Werner for another poststructuralist reading of the conjure tales and Duncan for an analysis of Chesnutt's own ambiguous authorial position. Myers's chapter on Chesnutt (87–110) and Mondie's essay both see Julius as engaged in part in an ecologically based struggle against John's environmental depredations. While I find both discussions useful, I read Julius's relation to the natural world as much more fraught than either critic. McElrath's recent book collects a good introductory survey of some of the most historically influential interpretations of Chesnutt's work.

6. Several recent essays on the gothic in Chesnutt suggest in a more limited way the traumatic reading I advance here. See especially Ianovici and Goldner.

7. In seeing conjuration as deeply connected to slavery as well as potentially liberating, I part somewhat with Houston Baker's greater emphasis on the empowering nature of conjuration. As Baker writes:

> [C]onjure is a power of transformation that causes definitions of "form" as fixed and comprehensible "thing" to dissolve. Black men, considered by slavery as "things" or "chattel personal," are transformed through conjure into seasonal vegetation figures, or trees, or gray wolves. White men, in turn, are transmuted into surly and abused "noo niggers." A black child is changed into a hummingbird and a mockingbird. A black woman becomes a cat, and an elderly man's clubfoot is a reminder of his transformation—under a conjurer's "revenge"—into a mule.
>
> The fluidity of *The Conjure Woman's* world, symbolized by such metamorphoses, is a function of the black narrator's mastery of form. The old man knows the sounds that are dear to the hearts of his white boss and his wife, and he presents them with conjuring efficaciousness. In effect, he presents a world in which "dialect" masks the drama of African spirituality challenging and changing the disastrous transformations of slavery. (*Modernism*, 44)

While I largely agree with Baker's interpretation of conjuration's emancipatory possibilities, I do read conjuration as considerably more double-edged than he does here.

8. I am indebted to Richard Brodhead's edition of *The Conjure Woman* that restores stories like "Dave's Neckliss" to the collection that were rejected by the first publisher. Brodhead's introduction to the tales and their publication history is essential reading for any scholar of Chesnutt.

9. The editor, Walter Hines Page, cut "Dave's Neckliss" from the collection and got Chesnutt to write six additional conjure tales in six weeks to round out the volume. The 1899 volume includes "The Goophered Grapevine" and "Po' Sandy" first, then inserts one of the six, "Mars Jeems's Nightmare" before "The Conjurer's Revenge." The last three tales, "Sis Becky's Pickaninny," "The Gray Wolf's Ha'nt," and "Hot-Foot Hannibal" were all written during that extraordinary six-week burst. See Brodhead 14–18 and 23–26 for more on the chronology of Chesnutt's composition and his relation to Page.

10. Note how John's subsequent exploitation of the land he buys mirrors the earlier pattern of northern white despoliation marked by the particularly environmentally destructive turpentine industry.

11. Here and throughout the essay, I use Julius's name—"Dugal'"—for his old master.

12. See Matthew Martin, 30, for a discussion of the significance of horse trading in southern culture.

13. Brodhead, for example, reads Julius's narratives as a form of conjuration: "Like the conjure woman working her roots or distributing her goopher mixtries, Julius's storytelling creates a zone of reality under his imaginative control, the space of a fictional reality. Casting his own kind of spell, the persuasion of his telling relocates his hearers' imaginations within this mind-managed world, where he can subject them to the counterforce of his different understanding" (10).

14. See Saxton, 69.

15. Angelina Weld Grimké's short story "Goldie" ends with a similarly nightmarish vision of a forest full of lynching trees. I discuss her story at some length in chapter eight.

6 STRANGE FRUIT

1. Ayers's study of Reconstruction provides an engaging introduction to the post-Reconstruction South.

2. Romine sees these sharply incompatible roles in terms of a "duel movement":

   On the one hand claimed as a devoted retainer and virtual member of the family (hence the master code, "we alone know the Negro") and on the other as an alien race and a threat to southern purity (hence their equation with contamination), African Americans existed on the margins of community. To put the matter another way, the Negro was rhetorically integrated into the community even as the African American was physically and symbolically separated from it. (21)

3. See Rachel Adams 36–37 for a discussion of the exhibit, and generally for an insightful analysis of so-called freak shows.

4. Saidaya Hartman notes how what she calls the "nonevent of Emancipation" (116) with its formal declaration of equality—and, I would argue here, the largely betrayed egalitarian possibilities of Darwin's work—made the sort of naturalized hierarchies represented by the What Is It? that much more important. She writes:

   The legacy of slavery was evidenced by the intransigence of racism, specifically the persistent declarations of inequality or violations of life, liberty, and property based on prior condition of servitude or race. On one hand, the constraints of race were formally negated by the stipulation of sovereign individuality and abstract equality, and on the other, racial discriminations and predilections were cherished and protected as beyond the scope of law. Even more unsettling was the instrumental role of equality in constructing a measure of man or descending scale of humanity that legitimated and naturalized subordination. (121)

5. While whites unsurprisingly dominated the "ethnological sciences," black writers and scientists also engaged in research and speculation on "innate" white savagery. See, for example, Hosea Easton's 1837 *Treatise on the*

Intellectual Character, and Civil and Political Condition of the Colored People of the United States, and James W.C. Pennington's 1841 *Text Book of the History of the Colored Race.* For more on Easton, Pennington, and others, Bay's work provides an invaluable reference, though Bay observes how the latest debates in ethnological theory were unlikely to be the main concern of largely uneducated slaves and ex-slaves, or, for that matter, for many of their ignorant owners. Bay insists, rightly I think, on the primacy of agricultural metaphors in the lived experience of degradation for most black people in this time:

> Steeped in a universalist understanding of Christianity and wholly unaware of scientific questions about the origins of the races, ex-slaves did not worry about tracing the biblical descent of their own race. Nor did they share the black intellectuals' anxieties about being mistaken for monkeys or apes—species largely unfamiliar to uneducated black Southerners. Instead, these African-Americans worried about being taken for animals of a different kind, complaining that whites made little distinction between black people and domestic animals. (119)

6. The full text of the first advertisement reads:
   "WHAT IS IT"?
   Is it a lower order of MAN? Or is it a higher order of MONKEY? None can tell! Perhaps it is a combination of both. It is beyond dispute THE MOST MARVELLOUS CREATURE LIVING. It was captured in a savage state in Central Africa, is probably about 20 years old, 4 feet high, intelligent, docile, active, sportive, and PLAYFUL AS A KITTEN. It has the skull, limbs and general anatomy of an ORANG OUTANG and the COUNTENANCE of a HUMAN BEING.

7. These quotes are taken from an advertisement for the exhibit in the March 1, 1860 *New York Tribune.* The CUNY Graduate School and the Center for History and New Media at George Mason University have constructed a website that provides invaluable information and images about Barnum's Museum of Wonders. The home page can be found at <http://www.lostmuseum.cuny.edu/home.html>.

8. The critical literature on the pervasive popular anti-black imagery in the nineteenth and twentieth century is far too substantial to note exhaustively here. Perhaps the best place to start is the online collection of the Jim Crow Museum of Racist Memorabilia at Ferris State, <http://www.ferris.edu/news/jimcrow/>. I found Hale's analysis as acute as the rest of her excellent book. See especially 121–97. Michael Harris's volume offers engaging interpretation and a wealth of reproductions of both racist imagery and African-American painting. Goings's book provides an invaluable introduction to the study of so-called collectables.

9. The full text of the cartoon reads: [Greeley]: "Gentlemen allow me to introduce to you, this illustrious individual in whom you will find combined all the intelligence and virtue of Black Republicanism, and whom we propose to you as the next Candidate for the Presidency." [What Is It?]: "What, can dey be!" [Lincoln]: "How fortunate! that this intelligent

and noble creature should have been discovered just at this time to prove to the world the superiority of the Colored over the Anglo Saxon race, he will be a worthy successor to carry out the policy which I shall inaugurate." Frost discusses this image on 7–9.

10. Before the war, the most influential polygenic theorists were Samuel Morton (whose research into race and cranial size led him to assemble the world's largest collection of human skulls, called the "American Golgotha" at the time), Josiah Nott and George Glidden (especially their 1854 *Types of Mankind)*, and Louis Agassiz, a Swiss naturalist who believed blacks and whites were different species altogether.

11 In Carroll's earlier work, *The Tempter of Eve*, the tempter is a black woman, thereby, at least in part, dodging the "unspeakable" possibility of Eve having sex with a black man, and, presumably, the question of why God "only" turned the tempter into a snake, rather than lynching him in the (southern) Garden.

12. Carroll's loathing for "mulattos" was also self-loathing, since, as Eric Sundquist claims, he was himself of "mixed" blood (395). Carroll's pathology then amounts to a re-externalization and further amplification of already internalized hate speech. Less intense varieties of this sort of mental illness recur in some members of minority communities to this day, as we see in the virulent homophobia of closeted right-wing activists, or in female antifeminist crusaders. Stokes discusses this issue on 104–7, and includes a photograph of Carroll that, perhaps predictably, fails to "establish" Carroll's racial essence. The question is both fascinating and finally beside the point. There is no biographical study of Carroll of which I am aware, an unfortunate absence given his importance in the development of the ideology of present-day hate groups like the Aryan Nations and the so-called Christian Identity movement. I certainly would admire the fortitude of any scholar willing to spend that much time with such a reprehensible figure.

13. Bay, for example, calls the book "probably the most egregiously racist production of the era" (95).

14. Note that "all other living things" includes all people of color since "they" are supposedly the result of ancient miscegenation, and therefore, are also Beasts with no souls. And since, as noted above, Carroll's own ancestry may well have been mixed, he was here declaring himself to be a Beast.

15. It is fascinating to observe how often anxiety about interracial sex was expressed in environmentally apocalyptic terms, not only in explicitly white supremacist postbellum work like Carroll's, but in antebellum abolitionist tracts as well. Take, for example, William Lloyd Garrison's 1853 outburst in the *Liberator*:

> There are in this country a million females who have no protection for their chastity, and who may be ravished by their masters or drivers with impunity!! There are born every year more than SIXTY THOUSAND infant slaves who are *illegitimate!* a large

proportion of whom have *white fathers*—some of these are the most distinguished men at the south—who sell them as they would pigs or sheep!! *Is not this perdition upon earth*—A BURNING HELL IN THE VERY BOSOM OF OUR COUNTRY—A VOLCANO OF LUST AND IMPURITY, *threatening to blast every plant of virtue, and to roll its lava tide over all that is beautiful to the eye, or precious in the sight of God.* (qtd. in Carby, *Reconstructing Womanhood*, 35. The various forms of emphases are in the original.)

And Garrison's imagery, of course, itself echoes Thoreau's in "Slavery in Massachusetts" that I discussed in the second chapter. Despite their sharp political differences, all three writers transform concerns about racially based violence into violence against the natural world.

16. As Grace Hale notes about this transition, commenting on the plot of Dixon's *Clansman*, "The fall from plantation grace, the loss of racial ease that makes segregation the only possible future, have been African Americans' fault all along. Beastlike blacks have destroyed the Old South's racial paradise and the North's idealistic if misguided attempt to lift up an 'inferior race'" (79).

17. Censer notes how the postbellum fear and hatred of black men was, initially, largely a white male problem, not appearing prominently in white women's writings until the end of the century when widespread fear of rape began to limit the independence some white women had enjoyed after the war:

> In the 1890s, southern women of all classes became more thoroughly enmeshed in the racial tragedy that came to characterize the twentieth-century South. The "great reaction" brought black disenfranchisement, the spread of segregation, and terroristic measures such as lynching and whitecapping. Earlier in the postwar years, racialist ideas had suffused white women's writings, but women had rarely displayed the contempt for blacks evident in southern white men's public and private utterances. By the end of the century, this had changed. Women were penning their share of the hate-filled articles and novels that characterized the period. A growing fear of blacks—especially black men—among white women was a critical factor in this development. The increased female autonomy of the postwar years had sparked a desire for greater freedom of movement and travel; racism compromised this freedom, with its constant warning that white women needed "protection" from black men, in the countryside or the city.
>
> These developments emerged from certain elements of the immediate postwar past. While discarding the kinds of interracial cooperation that had appeared after Reconstruction, a majority of Southerners from the old elite concentrated on celebrating their earlier history of slavery and the Confederacy. As they demanded and enforced white supremacy, these members of the old elite harkened back to an ideal, mythical antebellum regime in which racial hierarchy and harmony supposedly had prevailed. In this

re-creation of a past South, the only women celebrated were the plantation mistress and belle, and they primarily for their ornamental functions.... (279–80)

This shift suggests both the disciplinary function the Black Beast figure performed for the white patriarchy, as well as the connection of the Beast to the formation of the postbellum antebellum plantation pastoral.

18. For an acute discussion of interracial rape and lynching in this period see Gunning; she discusses Dixon specifically from 19–47.

19. This supplanting of rape by more straightforward physical violence also obtains in the rape scene of little Flora in Dixon's earlier novel, *The Leopard's Spots.* As Eby comments, "while Dixon is lavish with violent details, most of them point to murder, few to rape" (445).

20. For more on the dangers and critical promise of interracial intimacy in U.S. history and culture, see especially Sollors' collection, Hodes on the history of the nineteenth-century South specifically, and Randall Kennedy's work.

21. The reality that fathers can more easily deny their children than mothers can—just ask Hester Prynne—was a central part of the operation of slavery and the oppression of the black and white women (in much different ways) who lived under it. Slavery would have developed much differently, and ended much more quickly if white men had been minimally decent fathers. To compare the parental dedication of Harriet Jacobs and Mr. Sands, for example, underscores how central deadbeat white dads have been to the "problem" of race in American history.

22. As Eby notes generally "the 'beast' stereotype delineates a particular linking of eros and thanatos: the rape of a white woman as a prelude to her death and/or to the lynching of her accused rapist" (439).

23. This is same sort of white female landscape "blooming with flowers and overarched by a sunny sky" that Jacobs saw as the destiny of the little white girl in contrast to her darker sister that I discussed in chapter three.

24. Sappho not only survives the gang rape in a brothel in early adolescence that results in the conception of her child, she survives with her "natural" beauty intact. Indeed, in what seems to me an intervention on the postbellum association of the southern landscape and white female sexual purity, Sappho's "mulatto" beauty is portrayed as the produce of the southland:

Tall and fair, with hair of a golden cast, aquiline nose, rosebud mouth, soft brown eyes veiled by long, dark lashes which swept her cheek, just now covered with a delicate rose flush, she burst upon them—a combination of "queen rose and lily in one."

"Lord," said Ophelia Davis to her friend Sarah Ann, "I haven't see enything look like thet chile since I lef' home."

"That's the truth, 'Phelia," replied Sarah Ann; "that's somethin' God made, honey; thar ain't nothin' like thet growed outside o' Loosyannie." (107)

25. Carby writes about this cruel opposition between white and black women that patriarchy sets up, maintains, and from which it benefits: "Measured against the sentimental heroines of domestic novels, the

black woman repeatedly failed the test of true womanhood because she survived her institutionalized rape, whereas the true heroine would rather die than be sexually abused. Comparison between these figurations of black versus white womanhood also encouraged readers to conclude that the slave woman must be less sensitive and spiritually inferior" (*Reconstructing Womanhood*, 34).

26. As Stokes notes in his chapter on Dixon's *Leopard's Spots*, "White female bodies become sexual territory to be displayed, fought over, and protected" (133). Literally so, here.

27. All three are collected in the 2002 *On Lynching*.

28. Since between 75 and 90 percent of lynching's victims were black (Litwack, 12), and the vast majority of both victims and perpetrators were men, my focus on the practice risks occluding women's experience. Of greatest concern here, for me, is how black women's experience drops out in a focus on lynching, especially given that their experience is already suppressed in the historical record. On this issue, see Wiegman's "Anatomy." While lynching imagery might return traumatically, for example, to a contemporary black man walking alone in deep woods of the South in a way that imperiled the opportunity for natural communion, the equivalent traumatic return for a black woman walking alone might additionally include a historically justified anxiety over rape at the hands of white men. Discussing her fear of the wilderness, Evelyn White declares explicitly, "I was certain that if I ventured outside to admire a meadow or to feel the cool ripples in a stream, I'd be taunted, attacked, raped, maybe even murdered because of the color of my skin. I believe the fear I experience in the outdoors is shared by many African-American women and colors the decisions we make about our lives" (378).

29. Robert Snyder claims that over 50 million dollars worth of these photographs had been sold by 1909.

30. For a short and fascinating account of the history of the song's reception, see Margolick. See also Moore's "Introduction," especially 9.

31. The critical literature on lynching is enormous. For me the most useful texts have been Wells's early study, Hale's analysis of "spectacle lynching" (199–239), Apel's work on imagery, and the Allen *Without Sanctuary* collection of lynching photography (as well as Litwack's important introduction to the collection), and Gunning's and Jacquelyn Dowd Hall's work on women and lynching. Pinar's monumental (more than 1,200 pages) recent volume on same-sex desire and racial violence not only makes an important argument but offers an exhaustive reading of the relevant critical literature; see especially 183–234 for a summary of recent attempts to "explain" lynching.

32. As Saidiya Hartman pointedly asks in reference to the reproduction of, and critical commentary on, whipping scenes in the narratives:

At issue here is the precariousness of empathy and the uncertain line between witness and spectator. Only more obscene than the brutality unleashed at the whipping post is the demand that this suffering be materialized and evidenced by the display of the tortured body or endless recitations of the ghastly and terrible. In light of this, how does one give expression to these outrages without exacerbating the indifference to suffering that is the consequence of the benumbing spectacle or contend with the narcissistic identification that obliterates the other or the prurience that too often is the response to such displays? (4) Hartman responds to this genuine danger by focusing on "scenes in which terror can hardly be discerned.... the terror of the mundane and quotidian rather than...the shocking spectacle" (4). My approach is different—to draw a line that explicitly marks physically and emotionally the end of representation, of secondary trauma, and the beginning of the lynched subject's primary and unimaginable suffering. This line is intimately bound up with—and is as familiar as—the speechlessness of the nonhuman natural itself, the "thing" or context to which the human subject is both symbolically and literally reduced in the act of lynching.

33. For more on trauma in Morrison, see Bouson, Ramadanovic, and Spargo's article. For an explicitly ecocritical examination of Morrison's writing, see Wallace.

34. Professor Daniel Martin brought this quotation to my attention as part of his presentation, "Lynching Sites and the Trauma of Racial Violence: Richard Wright, Toni Morrison, Billy Holliday" at the 2003 Association for the Study of Literature and the Environment conference. The presentation was part of the panel "Racial Violence, Trauma, and the Experience of Nature" organized by my colleague at the University of Maine at Farmington, Michael Johnson. I contributed a paper to the panel, "Traumatic Metamorphosis in Charles Chesnutt," that not only formed the basis of chapter five but first got me thinking about the larger issue of the relation between natural experience and the construction of blackness and whiteness at the core of this book. Martin's invaluable essay in Ingram provides a fuller version of the conference paper.

7   WHITE FLIGHT

1. In this, my analysis compliments Amy Kaplan's recent work on U.S. imperialism, and her resistance to the Frontier as *the* explanatory master trope. As she insists in *The Anarchy of Empire*, an overemphasis on the Frontier, ...risks reproducing the teleological narrative that imperialism tells about itself, the inexorable westward march of empire. Furthermore, by taking as foundational the confrontation between white settlers and Native Americans, this approach also overlooks how intimately the issues of slavery and emancipation and relations between blacks and whites were intertwined with each stage of U.S. imperial expansion [....] [T]he representations of U.S. imperialism were mapped not through a West/East axis of frontier symbols and politics, but

instead through a North/South axis around the issues of slavery, Reconstruction, and Jim Crow segregation. The conquest of Indian and Mexican lands in the antebellum period cannot be understood separately from the expansion of slavery and the struggle for freedom. (17–18)

2. And note that it is the story of the frontier, the idea of the West, that matters in the production of the Western sublime, not necessarily actual frontier experience. It is not as if everyone who agreed with Turner's frontier thesis was or had been a cowboy.

3. In asserting the importance of this identification of whiteness and the Western landscape, I am not asserting of course that the West was, in reality, a space entirely without black people. For more on the African-American presence in the West and on the frontier see Michael Johnson's invaluable book.

4. See my discussion of Morrison in the introduction. The phrase is from *Playing in the Dark*.

5. As Houston Baker notes sharply in *Long Black Song:*

   The legends of men conquering wild and virgin lands are not the legends of black America; the stories of benevolent theocracies bringing light and salvation to pagans are not the stories of black America; and the tales of pioneers enduring the hardships of the West for the promise of immense wealth are not the tales of black America. When the black American reads Frederick Jackson Turner's *The Frontier in American History*, he feels no regret over the end of the Western frontier. To black America, *frontier* is an alien word; for, in essence, all frontiers established by the white psyche have been closed to the black man. (2)

6. See also, for example, De Luca, Braun, White, and Reed and Evans in Adamson. Rosendale's collection devotes a section to discussing the sublime in American and English Romantic contexts, see 181–245. Rozelle offers a spirited defense of sublimity as connecting us to a world, often toxic, Outside of human textuality, a textuality he associates with "a codependent, fetishistic relationship to the sign" (61).

7. The literature on the frontier's importance in the establishment of white and male identity is extensive. Slotkin's trilogy is a crucial starting point, especially *Regeneration* and *The Fatal Environment*. See also Rogin's *Fathers* and Drinnon on the role of antinative violence, and Takaki on race more generally in the nineteenth century. For a focus on race in the antebellum period, see Wrobel. Limerick's *Legacy of Conquest* is essential for an early "New West" critique of the frontier. I found Bederman's book on gender, race, and the West to be especially stimulating and useful.

8. Muir expands on this notion of nature as third term, a place outside of human history to which he and the reader share a privileged access in the book's final chapter, a natural version of what Nina Silber calls the "romance of reunion":

   In my walk from Indiana to the Gulf, earth and sky, plants and people, and all things changeable were constantly changing. Even in Kentucky nature and art have many a characteristic shibboleth. The people differ in language and in customs. Their architecture is generically different from that of their immediate neighbors in the north, not only in planters' mansions, but in barns and granaries and the cabins of the poor. But thousands of familiar flower faces looked from every hill and valley. I noted no difference in the sky, and the winds spoke the same things. I did not feel myself in a strange land. (171)

9. See the discussion of Emerson's famous "transparent eyeball" passage in chapter two.

10. The phrase is from Thoreau's "Slavery in Massachusetts," discussed in chapter two.

11. See chapter four for a discussion of Thomas Nelson Page, Joel Chandler Harris and their narrative strategies.

12. Smith's fascinating essay argues that the southern jungle, with its terrific heat, humidity, and rapid decomposition of everything organic, represents a deindividuating threat to the sublime and its "natural" setting in the sharply defined, cold, dry, and mountainous terrain of the north and west.

13. Muir often seems troubled by the degradation he perceives in some poor whites and natives who spend a great deal of time in nature, and is tempted to make a similar move, rendering them unnatural because they are subnatural, though not in the generalizing way he does with African Americans. See his descriptions of Billy and some natives in *My First Summer in the Sierras* for example, especially 199, 237–38, and 273 (*Eight Books*).

14. And Muir himself sounds very much like a Deep Ecologist at moments in the narrative. For example, he declares only half in jest: "But more than aught else mankind requires burning, as being in great part wicked, and if that transmundane furnace can be so applied and regulated as to smelt and purify us into conformity with the rest of the terrestrial creation, then the tophetisation of the erratic genus Homo were a consummation devoutly to be prayed for" (161). For more on Muir and Deep Ecology, see Devall, and Heffernan in Miller.

15. This division was a structural part of the division between "mainstream" environmentalism and the environmental justice movement that I discussed in the opening to this book, a division that mainstream environmentalism has, to its credit, moved to address subsequently.

16. Emancipation in Cuba did not occur until 1886, although importation of African slaves ended in 1865. Between 1800 and 1865, Cuba imported more than 600,000 African slaves, out of a total island population of 1.3 million in 1860 ("Cuba," *Britannica*).

17. Take for example, the two paragraphs that immediately precede this one in Muir's text:

Havana has a fine botanical garden. I spent pleasant hours in its magnificent flowery arbours and around its shady fountains. There is a palm avenue which is considered wonderfully stately and beautiful, fifty palms in two straight lines, each rigidly perpendicular. The smooth round shafts, slightly thicker in the middle, appear to be productions of the lathe, rather than vegetable stems. The fifty arched crowns, inimitably balanced, blaze in the sunshine like heaps of stars that have fallen from the skies. The stems were about sixty or seventy feet in height, the crowns about fifteen feet in diameter.

Along a stream-bank were tall, waving bamboos, leafy as willows, and infinitely graceful in wind gestures. There was one species of palm, with immense bipinnate leaves and leaflets fringed, jagged, and one-sided, like those of *Adiantum*. Hundreds of the most gorgeous-flowered plants, some of them large trees, belonging to the *Leguminosae*. Compared with what I have before seen in artificial flower-gardens, this is past comparison the grandest. It is a perfect metropolis of the brightest and most exuberant of garden plants, watered by handsome fountains, while graveled and finely bordered walks slant and curve in all directions, and in all kinds of fanciful playground styles, more like the fairy gardens of the Arabian Nights than any ordinary man-made pleasure ground. (169)

18. In general, discussions of Muir's explicit anti-black racism are almost nonexistent. Gifford's 2006 *Post-Pastoral*, for example, makes no mention of Muir's anti-black racism in his fairly extensive discussion of *1,000 Mile Walk to the Gulf*. See DeLuca and Demo's article for a discussion of Muir's role in creating a white wilderness at Yellowstone, though not one focused particularly on his racism.

19. Jon Smith's important essay argues that this rejection of the tropical in favor of the Western mountain sublime forms a critical part of how the nation was defined in this period: "I have been suggesting a more basic form of environmental determinism: that by speeding up the ontological transitions of both objects and subjects *as* objects, the greater heat and moisture found in the tropics have tended to make people more aware of materiality—of things themselves, and of themselves as things. Historically, people who like wilderness, who even invest their (usually 'American') identity in the idea of it—a roster of whom would include Muir, Miller, Frederick Jackson Turner, and a host of their intellectual disciples—have tended to marginalize the idea of jungle, even to define 'America in opposition to it'" (117).

20. See, for example, in *Sierras*, 243–44, 247–48 (*Eight Books*).

21. For more on Muir as a religious writer, see Gatta, especially 148–56.

8 MIGRATIONS

1. All told, between 1910 and 1970 more than 6.5 million African Americans left the south for the north (Lemann, 6).

2. In addition to Harrison, I found Lemann's history of the Great Migration particularly useful.

3. Only "Goldie" was published at the time, and neither story has attracted much critical attention subsequently, a neglect I think is very much unwarranted. Hirsch's important article is a notable exception. See also

Hull's chapter on Grimké, 107–52. I am indebted to Michael Johnson for bringing these stories to my attention.

4. Barbara Foley notes, for example, how the case "attracted attention because of its particular ferocity and inhumanity" and describes how *The Crisis* "continually reverted to the Turner case as an archetypical instance of Southern barbarism" (7).

5. Hirsch's comments on silence in the story are apposite to mine on how sublimity slips into trauma here: "Grimké's silence often has a different valence, a silence which...results from a confrontation with illogic, but this confrontation usually leads not to metaphysical understanding and communion but to a negation of meaning; it is a defeat rather than a triumph of attempted unification" (461).

6. In asserting that the reader and Reed are all-too-aware of the trees eco-historical context and signification, I differ with Hirsch's claim that "Reed does not know why he shudders listening to the hero's description of trees until he is presented with the 'speech' emanating from the trees themselves and becomes able to translate their 'words' significance" (469).

7. This nightmare forest was not unique to Grimké's imagination. See the discussion in chapter five of Chesnutt's story "Dave's Neckliss," where the delusional protagonist imagines a forest of ham trees (and recall that ham was a code for slave) as a prelude to his own self-lynching.

8. Foley is commenting specifically on Toomer's poems "Georgia Dusk" and "Song of the Sun" here, though she sees this issue pervading *Cane*.

9. As Foley summarizes in her essential essay on *Cane*: "Some scholars read the novel as a nostalgic celebration of a vanishing peasant existence close to the earth. If the text acknowledges the harshness of racism and poverty, it subordinates social protest to lyricism, the representation of the here and now to the search for prophetic truths beyond the limits of history" (181). Foley's article also offers a useful critical review of this fundamental debate: the question of whether Toomer's engagement with the landscape and the lyrical peasantry that he often celebrated served to obscure the history of racial violence, suffering, poverty, and hard labor that were certainly central to the experience of rural black southern life. In addition to Foley, for more on this question, see MacKethan, Kodat, Wardi, Van Mol, Ramsey, and Eldridge.

   Most critics seem to agree that Toomer sometimes, but not always, pastoralizes black suffering, poverty, and white violence. Historical references to lynching are certainly an explicit part of stories like "Blood Burning Moon" and "Kabnis," for example, but it also does seem undeniable that hard rural labor gets an obscuring aesthetic gloss in poems like "Georgia Dusk" and "Song of the Sun," and in stories like "Karintha." My point here is much more specific; given the history this book has been tracing, Toomer's invocation of pastoral lyricism was not simply an escape from history and the reality of black peasant life, but itself an intensely politicized intervention on the naturalizing tradition of racial identity formation.

10. As Kodat writes, "the difficulty, as *Cane* presents it, lies in finding an aesthetic approach to a history of exploitation and domination that does not itself partake of, or promote, such exploitation and domination in the aesthetic register.... The best that *Cane* can hope for, then, is a narrative that enacts the problem it is trying to solve" (13–14). While Kodat is discussing the "dialectic of expression and repression in modernist art" (13) here, that dialectic, it seems to me is reflected throughout *Cane* in Toomer's "uneasy suspension" between nature and the historical trauma that infects it.

11. The question of the interrelation between the pastoral and the rural history of racialized trauma permeates *Cane* and might well be the subject of its own chapter. I focus on "Kabnis" largely because in it, to my eye, Toomer engages most clearly and directly the danger of embracing the black southern pastoral and the cultural loss in rejecting it outright; and indeed, I argue that he makes his art out of that impossible choice.

12. See Carby, "Fiction, Anthropology and the Folk" and Wright's "Between." Barbara Johnson's essential article "Metaphor" takes Wright's review to task for discounting Janie's lived experience: "No message, no theme, no thought: the full range of questions and experiences of Janie's life are as invisible to a mind steeped in maleness as Ellison's Invisible Man is to minds steeped in whiteness" (241).

13. The critical literature on the novel is immense. Goldstein's article offers a very useful reception history of the novel. Awkward's "Introduction" in part discusses how the novel came to be "viewed by a multitude of readers as remarkably successful in its complex, satisfyingly realized depiction of its Afro-American female protagonist's search for self and community" (*New Essays*, 5). Cheryl Wall's chapter on Hurston in *Women* also provides a helpful summary of the critical conflicts over the novel; see especially 193–96. For views of the novel that see the book's natural imagery as part of a larger story of Janie's liberation, see especially Kathleen Davies, Awkward's *Inspiriting*, 15–57. Marks is more critical of what he calls Hurston's "organicist ideology." In an important article for my reading here, Curren also views the book as a gothic horror story as much as a novel of racial and female empowerment, concluding that "Hurston uses the gothic to inoculate black America against the infection of white prejudices" (24).

14. For more on Hurston and Boas, and the relationship of their association to Hurston's figuration of the Great Migration and black identity, see Krasner's Chapter Seven, 113–30, and Suzanne Clark.

15. See Kathleen Davies for a reading of this scene as fundamentally linguistic, a "metaphor for a metaphor," that "merges female orgasm—the pear tree's ecstatic shiver and Janie's simultaneous climax—with poetry to form a feminine poetics" (150–51).

16. Sivils reads Janie's relation to the pear tree and to other trees in the novel as "plac[ing] her within a natural ecological system, a situation that makes sense as Janie repeatedly fails to fit within human communities." See especially 95–99.

17. For Barbara Johnson, indeed, Janie's ability to speak "grows not out of her identity but out of her division into inside and outside. Knowing how not to mix them is knowing that articulate language requires the copresence of two distinct poles, not their collapse into oneness" (238).

18. My reading differs here from Lillios, who sees the hurricane as "the most powerful symbol in the book," that "symbolize[s] creation and regeneration, because it suggests the mingling of the elements," and that "suggests cosmic synergy" (89).

19. As Curren notes, "the title phrase, placed in the text at this particular point, demonstrates just how dependent on the master-slave dialectic and the principle of authority the Everglades folk community really is for Hurston" (17).

20. In a similar, though not environmentally specific, vein, Curren calls Tea Cake's rabies "social corruption...a metaphor for the infection of life-affirming black folk culture by the disease of deadly white prejudices—namely, the master-slave dialectic and the belief that racial hierarchy is justified by nature" (24).

21. Considered in itself, outside of the larger environmental context, the rabies incident is often read as a somewhat mechanical effort to express and contain Janie's anger at Tea Cake's abuse and her desire for independence. Alice Walker offers an early version of this in *Gardens*, 305–6. Marks sees Tea Cake's rabies as a "plot contrivance[] Hurston uses in order to justify his final fit of jealousy and his death" and thereby avoid recognizing the violence (supposedly) inherent in heterosexual unions (156). Kathleen Davies reads Tea Cake's transformation as "the hurricane's—and Hurston's—indirect punishment for his betrayal of Janie" (155). Cassidy sees the image of Janie clinging to the cow with the mad dog on top as a symbolic incarnation of Janie's psychology, both repressing and manifesting her anger (263).

22. Lillios offers a much more hopeful reading of the ending, in which Janie is "transform[ed]...from a woman whose fate depends on others to one who can forge her own destiny" (89).

WORKS CITED

Adams, Carol J. *The Sexual Politics of Meat: A Feminist-Vegetarian Critical Theory.* New York: Continuum, 1990.

Adams, Rachel. *Sideshow U.S.A.: Freaks and the American Cultural Imagination.* Chicago: U of Chicago P, 2001.

Adamson, Joni. *American Indian Literature, Environmental Justice, and Ecocriticism: The Middle Place.* Tucson: U of Arizona P, 2001.

Adamson, Joni, Mei Mei Evans, and Rachel Stein, eds. *The Environmental Justice Reader: Politics, Poetics, and Pedagogy.* Tucson: U of Arizona P, 2002.

Allen, James, Hilton Als, Congressman John Lewis, and Leon F. Litwack. *Without Sanctuary: Lynching Photography in America.* Sante Fe: Twin Palms P, 2000.

Althusser, Louis. "Ideology and Ideological State Apparatuses (Notes toward an Investigation)." Louis Althusser, *Lenin and Philosophy and Other Essays.* Trans. B. Brewster. New York: Monthly Review Press, 1971.

Ammons, A.R. "Giving up Words with Words." *The Selected Poems, Expanded Edition.* New York: W.W. Norton, 1986, 116.

Andrews, William L. "The Representation of Slavery and the Rise of Afro-American Literary Realism 1865–1920." McDowell, *Slavery,* 62–80.

Apel, Dora. *Imagery of Lynching: Black Men, White Women, and the Mob.* New Brunswick: Rutgers UP, 2004.

Arensberg, Mary, ed. *The American Sublime.* Albany: State U of New York P, 1986.

Armbruster, Karla and Kathleen R. Wallace, eds. *Beyond Nature Writing: Expanding the Boundaries of Ecocriticism.* Charlottesville: UP of Virginia, 2001.

Armstrong, Meg. " 'The Effects of Blackness:' Gender, Race, and the Sublime in Aesthetic Theories of Burke and Kant." *The Journal of Aesthetics and Art Criticism.* 54:3 (1996) 213–36.

Ashfield, Andrew and Peter de Bolla, eds. *The Sublime: A Reader in British Eighteenth-Century Aesthetic Theory.* Cambridge: Cambridge UP, 1996.

Awkward, Michael. *Inspiriting Influences: Tradition, Revision, and Afro-American Women's Novels.* New York: Columbia UP, 1991.

———, ed. *New Essays on "Their Eyes Were Watching God."* Cambridge: Cambridge UP, 1990.

Ayers, Edward L. *The Promise of the New South: Life after Reconstruction.* New York: Oxford UP, 1992.

Babb, Valerie. *Whiteness Visible: The Meaning of Whiteness in American Literature and Culture.* New York: New York UP, 1998.

Bagby, George W. *The Old Virginia Gentleman and Other Sketches.* Richmond: Dietz P, 1948.

Baker, Houston A., Jr. "Autobiographical Acts and the Voice of the Southern Slave." Davis, *Slave's Narrative.* 242–61.

———. "Figurations for a New American Literary History." Bercovitch, *Ideology,* 145–71.

———. *Long Black Song: Essays in Black American Literature and Culture.* Charlottesville: UP of Virginia, 1972.

———. *Modernism and the Harlem Renaissance.* Chicago: U of Chicago P, 1987.

Barnhill, David Landis, ed. *At Home On the Earth: Becoming Native to Our Place: A Multicultural Anthology.* Berkeley: U of California P, 1999.

Barringer, Tim. "The Course of Empires: Landscape and Identity in America and Britain, 1820–1880." Wilton, *American Sublime,* 39–65.

Bate, Jonathan. *Romantic Ecology: Wordsworth and the Environmental Tradition.* London: Routledge, 1991.

Bay, Mia. *The White Image in the Black Mind: African-American Ideas about White People, 1830–1925.* New York: Oxford UP, 2000.

Bederman, Gail. *Manliness & Civilization: A Cultural History of Gender and Race in the United States, 1880–1917.* Chicago: U of Chicago P, 1995.

Bennett, Michael. "Anti-Pastoralism, Frederick Douglass, and the Nature of Slavery." Armbruster and Wallace, *Beyond Nature Writing,* 195–210.

Bennett, Michael and David W. Teague, eds. *The Nature of Cities: Ecocriticism and Urban Environments.* Tuscon: U of Arizona P, 1999.

Bercovitch, Sacvan and Myra Jehlen, eds. *Ideology and Classic American Literature.* Cambridge: Cambridge UP, 1986.

Berger, James. *After the End: Representations of Post-Apocalypse.* Minneapolis: U of Minnesota P, 1999.

Bernhard, Virginia, Betty Brandon, Elizabeth Fox-Genovese, Theda Perdue, eds. *Southern Women: Histories and Identities.* Columbia: U of Missouri P, 1992.

Berry, Wendell. *The Hidden Wound.* Boston: Houghton Mifflin, 1970.

Bibb, Henry. *Narrative of the Life and Adventures of Henry Bibb, an American Slave, Written by Himself.* Osofsky, *Puttin' on,* 51–172.

Bickley Jr., R. Bruce, ed. *Critical Essays on Joel Chandler Harris.* Boston: G. K. Hall, 1981.

Bickley Jr., R. Bruce and Hugh T. Keenan, eds. *Joel Chandler Harris: An Annotated Bibliography of Criticism, 1977–1996, with Supplement, 1892–1976.* Westport, Connecticut: Greenwood, 1997.

Boesenberg, Eva. "The Color of Money: Economic Structures of Race and Gender under Slavery." Maria Diedrich, Henry Louis Gates, Jr., and Carl Pedersen, eds. *Black Imagination and the Middle Passage.* New York: Oxford UP, 1999, 117–26.

Bouson, J. Brooks. *"Quiet as It's Kept:" Shame, Trauma, and Race in the Novels of Toni Morrison.* Albany: State U of New York P, 2000.

Branch, Michael P. "Before Nature Writing: Discourses of Colonial American Natural History." Armbruster and Wallace, *Beyond Nature Writing*, 91–107.

———. "Indexing American Possibilities: The Natural History Writing of Bartram, Wilson, and Audubon." Glotfelty, *Ecocriticism Reader*, 282–302.

Branch, Michael P., Rochelle Johnson, and Daniel Patterson, eds. *Reading the Earth: New Directions in the Study of Literature and the Environment.* Moscow, ID: U of Idaho P, 1998.

Braun, Bruce. "'On the Raggedy Edge of Risk': Articulations of Race and Nature After Biology." Moore, *Race*, 175–203.

Brodhead, Richard H. "Introduction." Chesnutt, *Conjure Woman*, 1–21.

Buell, Lawrence. *Emerson.* Cambridge: Belknap P of Harvard UP, 2003.

———. *The Environmental Imagination: Thoreau, Nature Writing and the Formation of American Culture.* Cambridge: Belknap P of Harvard UP, 1995.

———. *Writing for an Endangered World: Literature, Culture, and the Environment in the U.S. and Beyond.* Cambridge: Belknap P of Harvard UP, 2001.

Bullard, Robert D. "Anatomy of Environmental Racism." Hofrichter, *Toxic Struggles*, 25–35.

Burke, Edmund. *A Philosophical Enquiry into the Origin of our Ideas of the Sublime and the Beautiful.* Ed. James T. Bouton. Notre Dame: U of Notre Dame P, 1986.

Butler, Judith. "Afterword: After Loss, What Then?" Eng, *Loss*, 467–73.

Carby, Hazel V. "Ideologies of Black Folk: The Historical Novel of Slavery." McDowell, *Slavery*, 125–43.

———. "The Politics of Fiction, Anthropology, and the Folk: Zora Neale Hurston." Awkward, *New Essays*, 71–93.

———. *Reconstructing Womanhood: The Emergence of the Afro-American Woman Novelist.* New York: Oxford UP, 1987.

Carroll, Charles. *The Negro a Beast, or "In the Image of God": The Reasoner of the Age, the Revelator of the Century! The Bible as It Is! The Negro and His Relation to the Human Family!* 1900. Salem, N.H.: Ayer, 1991.

———. *The Tempter of Eve; or, The Criminality of Man's Social, Political, and Religious Equality with the Negro, and the Amalgamation to Which These Crimes Inevitably Lead. Discussed in Light of the Scriptures, the Sciences, Profane History, Tradition, and the Testimony of the Monuments.* St. Louis: Adamic, 1902. Rpt. in *Anti-Black Thought, 1863–1925: "The Negro Problem."* Ed. John David Smith. Vol. 6. New York: Garland, 1993, 297–798.

Caruth, Cathy. "Trauma and Experience: Introduction." Caruth, *Trauma*, 3–12.

Caruth, Cathy, ed. *Trauma: Explorations in Memory*. Baltimore: Johns Hopkins UP, 1995, 3–12.

Cassidy, Thomas. "Janie's Rage: The Dog and the Storm in *Their Eyes Were Watching God*." *College Language Association Journal*. 36:3 (March 1993) 260–69.

Censer, Jane Turner. *The Reconstruction of White Southern Womanhood 1865–1895*. Baton Rouge: Louisiana State UP, 2003.

Cheng, Anne Anlin. *The Melancholy of Race*. New York: Oxford UP, 2000.

Chesnutt, Charles. *The Conjure Woman and other Conjure Tales*. Ed. Richard H. Brodhead. Durham: Duke UP, 1993.

Clark, Suzanne. "Narrative Fitness: Science, Nature, and Zora Neale Hurston's Folk Culture." Mayer, *Restoring*, 45–72.

Clifton, Spargo R. "Trauma and the Specters of Enslavement in Morrison's *Beloved*." *Mosaic: A Journal for the Interdisciplinary Study of Literature*. 35:1 (2002) 113–31.

Clinton, Catherine. *Tara Revisited: Women, War, & the Plantation Legend*. New York: Abbeville P, 1995.

Cole, Luke W. and Sheila R. Foster. *From the Ground Up: Environmental Racism and the Rise of the Environmental Justice Movement*. New York: New York UP, 2001.

Cone, James H. *Risks of Faith: The Emergence of a Black Theology of Liberation, 1968–1998*. Boston: Beacon P, 1999.

Cook, Barbara. "Enclosed by Racist Politics: Space, Place, and Power Dynamics in the Slave Narrative of Harriet Jacobs and in Environmental Justice Activism." Mayer, *Restoring*, 31–44.

Crawford, Margo. "Preface: Erasing the Commas: Race Gender Class Sexuality Region." *American Literature*. 77:1 (2005) 1–5.

Crèvecoeur , Hector St. John de. *Letters from an American Farmer*. 1782. London: J.M. Dent, 1912.

Cronon, William. "The Trouble with Wilderness; or, Getting Back to the Wrong Nature." Cronon, *Uncommon Ground*, 69–90.

———, ed. *Uncommon Ground: Rethinking the Human Place in Nature*. New York: W.W. Norton, 1996.

Curren, Erik D. "Should Their Eyes Have Been Watching God?: Hurston's Use of Religious Experience and Gothic Horror." *African American Review*. 29:1 (1995) 17–25.

Davie, Sharon. "Free Mules, Talking Buzzards, and Cracked Plates: the Politics of Dislocation in *Their Eyes Were Watching God*." *PMLA*. 108 (1993) 446–59.

Davies, Kathleen. "Zora Neal Hurston's Poetics of Embalmment: Articulating the Rage of Black Women and Narrative Self-Defense." *African American Review*. 26:1 (1992) 147–59.

Davis, Charles T. and Henry Louis Gates, Jr., eds. *The Slave's Narrative*. Oxford: Oxford UP, 1985.

de Bolla, Peter. *The Discourse of the Sublime: Readings in History: Aesthetics, and the Subject*. Oxford: B. Blackwell, 1989.

Debian, Marty. "White Antiracist Rhetoric as Apologia: Wendell Berry's *The Hidden Wound*." Nakayama and Martin, *Whiteness*, 51–68.

DeLuca, Kevin. "In the Shadow of Whiteness: The Consequences of the Destruction of Nature in Environmental Politics." Nakayama and Martin, *Whiteness*, 217–46.

—— and Anne Demo. "Imagining Nature and Erasing Class and Race: Carelton Watkins, John Muir and the Construction of Wilderness." *Environmental History*. 6:4 (2001) 541–60.

Devall, Bill. "John Muir as Deep Ecologist." *Environmental Review*. 6.1 (1982) 63–86.

—— and George Sessions, eds. *Deep Ecology*. Salt Lake City: Peregrine Smith Books, 1985.

Devine, Maureen. *Woman and Nature: Literary Reconceptualizations*. Metuchen: Scarecrow P, 1992.

Diamond, Irene and Gloria Orenstein, eds. *Reweaving the World: The Emergence of Ecofeminism*. Sierra Club Books, 1990.

Dixon, Melvin. *Ride Out the Wilderness: Geography and Identity in Afro-American Literature*. Urbana: U of Illinois P, 1987.

——. "Singing Swords: The Literary Legacy of Slavery." Davis, *Slave's Narrative*, 298–317.

Dixon, Thomas Jr. *The Clansman: An Historical Romance of the Ku Klux Klan*. 1905. Lexington: UP of Kentucky, 1970.

——. *The Leopard's Spots: A Romance of the White Man's Burden—1865–1900*. New York: Doubleday, Page, 1903.

Dodd, Elizabeth. "The Great Rainbowed Swamp: History as Moral Ecology in the Poetry of Michael S. Harper." Armbruster and Wallace, *Beyond Nature Writing*, 177–94.

Dollow, Gerard J. "Misogyny in the American Eden: Abbey, Cather, and Maclean." Branch, *Reading the Earth*, 97–105.

Douglass, Fredrick. *My Bondage and My Freedom*. 1855. *Fredrick Douglass: Autobiographies*. Ed. Henry Louis Gates, Jr. New York: Library of America, 1994, 105–452.

——. *Narrative of the Life of Frederick Douglass, an American Slave*. 1845. *Fredrick Douglass: Autobiographies*. Ed. Henry Louis Gates, Jr. New York: Library of America, 1994, 3–102.

Doyle, Laura. "The Racial Sublime." *Romanticism, Race, and Imperial Culture, 1780–1834*. Ed. Alan Richardson and Sonia Hofkosh. Bloomington: Indiana UP, 1996. 15–39.

Dreese, Donelle N. *Ecocriticism: Creating Self and Place in Environmental and American Indian Literatures*. New York: Peter Lang, 2002.

Drinnon, Richard. *Facing West: The Metaphysics of Indian-Hating and Empire-Building*. New York: New American Library, 1980.

DuBois, William Edward Burghardt. *The Souls of Black Folk*. 1903. New York: Dover, 1994.

Duncan, Charles. *The Absent Man: The Narrative Craft of Charles W. Chesnutt*. Athens: Ohio UP, 1998.

Dyer, Richard. *White*. London: Routledge, 1997.

Eby, Clare. "Slouching towards Beastliness: Richard Wright's Anatomy of Thomas Dixon." 35:3 (2001) 439–58.

Eldridge, Richard. "The Unifying Images in Part One of Jean Toomer's *Cane*." *College Language Association Journal*. 22 (1979) 187–214.

Emerson, Ralph Waldo. *The Essential Writings of Ralph Waldo Emerson*. Ed. Brooks Atkinson. New York: Modern Library, 2000.

Eng, David L. and David Kazanjian, "Introduction: Mourning Remains." Eng, *Loss*, 1–25.

———. eds. *Loss: The Politics of Mourning*. Berkeley: U of California P, 2003.

Erikson, Kai. "Notes on Trauma and Community." Caruth, *Trauma*, 183–99.

Evans, Mei Mei. "'Nature' and Environmental Justice." Adamson, *Environmental Justice Reader*, 181–93.

Evernden, Neil. *The Natural Alien: Humankind and Environment*. Toronto: U of Toronto P, 1985.

——— *The Social Creation of Nature*. Baltimore: Johns Hopkins UP, 1992.

Eyerman, Ron. *Cultural Trauma: Slavery and the Formation of African American Identity*. Cambridge: Cambridge UP, 2001.

Eze, Emmanuel Chukwudi. *Race and the Enlightenment: A Reader*. Oxford: Blackwell, 1997.

Faber, Daniel and James O'Connor. "Capitalism and the Crisis of Environmentalism." Hofrichter, *Toxic Struggles*, 12–24.

Fabre, Geneviève, and Robert O'Meally, eds. *History and Memory in African-American Culture*. New York: Oxford UP, 1994.

Ferguson, Frances. *Solitude and the Sublime: Romanticism and the Aesthetics of Individuation*. New York: Routledge, 1992.

Foley, Barbara. "'In the Land of Cotton': Economics and Violence in Jean Toomer's Cane." *African American Review*. 32:2 (1998) 181–98.

Fox-Genovese, Elizabeth. *Within the Plantation Household: Black and White Women of the Old South*. Chapel Hill: U of North Carolina P, 1988.

Fredrickson, George M. *The Black Image in the White Mind: The Debate on Afro-American Character and Destiny, 1817–1914*. New York: Harper and Row, 1971.

Freeman, Barbara Claire. *The Feminine Sublime: Gender and Excess in Women's Fiction*. Berkeley: U of California P, 1995.

Frost, Linda. *Never One Nation: Freaks, Savages, and Whiteness in U.S. Popular Culture 1850–1877*. Minneapolis: U of Minnesota P, 2005.

Gaard, Greta, ed. *Ecofeminism: Woman, Animals, Nature*. Philadelphia: Temple UP, 1993.

Gaard, Greta and Patrick D. Murphy, eds. *Ecofeminist Literary Criticism: Theory, Interpretation, Pedagogy*. Urbana: U of Illinois P, 1998.

Gates, Henry Louis, Jr., ed. *Reading Black, Reading Feminist: A Critical Anthology*. New York: Meridian, 1990.

———, ed. *Six Women's Slave Narratives*. New York: Oxford UP, 1988.

Gatta, John. *Making Nature Sacred: Literature, Religion, and Environment in America from the Puritans to the Present*. New York: Oxford UP, 2004.

Genovese, Eugene. *The Political Economy of Slavery*. Middletown, CT: Wesleyan UP, 1989.

Gerhardt, Christine. "Border Ecology: The Slave Narrative of Henry Bibb, Nature, and the Frontier Myth." Mayer, *Restoring*, 11–30.

———. "The Greening of African-American Literary Landscapes: Where Ecocriticism Meets Postcolonial Theory." *Mississippi Quarterly: The Journal of Southern Cultures*. 55 (2002) 515–33.

Gifford, Terry. "Introduction." Muir, *Eight Books*, 13–20.

———. *Reconnecting with John Muir: Essays in Post-Pastoral Practice*. Athens: U of Georgia P, 2006.

Gilroy, Paul. "After the Great White Error...the Great Black Mirage." Moore, *Race*, 73–98.

———. *Against Race: Imagining Political Culture beyond the Color Line*. Cambridge: Belknap P of Harvard UP, 2000.

———. *The Black Atlantic: Modernity and Double Consciousness*. Cambridge: Harvard UP, 1993.

Glasrud, Bruce A. and Alan M. Smith, eds. *Race Relations in British North America, 1607–1783*. Chicago: Nelson Hall, 1982.

Glotfelty, Cheryll and Harold Fromm. *The Ecocriticism Reader: Landmarks in Literary Ecology*. Athens: U of Georgia P, 1996.

Goings, Kenneth W. *Mammy and Uncle Mose: Black Collectibles and American Stereotyping*. Bloomington: Indiana UP, 1994.

Goldner, Ellen J. "Other(ed) Ghosts: Gothicism and the Bonds of Reason in Melville, Chesnutt, and Morrison." *MELUS*. 24:1 (Spring 1999) 59–83.

Goldstein, Philip. "Critical Realism or Black Modernism?: The Reception of *Their Eyes Were Watching God*." *Reader*. 41 (1999) 54–73.

Gossett, Thomas F. *Race: The History of an Idea in America*. Dallas: Southern Methodist UP, 1963.

Grimké, Angelina Weld. *Selected Works of Angelina Weld Grimké*. Ed. Henry Louis Gates, Jr. The Schomburg Library of Nineteenth-Century Black Women Writers. New York: Oxford UP, 1991.

Gubar, Susan. *Racechanges: White Skin, Black Face in American Culture*. New York: Oxford UP, 1997.

Guha, Ramachandra, and Juan Martinez-Alier. *Varieties of Environmentalism: Essays North and South*. London: Earthscan, 1997.

Gunning, Sandra. *Race, Rape, and Lynching: The Red Record of American Literature, 1890–1912*. New York: Oxford UP, 1996.

Hagood, Taylor. " 'Prodjickin', or mekin' a present to yo' fam'ly': Rereading Empowerment in Thomas Nelson Page's Frame Narratives." *Mississippi Quarterly*. 57:3 (2004) 423–40.

Hale, Grace Elizabeth. *Making Whiteness: The Culture of Segregation in the South, 1890–1940*. New York: Vintage, 1999.

Hall, Jacquelyn Dowd. *Revolt against Chivalry: Jessie Daniel Ames and the Women's Campaign against Lynching.* New York: Columbia UP, 1979.

Hall, Stuart. "The Toad in the Garden: Thatcherism among the Theorists." *Marxism and the Interpretation of Culture.* Ed. Cary Nelson and Lawrence Grossberg. Champaign-Urbana: U of Illinois P, 1998. 35–57.

Haraway, Donna. *Primate Visions: Gender, Race, and Nature in the World of Modern Science.* New York: Routledge, 1989.

———. *Simians, Cyborgs, and Women: The Reinvention of Nature.* New York: Routledge, 1991.

Harris, Joel Chandler. *The Complete Tales of Uncle Remus.* Boston: Houghton Mifflin, 1955.

Harris, Michael D. *Colored Pictures: Race and Visual Representation.* Chapel Hill: U of North Carolina P, 2003.

Harrison, Alferdteen, ed. *Black Exodus: The Great Migration from the American South.* Jackson: UP of Mississippi, 1991.

Hartman, Geoffrey H. "On Traumatic Knowledge and Literary Studies." *New Literary History.* 26 (1995) 537–63.

Hartman, Saidiya, V. *Scenes of Subjection: Terror, Slavery, and Self-Making in Nineteenth-Century America.* New York: Oxford UP, 1997.

Hass, Robert. "Might Zora Neale Hurston's Janie Woods Be Dying of Rabies? Considerations from Historical Medicine." *Literature and Medicine.* 19:2 (Fall 2000) 205–28.

Heffernan, James D. "Why Wilderness? John Muir's 'Deep Ecology.'" *John Muir, Life and Work.* Ed. Sally M. Miller. Albuquerque: U of New Mexico P, 1993. 102–116.

Herzogenrath, Bernd, ed. *From Virgin Land to Disney World: Nature and its Discontents in the USA of Yesterday and Today.* Amsterdam: Rodopi, 2001.

Hicks, Scott. "W.E.B. DuBois, Booker T. Washington and Richard Wright: Towards an Ecocriticism of Color." *Callaloo.* 29:1 (2006) 202–22.

Hill, Mike. *After Whiteness: Unmaking an American Majority.* New York: New York UP, 2004.

———. "Introduction: Vipers in Shangri-la: Whiteness, Writing, and Other Ordinary Terrors." Hill, *Whiteness: A Critical Reader,* 1–18.

———, ed. *Whiteness: A Critical Reader.* New York: New York UP, 1997.

Hirsch, David A. Hedrich. "Speaking Silences in Angelina Weld Grimké's 'The Closing Door' and 'Blackness.'" *African American Review.* 26:3 (Autumn 1992) 459–74.

Hitt, Christopher. "Toward an Ecological Sublime." *New Literary History: A Journal of Theory and Interpretation.* 30:3 (1999) 603–23.

Hodes, Martha. *White Women, Black Men: Illicit Sex in the 19th Century South.* New Haven: Yale UP, 1997.

Hofrichter, Richard. *Toxic Struggles: The Theory and Practice of Environmental Justice.* Salt Lake City: U of Utah P, 1993, 2002.

hooks, bell. "Touching the Earth." Barnhill, *At Home,* 51–56.

Hopkins, Pauline E. *Contending Forces: A Romance Illustrative of Negro Life North and South.* 1900. New York: Oxford UP, 1988.

Horsman, Reginald. *Race and Manifest Destiny: The Origins of American Racial Anglo-Saxonism.* Cambridge: Harvard UP, 1981.

Hull, Gloria T. *Color, Sex, and Poetry: Three Women Writers of the Harlem Renaissance.* Bloomington: Indiana UP, 1987.

Huntington, Ellsworth. *Climate and Civilization. Third Edition, Revised and Rewritten with Many New Chapters.* New Haven: Yale UP, 1924.

Hurston, Zora Neale. *Their Eyes Were Watching God.* 1937, New York: HarperCollins, 2000

Ianovici, Gerald. "'A Living Death': Gothic Signification and the Nadir in *The Marrow of Tradition.*" *MELUS.* 27:4 (Winter 2002) 33–58.

Ignatiev, Noel. *How the Irish Became White.* New York: Routledge, 1995.

Ingram, Annie Merrill, Ian Marshall, Daniel J. Philippon, and Adam W. Sweeting, eds. *Coming into Contact: Explorations in Ecocritical Theory and Practice.* Athens: U of Georgia P, 2007.

Jacobs, Harriet. *Incidents in the Life of a Slave Girl, Written by Herself.* 1861. *Narrative of the Life of Frederick Douglass, an American Slave & Incidents in the Life of a Slave Girl.* New York: Modern Library, 2000. 114–353.

Johnson, Barbara. "Metaphor, Metonymy, and Voice in Zora Neale Hurston's *Their Eyes Were Watching God.*" *Textual Analysis: Some Readers Reading.* Ed. Mary Ann Caws. New York: Modern Language Association of America, 1986. 232–44.

Johnson, Michael K. *Black Masculinity and the Frontier Myth in American Literature.* Norman: U of Oklahoma P, 2002.

Johnson, Walter. *Soul by Soul: Life Inside the Antebellum Slave Market.* Cambridge: Harvard UP, 1999.

Judy, Ronald A. T. *(Dis)Forming the American Canon: African-Arabic Slave Narratives and the Vernacular.* Minneapolis: U of Minnesota P, 1993.

Kant, Immanuel. *Critique of Judgment.* Trans. J.H. Bernard. New York: Hafner P, 1951.

———. "Observations on the Feelings of the Beautiful and Sublime." Trans. John T. Goldthwaite: U of California P, 1960.

Kaplan, Amy. *The Anarchy of Empire in the Making of U.S. Culture.* Cambridge: Harvard UP, 2002.

Kawash, Samira. *Dislocating the Color Line: Identity, Hybridity, and Singularity in African-American Literature.* Stanford: Stanford UP, 1997.

Kazanjian, David. *The Colonizing Trick: National Culture and Imperial Citizenship in Early America.* Minneapolis: U of Minnesota P, 2003.

Kennedy, John Pendleton. *Swallow Barn; or, a Sojourn in the Old Dominion.* 1832. Baton Rouge: Louisiana State UP, 1986.

Kennedy, Randall. *Interracial Intimacies: Sex, Marriage, Identity, and Adoption.* New York: Pantheon Books, 2003.

King, Ynestra. "The Ecology of Feminism and the Feminism of Ecology." Plant, *Healing the Wounds,* 18–28.

Klein, Richard. *Cigarettes Are Sublime*. Durham: Duke UP, 1993.

Kodat, Catherine Gunther. "To 'Flash White Light from Ebony': The Problem of Modernism in Jean Toomer's *Cane*." *Twentieth-Century Literature*. 46:1 (2000) 1–19.

Kolodny, Annette. *The Land before Her: Fantasy and Experience of the American Frontiers, 1630–1860*. Chapel Hill: U of North Carolina P, 1984.

———. *The Lay of the Land: Metaphor as Experience and History in American Life and Letters*. Chapel Hill: U of North Carolina P, 1975.

Krasner, David. *A Beautiful Pageant: African American Theatre, Drama, and Performance in the Harlem Renaissance, 1910–1927*. New York: Palgrave Macmillan, 2004.

LaCapra, Dominick. *Representing the Holocaust: History, Theory, Trauma*. Ithaca: Cornell UP, 1994.

Latour, Bruno. *We Have Never Been Modern*. Trans. Catherine Porter. Cambridge: Harvard UP, 1993.

Laub, Dori. "Truth and Testimony: The Process and the Struggle." Caruth, *Trauma*, 61–75.

Lemann, Nicholas. *The Promised Land: The Great Black Migration and How It Changed America*. New York: Knopf, 1991.

Leopold, Aldo. *A Sand County Almanac and Sketches Here and There*. New York: Oxford UP, 1987.

Levin, Jonathan. "Forum on Literatures of the Environment." *PMLA*. 114 (1999) 1097–98.

Leys, Ruth. *Trauma: A Genealogy*. Chicago and London: U of Chicago P, 2000.

Lillios, Anna. "'The Monstropolous Beast': The Hurricane in Zora Neale Hurston's *Their Eyes Were Watching God*." *Southern Quarterly: A Journal of Arts in the South*. 36:3 (1998) 89–93.

Limerick, Patricia Nelson. *The Legacy of Conquest: The Unbroken Past of the American West*. New York: Norton, 1987.

Lipsitz, George. *The Possessive Investment in Whiteness: How White People Profit from Identity Politics*. Philadelphia: Temple UP, 1998.

Litwack, Leon F. "Hellhounds." Allen, *Without Sanctuary*, 8–37.

Lott, Eric. *Love and Theft: Blackface Minstrelsy and the American Working Class*. New York: Oxford UP, 1993.

Lyotard, Jean-François. *The Inhuman: Reflections on Time*. Trans. Geoffrey Bennington and Rachel Bowlby. Stanford: Stanford UP, 1991.

———. *Lessons on the Analytic of the Sublime: Kant's Critique of Judgment, [sections] 23–29*. Trans. Elizabeth Rottenberg. Stanford: Stanford UP, 1994.

MacKethan, Lucinda H. "Jean Toomer's *Cane*: A Pastoral Problem." *Mississippi Quarterly*. 28 (1975) 423–34.

Margolick, David. *Strange Fruit: Billie Holiday, Café Society, and an Early Cry for Civil Rights*. Philadelphia: Running P, 2000.

Marks, Donald R. "Sex, Violence, and Organic Consciousness in Zora Neale Hurston's *Their Eyes Were Watching God*." *Black American Literature Forum*. 19:4 (Winter 1985) 152–57.

Martin, Daniel J. "Lynching Sites: Where Trauma and Pastoral Collide."
Ingram, *Coming*, 93–108.

Martin, Matthew R. "The Two-Faced New South: The Plantation Tales of
Thomas Nelson Page and Charles W. Chesnutt." *Southern Literary
Journal*. 30:2 (Spring 1998) 17–36.

Marx, Leo. "Pastoralism in America." Bercovitch, *Ideology*, 36–69.

———. *The Machine in the Garden: Technology and the Pastoral Ideal in
America*. New York: Oxford UP, 1964.

Mayer, Sylvia. *Restoring the Connection to the Natural World: Essays on the
African American Environmental Imagination*. Munster: Lit Verlag,
2003.

Mazel, David. *American Literary Environmentalism*. Athens: U of Georgia
P, 2000.

McDowell, Deborah E. and Arnold Rampersad, eds. *Slavery and the Literary
Imagination: Selected Papers from the English Institute, 1987 New Series,
no. 13*. Baltimore: Johns Hopkins UP, 1989.

McElrath, Joseph R., Jr., ed. *Critical Essays on Charles W. Chesnutt*. New
York: G.K. Hall, 1999.

McPherson, Tara. *Reconstructing Dixie: Race, Gender, and Nostalgia in the
Imagined South*. Durham: Duke UP, 2003.

McWilliams, Dean. *Charles W. Chesnutt and the Fictions of Race*. Athens: U
of Georgia P, 2002.

Melville, Herman. *The Poems of Herman Melville*. Ed. Douglas Robillard.
Albany: New College and University P, 1976.

Mies, Maria and Vandana Shiva. *Ecofeminism*. London: Zed Books,
1993.

Mixon, Wayne. "The Ultimate Irrelevance of Race: Joel Chandler Harris and
Uncle Remus in Their Time." *The Journal of Southern History*. 56 (1990)
457–80.

Mondie, Levita. "MFINDA—Beyond an Ecocritical Discourse in the
African American Literary Tradition: The Case of Charles Chesnutt's *The
Conjure Woman*." *In Process: A Graduate Student Journal of African-
American and African Diasporan Literature and Culture*. 2 Spring
(2000) 155–77.

Montag, Warren. "The Universalization of Whiteness: Racism and
Enlightenment." Hill, *Whiteness: A Critical Reader*, 281–93.

Moore, Donald S., Anand Pandian, and Jake Kosek. "Introduction. The
Cultural Politics of Race and Nature: Terrains of Power and Practice."
Moore, *Race*, 1–70.

Moore, Donald S., Jake Kosek, and Anand Pandian, eds. *Race, Nature and
the Politics of Difference*. Durham: Duke UP, 2003.

Morrison, Toni. *Beloved*. New York: Knopf, 1987.

———. *Playing in the Dark: Whiteness and the Literary Imagination*.
New York: Vintage, 1993.

Muir, John. *John Muir: The Eight Wilderness Discovery Books*. Ed. Terry
Gifford. London: Diadem, 1992.

Murphy, Patrick D. *Literature, Nature, and Other: Ecofeminist Critiques.* Albany: State U of New York P, 1995.

Myers, Jeffrey. *Converging Stories: Race, Ecology, and Environmental Justice in American Literature.* Athens: U of Georgia P, 2005.

Nakayama, Thomas K. and Judith N. Martin, eds. *Whiteness: The Communication of Social Identity.* Thousand Oaks: Sage, 1999.

Nash, Roderick F. *Wilderness and the American Mind.* 1967. New Haven: Yale UP, 2001.

Newitz, Annalee and Matthew Wray, eds. "What is 'White Trash'? Stereotypes and Economic Conditions of Poor Whites in the United States." Hill, *Whiteness: A Critical Reader*, 168–84.

Northup, Solomon. *Twelve Years a Slave: The Narrative of Solomon Northup.* Osofsky, *Puttin' on*, 225–406.

Norwood, Vera. *Made From this Earth: American Woman and Nature.* Chapel Hill: U of North Carolina P, 1993.

Olney James. " 'I Was Born': Slave Narratives, Their Status as Autobiography and as Literature." Davis, *Slave's Narrative*, 148–75.

O'Meally, Robert and Geneviève Fabre. "Introduction." Fabre, *History and Memory*, 3–17.

Osofsky, Gilbert. "Introduction: Puttin' On Ole Massa: The Significance of Slave Narratives." Osofsky, *Puttin' On*, 9–44.

———. ed. *Puttin' On Ole Massa: The Slave Narratives of Henry Bibb, William Wells Brown, and Solomon Northup.* New York: Harper & Row, 1969.

Outka, Paul. "Whitman and Race ('He's Queer, He's Unclear, Get Used To It...')." *Journal of American Studies.* 36 (2002) 293–318.

Page, Thomas Nelson. *In Ole Virginia, or Marse Chan and Other Stories.* 1887. Nashville: J.S. Sanders, 1991.

———. "Social Life in Old Virginia before the War." Thomas Nelson Page, *The Old South: Essays Social and Political.* New York: Charles Scribner's Sons, 1892. 143–88.

Pease, Donald. "Sublime Poetics." Arensberg, *American Sublime*, 29–41.

Pinar, William F. *The Gender of Racial Politics and Violence in America: Lynching, Prison Rape, and the Crisis of Masculinity.* New York: Peter Lang, 2001.

Plant, Judith, ed. *Healing the Wounds: The Promise of Ecofeminism.* Philadelphia: New Society Publishers, 1989.

Plumwood, Val. *Feminism and the Mastery of Nature.* New York: Routledge, 1993.

Prince, Mary. *The History of Mary Prince, a West Indian Slave.* 1831. Gates, *Six Women's Slave Narratives*.

Pulido, Laura. *Environmentalism and Economic Justice: Two Chicano Struggles in the Southwest.* Tucson: U of Arizona P, 1996.

Rable, George C. *Civil Wars: Women and the Crisis of Southern Nationalism.* Urbana: U of Illinois P, 1989.

Ramadanovic, Petar. *Forgetting Futures: on Memory, Trauma, and Identity.* Lanham: Lexington Books, 2001.

Ramsey, William M. "Jean Toomer's Eternal South." *Southern Literary Journal.* 36:1 (2003) 74–89.

Reed, T.V. "Toward an Environmental Justice Ecocriticism." Adamson, *Environmental Justice Reader*, 145–62.

Rhodes, Edwardo Lao. *Environmental Justice in America: A New Paradigm.* Bloomington: Indiana UP, 2003.

Ritterhouse, Jennifer. "Reading, Intimacy and the Role of Uncle Remus in White Southern Social Memory." *The Journal of Southern History.* 69 (2003) 585–622.

Robbins, Bruce. "The Sweatshop Sublime." *PMLA.* 117:1 (2002) 84–97.

Roediger, David R. *The Wages of Whiteness: Race and the Making of the American Working Class.* London: Verso, 1991.

Rogin, Michael. *Fathers and Children: Andrew Jackson and the Subjugation of the American Indian.* New York: Random House, 1975.

Romine, Scott. *The Narrative Forms of Southern Community.* Baton Rouge: Louisiana State UP, 1999.

Rosendale, Steven, ed. *The Greening of Literary Scholarship: Literature, Theory, and the Environment.* Iowa City: U of Iowa P, 2002.

Ross, Andrew. *The Chicago Gangster Theory of Life: Nature's Debt to Society.* London: Verso, 1994.

Rozelle, Lee. *Ecosublime: Environmental Awe and Terror from New World to Oddworld.* Tuscaloosa: U of Alabama P, 2006.

Sarver, Stephanie L. *Uneven Land: Nature and Agriculture in American Writing.* Lincoln: U of Nebraska P, 1999.

Saxton, Alexander. *The Rise and Fall of the White Republic: Class Politics and Mass Culture in Nineteenth-Century America.* London: Verso, 1990.

Shiva, Vandana. *Staying Alive: Women, Ecology and Development.* London: Zed Books, 1988.

Shrader-Frechette, Kristin. *Environmental Justice: Creating Equality, Reclaiming Democracy.* Oxford: Oxford UP, 2002.

Silber, Nina. *The Romance of Reunion: Northerners and the South, 1865–1900.* Chapel Hill: U of North Carolina P, 1993.

Silko, Leslie Marmon. "Landscape, History, and the Pueblo Imagination." Glotfelty, *Ecocriticism Reader*, 264–81.

Sivils, Matthew Wynn. "Reading Trees in Southern Literature." *Southern Quarterly.* 44:1 (2006) 88–102.

Slotkin, Richard. *The Fatal Environment: The Myth of the Frontier in the Age of Industrialization, 1800–1890.* New York: Atheneum, 1985.

———. *Gunfighter Nation: The Myth of the Frontier in Twentieth-Century America.* New York: Atheneum, 1992.

———. *Regeneration Through Violence: The Mythology of the American Frontier, 1600–1860.* Middletown, CT: Weslyan UP, 1973.

Smith, Jon. "Hot Bodies and 'Barbaric Tropics': The U.S. South and New World Natures." *The Southern Literary Journal.* 36.1 (2003) 104–20.

Smith, Valerie. "'Loopholes of Retreat:' Architecture and Ideology in Harriet Jacobs's *Incidents in the Life of a Slave Girl.*" Gates, *Reading Black*, 212–26.

Snyder, Robert E. "Without Sanctuary: An American Holocaust?" *Southern Quarterly.* 39:3 (2001) 162–71.

Sollors, Werner, ed. *Interracialism: Black-White Intermarriage in American History, Literature, and Law.* New York: Oxford UP, 2000.

Solnit, Rebecca. *Savage Dreams.* New York: Vintage, 1994.

Soulé, Michael E. and Gary Lease, eds. *Reinventing Nature? Responses to Postmodern Deconstruction.* Washington, D.C.: Island P, 1995.

Spillers, Hortense J. "Mama's Baby, Papa's Maybe: An American Grammar Book." *Diacritics.* 17:2 (1987) 65–81.

———. "Changing the Letter: The Yokes, the Jokes of Discourse, or, Mrs. Stowe, Mr. Reed." McDowell, *Slavery*, 25–61.

Steinberg, Ted. *Down to Earth: Nature's Role in American History.* New York: Oxford UP, 2002.

Stokes, Mason. *The Color of Sex: Whiteness, Heterosexuality, and the Fictions of White Supremacy.* Durham: Duke UP, 2001.

Stoll, Steven. *Larding the Lean Earth: Soil and Society in Nineteenth-Century America.* New York: Hill and Wang, 2002.

Sundquist, Eric. J. *To Wake the Nations: Race in the Making of American Literature.* Cambridge: Belknap P of Harvard UP, 1993.

Sweet, John Wood. *Bodies Politic: Negotiating Race in the American North, 1730–1830.* Baltimore: Johns Hopkins UP, 2003.

Sweet, Timothy. *American Georgics: Economy and Environment in Early American Literature.* Philadelphia: U of Pennsylvania P, 2002.

Takaki, Ronald. *Iron Cages: Race and Culture in Nineteenth-Century America.* New York: Knopf, 1979.

Tallmadge, John and Henry Harrington, eds. *Reading under the Sign of Nature: New Essays in Ecocriticism.* Salt Lake City: U of Utah P, 2000.

Taylor, Gary. *Buying Whiteness: Race, Culture, and Identity from Columbus to Hip Hop.* New York: Palgrave Macmillan, 2005.

Thoreau, Henry David. *Collected Essays and Poems.* New York: The Library of America, 2001.

———. "Slavery in Massachusetts." *Collected*, 333–47.

———. "Walking." *Collected*, 225–55.

Tompkins, Jane P. *West of Everything: The Inner Life of Westerns.* New York: Oxford UP, 1992.

Toomer, Jean. *Cane.* 1923. New York: Harper and Row, 1969.

Turner, Fredrick Jackson. *Rereading Frederick Jackson Turner: "The Significance of the Frontier in American History" and other Essays.* New York: Henry Holt, 1994.

Twain Mark. *The Adventures of Huckleberry Finn.* New York: Oxford UP, 1999.

Van Mol, Kay R. "Primitivisim and Intellect in Toomer's *Cane* and McKay's *Banana Bottom*: The Need for an Integrated Black Consciousness." *Negro American Literature Forum*. 10:2 (1976) 48–52.

Walker, Alice. *In Search of Our Mother's Gardens*. New York: Harcourt, 1983.

———. "The Universe Responds: Or, How I Learned We Can Have Peace on Earth." Barnhill, *At Home*, 307–12.

Walker, David. *David Walker's Appeal to the Coloured Citizens of the World*. 1829. Ed. Peter P. Hinks, University Park: Pennsylvania State UP, 2000.

Wall, Cheryl A. *Women of the Harlem Renaissance*. Bloomington: Indiana UP, 1995.

Wallace, Kathleen R. "The Novels of Toni Morrison: 'Wild Wilderness Where There Was None." Armbruster and Wallace, *Beyond Nature Writing*, 211–30.

Wardi, Anissa Janine. *Death and the Arc of Mourning in African American Literature*. Gainsville: UP of Florida, 2003.

Ware, Vron and Les Back. *Out of Whiteness: Color, Politics, and Culture*. Chicago: U of Chicago P, 2002.

Washington, Booker T. *Up from Slavery*. 1901. New York: Dover, 1995.

Weiskel, Thomas. *The Romantic Sublime: Studies in the Structure and Psychology of Transcendence*. Baltimore: Johns Hopkins UP, 1976.

Wells-Barnett, Ida B. *On Lynchings*. Amherst: Humanity Books, 2002.

Wheeler, Roxann. *The Complexion of Race: Categories of Difference in Eighteenth-Century British Culture*. Philadelphia: U of Pennsylvania P, 2000.

White, Evelyn C. "Black Women and the Wilderness." *The Stories that Shape Us: Contemporary Women Write about the West*. Ed. Theresa Jordan and James Hepworth. New York: Norton, 1995. 376–83.

Wiegman, Robyn. "The Anatomy of Lynching." *Journal of the History of Sexuality*. 3 (1993) 445–67.

———. "Whiteness Studies and the Paradox of Particularity." *boundary 2*. 26:3 (1999) 115–50.

Wilson, Clyde N. "Introduction." Page, *In Ole Virginia*, xi–xxi.

Wilson, Rob. *American Sublime: The Genealogy of a Poetic Genre*. Madison: U of Wisconsin P, 1991.

Wilton, Andrew, "The Sublime in the Old World and the New." Wilton, *American Sublime*, 11–37.

Wilton, Andrew and Tim Barringer, eds. *American Sublime: Landscape Painting in the United States, 1820–1880*. Princeton: Princeton UP, 2002.

Winston, George T. "The Relation of the Whites to the Negroes." *America's Race Problems: Addresses at the Annual Meeting of the American Academy of Political and Social Science, Philadelphia, April Twelfth and Thirteenth, MCMI*. New York: Negro Universities P, 1969. 105–18.

Wolf, Bryan Jay. *Romantic Re-vison: Culture and Consciousness in Nineteenth-Century American Literature and Painting*. Chicago: U of Chicago P, 1982.

Wolfe, Cary. *Animal Rites: American Culture, the Discourse of Species, and Posthumanist Theory.* Chicago: U of Chicago P, 2003.

Wright, Richard. "Between Laughter and Tears." *New Masses*, October 5, 1937, 22–23.

Wrobel, David M. *The End of American Exceptionalism: Frontier Anxiety from the Old West to the New Deal.* Lawrence: UP of Kansas, 1993.

Yancy, George. "Introduction: Fragments of a Social Ontology of Whiteness." *What White Looks Like: African-American Philosophers on the Whiteness Question.* Ed. George Yancy. New York: Routledge, 2004. 1–23.

———, ed. *White on White/Black on Black.* Lanham: Rowman & Littlefield, 2005.

Yellin, Jean Gagan. *The Intricate Knot: Black Figures in American Literature, 1776–1863.* New York: New York UP, 1972.

Žižek, Slavoj. *The Sublime Object of Ideology.* London: Verso, 1989.

Zwarg, Christina. "The Work of Trauma: Fuller, Douglass, and Emerson on the Border of Ridicule." *Studies in Romanticism.* 41.1 (2002) 65–88.

INDEX

Boldfaced entries indicate subjects; name references are in regular type. Page ranges for more extensive discussions under a given heading are also in boldface. An "n." before a page number indicates that the reference is found in the endnotes.